THE GROWING CHURCH
LOBBY IN WASHINGTON

THE GROWING CHURCH LOBBY IN WASHINGTON

James L. Adams

WILLIAM B. EERDMANS PUBLISHING COMPANY
GRAND RAPIDS, MICHIGAN

*To Phyllis
and our daughters
Jeanne, Pamela and Cheryl
who never lost faith*

ACKNOWLEDGMENTS

The idea for this book germinated in the spring of 1967 while I was a Fellow at the Washington (D.C.) Journalism Center (WJC). The Center, a non-profit institution founded by educators and professional journalists in 1965, enrolls ten Fellows in each of two semesters a year. In a conversation with Louis Cassels, Senior Editor of UPI, I was encouraged to proceed but also warned: "Writing a book is a little like having a baby — easier conceived than to give birth to."

Now that the labor pains are over, I can better appreciate Mr. Cassel's biological analogy. And if it hadn't been for the advice, direction and support I was given by so many, this book would have remained only a glint in a reporter's eye.

Dr. Ray E. Hiebert, the Center's patient director, gently prodded when I seemed to waver. The schedule at the Center called for morning lectures and afternoon assignments with a daily newspaper, magazine, radio or television station. I "interned" at *Christianity Today* magazine. I am deeply grateful to Dr. Carl F. H. Henry, who was then editor; David E. Kucharsky, associate editor, and Richard Osling, then news editor but now with *Time* magazine, for permitting me to pursue my investigation of the church lobbyist. Two articles appeared in the magazine based on my research.

I spent hours compiling notes and collecting documents, doing taped interviews, poring over committee reports and the *Congressional Record,* and rather brashly invading the offices of Congressmen and Senators for interviews. I shall always remember the kindness of Senator John Sherman Cooper of Kentucky — my native state — who left the Senate floor in the midst of an important debate on the draft law to talk with "an old boy from Casey County." The Senator rushed back on the floor and cast his vote. Both Congressmen Charles E. Goodell of New York and

Albert H. Quie of Minnesota graciously granted me interviews. An old friend from Northern Illinois, U. S. Rep. John N. Erlenborn, provided me with material and gave me invaluable background information.

Almost without exception, the church bureaucrats took time out to talk about their jobs. I am deeply indebted to James Hamilton, the affable director of the National Council of Churches (NCC) Washington office. Dr. Lewis I. Maddocks of the United Church of Christ went the second mile in explaining the role of a church secretary in the nation's Capital.

My interview with Dean M. Kelley, director of the Commission on Religious Liberty of the NCC, was brief but invaluable, and the written material he gave me was indispensable for interpreting the Elementary and Secondary Act of 1965. I remember with warm affection my lively sessions with Rabbi Richard G. Hirsch of the Religious Action Center.

After I began writing, my former city editor, Leo Hirtl, played a supportive role with his comments and criticisms.

Special acknowledgment is due my sister, Miss June Adams, a typist without peer, and my mother, Mrs. James B. Adams, who went over each page with dictionary in hand to catch and correct errors. Their labor of love made this book possible. For the help of all these mentioned and those unfortunately overlooked, I am profoundly grateful.

— JAMES L. ADAMS

Foreword

The Growing Church Lobby in Washington is a very useful
compilation of information not available elsewhere. It covers the
operations of the churches in connection with the Civil Rights
Act of 1964 and the first really big and important and successful
invocation of cloture on Civil Rights. It covers in important
detail the big fight about the Delta Ministry and OEO headed
by Sargent Shriver. It has the fullest account of the most recent
and modern Church-State battle among religious forces. It out-
lines the operations of the official and semi-official church groups
on world peace and especially Vietnam. It has a full description
of the presently active church lobbying organizations.

Now I'm not exactly unbiased in this area. I am a registered
lobbyist (which means paid) for the Committee for a National
Trade Policy, the business-oriented group that co-ordinates the
efforts of many national and local groups in support of the Re-
ciprocal Trade Agreements Policy. The church groups work with
us on that, like many of the other groups mentioned in this book
as backing Civil Rights.

It is perhaps of some interest that we report only expenditures
that are aimed at pressures on members of Congress in support of
or against specific pending legislation. We raise non-exempt
money for that. Most of our expenses are clearly such as to permit
contributions of businesses to be deducted as business expense,
even before the more recent amendments to lobbying legislation.
This is quite different from the procedures Mr. Adams mentions
for the U. S. Chamber of Commerce and other business groups
("It's only a small part of our total job").

Mr. Adams asked me to do this foreword because of several
broadcasts I did in 1969 around the problems raised in churches

by the Black Manifesto. I hope he does a sequel on what has happened in twelve months or more in that area. I mention this because I don't think he has emphasized enough the absence of real lay participation in the church operations he describes. One of my broadcasts came in our City Council campaign in the fall of 1969. It was then condensed and given to the press. I believe it is directly relevant in giving a little different slant to the contents of this book.

"There is today a sharp division between the clergy and the laity in most Christian churches.

"There is little sense of a common enterprise in Christ's army, because there is no adequate understanding between laity and clergy as to what the church's objectives are in a secular community.

"A sound doctrine in Protestant churches, accepted by leading Roman Catholic archbishops, states that the church is the Laos, the People of God: that includes both clergy and laity. But the operation of our churches appears to be placed entirely in the clergy.

"In a National Council of Churches' poll, 58.6% of the people questioned said the church should not become involved in social and political issues. These people are alarmed by rapid social change, and take a dim view of the church serving as agent in the process they find so disturbing, according to Louis Cassels, who conducted the poll.

"I don't agree with the conservative groups, but I wonder if it is the job of the clergy to be out in front in religious enterprises without securing real lay understanding and backing.

"Clerical leaders have deep reasons of conscience for seeking their objectives, but they dare not leave their laity behind when it insists upon being part of the action. An effort must be made to bring both clergy and laymen to accept their respective responsibilities.

"I am a public official, a public servant. I do not order my opinion on the basis of political pressure, or a Gallup poll. But my responsible duty is to carry my constituency with me in such a way as to accomplish my objective in the human process of politics.

"When the laity has not been part of the action early enough, they are unwilling to accept any responsibility. The clergy has a difficult, if not impossible, task to educate after the fact.

"This is the lay-clergy rift we face today."

So you see perhaps why the Civil Rights Act of 1964, coming after all the secular publicity and religious comment on the situation in the South, received such widespread lay backing. The clergy did not do that, and when other enterprises have come in and the clergy failed really to educate their lay people, they did not get the same results.

I was brought up and trained in the YMCA. A Y secretary, so the late Judson McKim, General Secretary in Cincinnati, said once, is like Noah's dove; he is sent out to light on the first green thing he sees. He is trained to push his laymen out front. I wish they had a course in every seminary of every denomination teaching that relation between clergymen and lay leaders. Of course it takes more time. Of course the job is not as well done at first. But the man multiplies himself, and the image of the operation is the right one, that of the Laos of God, the laity *and* the clergy as the church.

I am happy to commend this book, though I don't agree with all of it. But read it and do some real thinking, and then insist on talking about it, in the right places.

— CHARLES P. TAFT*

*Charles P. Taft is a Cincinnati lawyer, serving his twenty-second year in City Council, and even longer as Senior Warden of Christ Church, Cincinnati, one of the strongest Episcopal parishes in the country. He does a five-minute radio commentary five days a week. For twenty years he served the National Council of Churches Department of Church and Economic Life, most of the time as chairman.

Preface: The Religious Lobbyist

This is an irreverent look at a religious reality — the church lobby in the nation's Capital.

Church officials practice the ancient art of lobbying with a fervor peculiar to the dedicated. They obviously feel that they are manning the most important outposts in the legions of the Lord. "There's no question about the fact we lobby," Dr. Grover C. Bagby of the Division of Human Relations and Economic Affairs for the United Methodist Church admitted to me in his office in the Methodist Building. (The building sits circumspectly on the edge of the Capitol grounds.) The major Protestant denominations — not to mention several minor ones — and the Roman Catholic Church spend more than a million dollars annually to operate their Washington offices and pay their professional staffs.

Religious lobbyists are not noticeably bothered about possible Constitutional infringements. One gets the impression that church activists regard the wall of separation between church and state as a kind of political aberration on the part of Thomas Jefferson. (Every man has his blind spots. And after all Jefferson did own slaves while writing the Declaration of Independence.) The rationale of the religious lobbyist, in brief, is that modern man lives in a complex, highly structured society made up of pressure groups. Political pressure peaks under the Capitol dome in the halls of Congress. Therefore, the church should make its muscle felt at this vital pressure point. Politics involves people and the church's primary purpose is to serve people.

The argument appears sound. Who wants to be placed in the position of being against people? But nagging doubts keep cropping up. Did Jesus Christ found a political pressure group or a church? Where does the church show up on the political spectrum — on the Democratic side of the aisle or on the Republican? Is the church getting involved in socio-economic issues in which it has no expertise? Is the church substituting the power of moral persuasion — supposedly its stock in trade — for power politics?

The church lobby is as firmly entrenched now on the capital landscape as the Washington Monument. Yet the man in the pew is abysmally unaware of what his denomination is doing there. A Presbyterian church elder I know in Cincinnati — more astute than the average elder — did not even know that his communion operates a Washington Office for Public Affairs. Church lobbyists form a kind of self-perpetuating religious curia operating in a free-wheeling fashion with no accounting to the people they supposedly represent and who incidentally pay their salaries.

Most church lobbyists prefer to be called social action secretaries or public affairs officials. Others hedge, or verbally camouflage, their roles by arguing that they spend most of their time educating constituents on the moral implications of political issues rather than in actual lobbying.

This exercise in semantics is not without its practical reasons. Lobbying has a mercenary connotation to most. It also has implications for the church's tax standing before the Internal Revenue Service. The Federal Regulation of Lobbying Act of 1946 is so loosely worded, however, that churches can ignore it without so much as a nod in its direction. (They are not alone. The National Association of Manufacturers and the U. S. Chamber of Commerce also do not file spending reports, on the ground that lobbying isn't their principal purpose, the law's test of who must file.)

Religious lobbying has taken an ecumenical turn in conformity with recent church trends. A generation ago, Protestants acted as if their primary mission was to counter, and if possible cancel, the Catholic influence on government. The laboriously titled Protestants and Other Americans United for Separation of Church and State (POAU) made its appearance in Washington over twenty years ago when a group of national Protestant leaders banded together to block federal aid to parochial schools and the appointment of an ambassador to the Vatican.

But the primary difference between the church lobbyist of the Seventies and his counterpart of the Twenties is the modern-day lobbyist's determination to leave a church imprint on nearly every issue introduced on the floor of Congress. The mobilizing of the church to bring pressure to bear only on a single issue and then leave town went out with bathtub gin and the Anti-Saloon League.

The new-breed church lobbyist likes the feel of power as much as the old-line politician. It's apparently a universal urge to which churchmen are not immune. Albert Saunders, young secretary for national affairs of the United Presbyterian Church U. S. A., bluntly informed me: "Suddenly we in the field of religious social action found ourselves playing the role of political power groups — and many of us liked it."

Saunders was referring to the sustained effort of church activists who joined with liberal labor and civil rights organizations to lobby for the passage of the Civil Rights Act of 1964. The merging of labor, church, and civil rights forces for one common goal produced the short-lived coalition of "conscience and power" of the Kennedy-Johnson administrations. The role of the church in the bill's passage was a key one, and church lobbyists, for weal or woe, have never been the same. Having drunk of the heady wine of politics and power, they began eagerly flexing their moral muscles in anticipation of even bigger and more successful struggles.

The involvement of church activists in the thorny issues of the 1960's — the decade of great social change — gave the church a new political dimension. It's a story that needs telling if we are to understand the internal stresses now threatening to split the church's superstructure and rip the pulpit from the pew.

Contents

	Foreword	v
	Preface: The Religious Lobbyist	xi
I.	An Idea Whose Time Has Come	1
II.	Stronger Than an Army	21
III.	The Churches War on Shriver	44
IV.	Where the Action Is	64
V.	Scaling the Church-State Wall of Separation	89
VI.	A Split in the Ranks	101
VII.	A New Concept in Education	113
VIII.	HR 2362: An Instrument of Reconciliation	126
IX.	A Dubious Consensus	145
X.	A Second Look at the Church-State Settlement	178
XI.	Priority for Peace	204
XII.	Generals Without Armies	231
XIII.	Registering Christian Opinion	245
XIV.	Closing the Lobbying Gap	281
	Index	289

CHAPTER I

An Idea Whose Time Has Come

The excited whispering in the packed U. S. Senate gallery stopped as if on signal. Senator Clair Engle, Democrat of California, unable to speak because of a brain operation and still wearing a bandage around his head, was being pushed onto the floor in a wheelchair by an aide. The Administration leadership was taking no chances on June 30, 1964. Every loyal Democrat would be needed to help choke a Southern filibuster zeroed in on one target — the 1964 Civil Rights Bill. The battle lines already were drawn and all 100 Senators were present — a rarity in itself — and ready to cast their votes. Senator Mike Mansfield, the stone-faced majority leader, reminded his colleagues in flat, nasal tones which only added to the tension that "the Senate now stands at the crossroads of history, and the time for decision is at hand."

With the full complement of senators present, sixty-seven votes were needed to stop the Southern talkathon by activating Rule 22, which critics refer to as the "gag rule" and its advocates call cloture. Of the eleven cloture votes taken on civil rights legislation since Rule 22 was adopted by the Senate in 1917, all had failed to win the necessary two-thirds majority. Only four of the cloture resolutions had produced even a simple majority. History was on the side of the South in June of 1964.

Senator Carl Hayden, Democrat of Arizona, was the only member not in his seat when voting began. The aged dean of the Senate was fighting a personal battle in the Senate lobby. Senator Hayden feared that for the first time in his thirty-eight years in the Senate, he was going to be forced into voting for cloture. The former Western sheriff who came to Washington when Arizona was admitted to the Union in 1912, strongly believes that the filibuster is a legitimate parliamentary tactic to prevent small

1

states from being overwhelmed by the political strength of the large. He had hedged his promise to the leadership — he would vote for cloture only if his vote was absolutely necessary to achieve the two-thirds majority.

Senator Richard B. Russell, Democrat of Georgia, led the Senate's Southern bloc in the fight to knock out the cloture vote, taking the floor to protest the involvement of a group he considered guilty of having sold its spiritual birthright to play power politics in getting the Civil Rights Act approved.

"I have observed with profound sorrow," he began in his rich Georgian accent, "the role that many religious leaders have played in urging passage of this bill, because I can not make their activities jibe with my concept of the proper place of religious leaders in our national life.

"During the course of this debate, we have seen cardinals, bishops, elders, stated clerks, common preachers, priests and rabbis come to Washington to press for the passage of this bill. They have sought to make its passage a moral issue. If it is a great moral issue today, it was a greater moral issue on the day of the ratification of the Constitution of the United States."

The Senator stopped and looked up at the crowded gallery with its galaxy of clerical collars.

"This is not, and cannot be, a moral question," he explained as if he were giving the spectators a lecture on Political Science. "However it may be considered, it is a political question.

"Day after day men of the cloth have been standing on the mall urging a favorable vote on the bill. They have encouraged and prompted thousands of good citizens to sign petitions supporting the bill — but all without knowledge of the effect of what they are demanding of the representatives in the Congress of the United States.

"This is the second time in my lifetime," he concluded, "that an effort has been made by the clergy to make a moral question of a political issue. The other was Prohibition. We know something of that."

Senator Russell's critical comments caused scarcely a murmur among the clergymen and other church functionaries lining the gallery. Rather than feeling chastised, they were elated that one of the most influential men in the U. S. Senate publicly recognized the part they had played in pushing for passage of the bill. Scorn from an enemy often points to a higher degree of success than praise from a friend.

Political history was being made that hot day in June on the floor of the U. S. Senate. A deprived minority was on its way to achieving legal rights denied for more than 300 years. But the impact of the Civil Rights Act may have done more TO the church than it did FOR the Negro. Activist churchmen, having tasted the sweet fruits of a political victory, would no longer rely on moral suasion as the best means to achieve social justice.

In the summer of 1963, in a belated spurt of moral zeal and energy, liberal churchmen left pulpits and church studies to hustle votes for the Civil Rights Bill. They marched in Washington, led political workshops across the the nation, button-holed Congressmen and Senators, urged church members to deluge their elected representatives with mail backing the bill, participated in around-the-clock vigils at the Lincoln Memorial, and printed and distributed literature explaining the purpose of the bill and why it should be enacted into law.

For the first time, organized religion joined with labor and civil rights organizations to form a powerful coalition of "conscience and power." Never were clergymen so convinced of the rightness — or righteousness — of their cause. The issue was clear-cut. God's laws and the American Constitution both demanded that the Negro be accorded full human dignity and all rights as a citizen in a democratic society. To gainsay this argument would be not only un-American but also un-Christian. Both church and country could redeem themselves for their silence of the past in failing to speak out against the harsh treatment of Negroes by passing the Civil Rights Bill.

Even the world's greatest deliberative body must sooner or later take action. Senator Everett M. Dirksen, the Minority Leader, held the legislative key which could turn off the Southern filibuster. Obviously savoring his important role, he rose to his feet to bring the issue to a decision.

"Mr. President," he began in his dramatic baritone, "there are many reasons why cloture should be invoked and a good civil rights measure enacted. It is said that on the night he died, Victor Hugo wrote in his diary, substantially this sentiment: 'Stronger than all the armies is the idea whose time has come.'

"The time has come for equality of opportunity in sharing in government, in education and in employment. It will not be stayed or denied. It is here. I appeal to all Senators. We are confronted with a moral issue. Today let us not be found wanting in whatever it takes by way of moral and spiritual substance to face up to the issue and vote cloture."

The clerk in the well of the Senate began calling the roll.

* * * * *

The precise point of the start of the civil rights revolution is difficult to determine. It received a major impetus on December 5, 1955. A Negro seamstress, Mrs. Rosa Parks, refused to give up her seat on a city bus to a white person in Montgomery, Alabama. She was arrested and fined $10, but her defiant act triggered a year-long boycott of public transportation and, even more importantly, set free an idea which would sweep across the nation.

In 1954 the U. S. Supreme Court handed down its historic desegregation ruling in Brown vs. The Board of Education of Topeka, Kansas. In his 1955 State of the Union speech, President Eisenhower talked about eliminating demeaning practices based on race or color. A cautious Congress, however, waited until 1957 before enacting the first piece of civil rights legislation since the post-Civil War Reconstruction period. Three years later the Civil Rights Act of 1960 was approved. Both acts dealt primarily with voting rights and were far short of striking the chains of second-class citizenship from a determined minority.

In September of 1957, Governor Orval E. Faubus of Arkansas forced a showdown with the Federal government by refusing to obey a school integration court order. Nine Negro students were prevented by the Arkansas National Guard from entering the all-white Central High School in Little Rock. When the guardsmen were withdrawn, mob violence took over. President Eisenhower federalized the guard and then ordered the 101st Airborne Division into Little Rock to restore order and to escort frightened Negro students to and from school.

The Rev. John F. Cronin, assistant director of the Social Action Department of the National Catholic Welfare Conference — later to become the U. S. Catholic Conference — was appalled by pictures of Negro children beaten as they attempted to attend white schools in the South. He was doubly dismayed because the pictures were in the French and Italian newspapers he read while visiting Europe in the fall of 1957.

Upon his return to the United States, the mild-mannered priest requested the National Catholic Welfare Conference — the ad-

ministrative arm of the American Catholic Bishops — to issue a
denunciation of discrimination in its annual statement of 1957.
The statement already had been drawn up, however, and no
changes could be made at that late date. But a year later, in
November 1958, the American Catholic Bishops, prodded by
Father Cronin, became one of the first major religious groups to
verbally attack racial discrimination. Their statement declared:

> The heart of the race question is moral and religious. It con-
> cerns the rights of man and our attitude toward our fellow
> man. Discrimination based on the accidental fact of race or
> color, and as such injurious to human rights, regardless of personal
> qualities of achievements, cannot be reconciled with the truth
> that God has created all men with equal rights and equal dignity.

It would be four more years before the churches would give
substance to their statements through concerted action, but the
rallying cry had been sounded. It would be taken up across the
land.

Protestant denominations moved into the civil rights struggle
at differing speeds. The liberal, free-wheeling United Church
of Christ had had a long history of concern for racial justice,
reaching far back into the life of the uniting denominations —
Congregational and Evangelical and Reformed. The General
Synod in 1959 called upon the churches and their members to
pray and work for "the end of racial segregation and discrimination in our communities — in church life, in housing, in employment, in education, in public accommodations and services, and
in the exercise of political rights."

The Methodist Church, one of the nation's largest Protestant
communities, had built-in reasons for its hesitant approach to
civil rights. One third of the denomination's membership lived
in the South, and one of its six divisions was the all-Negro
Central Jurisdiction. It was the only division in the church
structure based on color rather than geography. The Central
Jurisdiction had twelve annual conferences (groups of churches),
2,030 congregations, and 231,000 members. It made up 2.2 percent of the Methodist membership.

In 1958, however, feeling the squeeze of public pressure, the
Methodist Church made it constitutionally possible for congregations and annual conferences to move across jurisdictional
lines, the purpose being to abolish the Central Jurisdiction. The
church, in a sudden seizure of conscience, set 1968 as the definite
date for eliminating the racially based jurisdiction, and the tar-

get date of 1972 for the end of segregated annual conferences. But the Methodists had their own long, hot summer to sweat out before taking their rightful place in the ranks of those ready to embark on a crusade to secure equal rights for all citizens. The United Presbyterian Church, U. S. A., was one of the first communions to form a Commission on Religion and Race. And in 1960, the church came out with its controversial endorsement of civil disobedience:

> Some laws and customs requiring racial discriminations are, in our judgment, such serious violations of the law of God as to justify peaceable and orderly disobedience or disregard of these laws.

The church's highest official, the Rev. Eugene Carson Blake, Stated Clerk, later would put these words to test and attract national headlines by being arrested and jailed in Baltimore.

* * * * *

Father Cronin, encouraged by the statement issued by the National Catholic Welfare Conference, believed that the time was ripe for all churches to join in an interfaith attempt to eradicate racial discrimination in America. The NCWC Conference of Interracial Justice proposed a national conference on religion and race to be held in Chicago in January of 1963 and attended by representatives from the major faiths. The conference attracted 700 delegates from sixty-seven major religious bodies — Protestant, Roman Catholic, and Jewish. Resources and ideas were pooled, and church leaders left Chicago imbued with enthusiasm and the determination to work together for harmonious race relations. The church was on the march.

* * * * *

On April 3, 1963, the Rev. Martin Luther King, Jr., president of the Southern Christian Leadership Conference (SCLC), and his fiery assistant, the Rev. Fred L. Shuttlesworth, pastor of the Revelation Baptist Church in Cincinnati and head of the Alabama Christian Movement for Human Rights, began mass demonstrations in Birmingham, Alabama. Hundreds of clergymen and laymen flew to Birmingham to walk shoulder to shoulder with the Negro leaders. "We believe the success of Martin Luther King in Birmingham was made partly possible by the Chicago conference in January," Father Cronin said. "This was the first time the Negro civil rights leaders, particularly the religious ones, felt that the position of the white power structure was one of support."

Birmingham police responded to the marches with high-pressure water hoses and snarling German Shepherd dogs. A temporary truce was called May 10. Negro leaders said they had been promised by city officials that public accommodations would be desegregated within ninety days, that Negroes would be offered better jobs, and that the Negro and white communities would work out some means of communicating. The truce lasted one day. Bombs were thrown at the home of Dr. King's brother, the Rev. A. D. King, and at the motel room where the SCLC leader himself was staying. President Kennedy instructed the Defense Department to alert military units for quick dispatch to Birmingham. Racial tensions slowly died down and the troops were never sent.

* * * * *

In June of 1963, the politically oriented National Council of Churches began mobilizing its vast resources for passage of a Civil Rights Act. The Council has over thirty member communions with a combined membership of more than 40 million. In a crash program the NCC General Board created a Commission on Religion and Race. A former NCC president and Stated Clerk of the United Presbyterians, Dr. Eugene Carson Blake, was named chairman of the commission. Dr. Robert Spike, a United Church of Christ avant-garde theologian and minister, was appointed executive secretary. They would soon become the two most influential Protestant leaders in the civil rights struggle. James Hamilton, an attorney and member of the NCC Washington staff, was assigned to work full-time on civil rights. Hamilton was slated to become one of the key liaison men for the church lobbyists.

By now the aggressive United Church of Christ began getting specific in its campaign against racial bigotry, calling upon its members "to urge your Senators and Representatives to support such legislation on a non-partisan basis in this session of Congress." The denomination also authorized its Council for Christian Social Action to present testimony in support of civil rights and asked members for the first time to support specific legislation in Congress. It further established the Committee on Racial Justice Now to guide the United Church program for racial justice and requested congregations to back the program with dollars from their collection plates.

The steady stream of pronouncements on civil rights from the churches, coupled with political action to seek passage of a specific bill in Congress, represented a radical departure from the traditional role of the clergy. The minister, in effect, albeit for a good cause, exchanged his role of pastor-preacher to ecclesiastical lobbyist. For better or worse, the church would never be the same.

In a nationwide television address on June 11, President Kennedy appealed for backing of the bill he would submit to Congress:

> We are confronted primarily with a moral issue. . . . The fires of frustration and discord are burning in every city, North or South, where legal remedies are not at hand. Redress is sought in the streets, in demonstrations, parades and protests which create tensions and threaten violence — and threaten lives.

Lives were more than threatened. The next day, a deranged sniper's bullet probably did more to get a comprehensive civil rights bill before Congress than all the marches and demonstrations. Medgar Evers, NAACP State Chairman in Mississippi, was shot down as he entered his home at Jackson. He had been leading a series of sit-ins and other demonstrations for the past two weeks in Jackson. The Civil Rights movement now had a martyr. It would not be denied.

President Kennedy began holding meetings with labor and religious leaders, with lawyers and with civil rights leaders. He drew up a broad bill covering voting rights, school desegregation, employment, the use of federal funds without discrimination and access to public accommodations — the latter often called the "symbolic heart" of the President's bill. (In 1963, the major demonstrations centered on the exclusion of Negroes from restaurants, theaters, lunch counters, amusement parks, hotels, and other public places.) The public accommodations provisions and the federal funds section were considered the titles which would be most difficult to get through Congress. Senator Dirksen made it known that he would support only a voluntary public accommodations provision. And without the support of the Republicans, the chances of getting the bill past Southern and border-state members were nil.

In a meeting in the White House with the backers of the Civil Rights Bill — including seven clergymen — President Kennedy made it clear that he was going to rely heavily on their support. The question arose as to which group would serve as the chief lobbying apparatus for the bill. At the suggestion of Roy

Wilkins, NAACP national executive secretary, the assignment was given to the Leadership Conference on Civil Rights. The Conference had been formed in 1949, with an initial membership of twenty organizations, as an umbrella agency for nongovernmental organizations interested in civil rights legislation. Arnold Aronson, secretary of the Conference, directed its permanent Washington office. Marvin Kaplan, loaned from the Industrial Unions Department of the AFL-CIO, served as associate director. And Violet Gunther, formerly of Americans for Democratic Action, was legislative consultant. The Leadership Conference was the logical vehicle to help push the bill through Congress, since it had gained experience by mobilizing support for the 1957 and 1960 civil rights laws.

Because of its size — now grown to over seventy-five participating groups — the Leadership Conference had to select a limited number from its own ranks to work with the Administration forces on the floors of the House and Senate. Veteran lobbyists Clarence Mitchell of the NAACP and Joseph Rauh, vice chairman of Americans for Democratic Action, were obvious choices. Both were battle-scarred fighters in the political arena. Andrew Biemiller, legislative director for the AFL-CIO, and Jack Conway, close associate of Walter Reuther of the United Auto Workers, were named to represent labor.

The church joined the ranks. James Hamilton, a husky 1956 graduate of George Washington Law School and a six-year veteran of the Washington staff, was drafted by the National Council of Churches to work full-time on the Civil Rights Bill. Hamilton teamed up with civil rights leader Mitchell, labor's Conway and Biemiller and Rauh of ADA to form the key group within the Leadership Conference.

President Kennedy assigned Deputy Attorney General Nicholas deB. Katzenbach and Burke Marshall, head of the Justice Department's Civil Rights Division, as Administration liaison men with lobbying groups and with Congress. U. S. Rep. William M. McCulloch of Ohio, ranking minority member of the Judiciary Committee, led the Republicans backing the bill. McCulloch kept in close contact with Minority Leader Charles A. Halleck of Indiana and in return received his general support, although Halleck hardly could be called a zealous civil rights man. He was seldom on the floor during debate, and he participated in only a few of the standing and teller votes.

The Leadership Conference set up its field headquarters in

the Mills Building at Seventeenth Street and Pennsylvania Avenue, a block from the White House, in preparation for battle
with the powerful foes of the Civil Rights Act.

The church quickly became visible in its support of the bill.
On his first visit to House Judiciary Subcommittee No. 5, which
held hearings from May 8 through August 2, Joe Rauh of ADA
describes this scene in the House corridor:

> Standing outside the Committee Room was the most beautiful
> sight I had ever seen — twenty Episcopal priests, fully garbed,
> all young beautiful WASPS. I used to think that the only two
> people out in front for civil rights were a Negro and a Jew —
> Mitchell and myself. But this was something the committee mem-
> bers had never seen before. I knew then we really were in business.
>
> Indeed, I had the feeling that as the committee members filed
> past the priests into the Committee Room that they were going
> through a cheering section the way a football team runs out on
> the field through a band formation. It was a thrilling sight and
> dramatic evidence of the church's activity.

The National Council of Churches developed a four-pronged
campaign to help push the bill through Congress — cooperating
with the Leadership Conference, forming alliances with individual denominations, bringing national religious leaders to
Washington to visit key legislators, and dispatching four-man
teams into the Midwest and Rocky Mountain regions where labor
and civil rights groups were ineffective and the churches strong.

The church lobbyists adopted a rigorous selection of targets.
It was generally agreed that it would be futile to try to persuade
Congressmen or Senators from the Deep South not to oppose the
bill. On the other hand, it would not be necessary to waste
energy on those Congressmen who were strong advocates of civil
rights and who had a long voting record supporting such legislation. The targets, then, were those Congressmen and Senators
who had ambiguous attitudes toward civil rights or who would
support the bill if they believed their constituents favored it. It
was the church's job to convince the Congress that the majority
of voters and party workers in their districts favored the bill.

*   *   *   *   *

The big, broad-shouldered man wearing a clerical collar
hunched forward as he began reading his testimony to members
of the House Judiciary Committee on July 24, 1963.

"Mr. Chairman and members of the Committee," he said,
looking up at Chairman Emanuel Celler, Democrat of New

York, "my name is Dr. Eugene C. Blake. Accompanying me are Rabbi Irving Blank and Father John Cronin.

"It is an unprecedented and indeed historic event that I speak for the social action, and racial action departments of the National Council of Churches, the National Catholic Welfare Conference and the Synagogue Council of America."

The role was not a new one for Dr. Blake, who more and more was calling the signals in the civil rights struggle as chairman of the National Council of Churches' Commission on Race and Religion. Dr. Blake told the committee that more than thirty Jewish, Catholic, and Protestant organizations joined in presenting the statement he was reading and gave the rationale for their involvement:

"The religious conscience of America condemns racism as blasphemy against God. It recognizes that the racial segregation and discrimination that flow from it are a denial of the worth which God has given to all persons. We hold that God is the Creator of all men. 'In the image of God created He them.' Consequently in every person there is an innate dignity which is the basis of human rights. These rights constitute a moral claim which must be honored both by all persons and the state. Denial of such rights is immoral."

After defining the moral principle on which the religious groups based their beliefs, Dr. Blake referred to the President's civil rights message of the preceding month: "The message clearly sets forth the need for legislation to guarantee the availability of voting rights; to assure equal accommodation in public facilities; to facilitate desegregation of schools; to achieve fair and full employment and to establish a community relations service. . . . As churches, synagogues and religious leaders, our concern is with the purpose of civil rights legislation and with the moral principles that indicate the necessity of enacting such legislation," Dr. Blake said. He then listed the specifics of the President's bill and cited the reasons the religious groups favored their enactment.

Dr. Blake closed his testimony with a warning:

"In spite of these principles, there have been times in history when men of good will were compelled to move slowly in securing rights and privileges. No such attenuating circumstances exist today. We are in the midst of a social revolution. *Please God it will remain a social revolution and not degenerate into civil chaos.* But let us not underestimate the demand for justice regardless of color, race or national origin. What is right, both in terms of basic morality and in terms of democratic ideals, must be granted without delay. The time is past for tokenism or demands for endless patience. We must move firmly, rapidly and courageously toward goals which our consciences assure us are right and necessary. We can do no less for God and country."

Dr. Blake's warning of civil chaos came to pass in the bloody race riots of Detroit, Newark, Cincinnati and Houston three years later.

The hot summer of 1963 was made even warmer for many Congressmen by the incessant activities of church officials pressuring for passage of the bill. Church leaders were determined to quicken the pace of Congress by lighting political fires under the feet of members. The demonstrations of the summer would climax in a gigantic, dramatic "March on Washington for Jobs and Freedom" on August 28. The demonstration provided a natural outlet for many churchmen frustrated by their personal inability to correct the injustices of society. The National Council of Churches summoned its member-communions to put feet to their faith, and the response was spectacular, with more than 200,000 persons marching. The theologically uninhibited Unitarian-Universalist Association was represented by 1,500 of its members — one tenth of the group's entire membership.

Once again one of the most enthusiastic and best organized churches supporting the March on Washington was the 2-million-member United Church of Christ. A case history of how this denomination set its machinery in motion indicates how deeply committed liberal churches were to racial justice in 1963. The United Church of Christ began its enthusiastic support of the March on Washington with a six-page letter sent to pastors, social action chairmen, executives, religious educators, and members of the Fellowship of the Committed. The letter described the march as a "massive, and democratic demonstration in the nation's capital . . . to provide evidence of the need for the Federal Government to take effective and immediate action to deal with the national crisis in civil rights." The letter suggested that those unable to march could at least write their Congressmen on behalf of strong civil rights legislation.

The church's Council for Christian Social Action, under the direction of Dr. Ray Gibbons, focused its efforts on twenty-three cities with more than 100,000 population in which there were member churches. This included cities from Boston in the Northeast to Greensboro, N. C., in the Southeast and as far west as Des Moines, Iowa. The Moderator of the New York Association sent a letter to all pastors in the association urging them to join the march, and Council staff members telephoned each pastor and church repeatedly.

On August 27, the Council for Christian Social Action held a midnight service at the Broadway Congregational Church in New York City. The sanctuary was filled with marchers and other worshippers, as television cameras peered from the balcony and newspapermen covering the service mingled with the audience. Following the service, the 400 volunteer marchers ate a sandwich lunch and then boarded eleven buses for Washington. Scores of placards and huge banners were fastened on the sides of the buses, and as the caravan pulled away from the church, it resembled more a group of excited college students bound for the Rose Bowl than churchgoers on their way to protest discrimination against American Negroes.

The buses arrived in Washington at 7 A.M. on the day of the march. Breakfast was served at the Lincoln Temple Church. The New York delegation was joined by hundreds of other volunteers from the churches in the Washington area and elsewhere. And after a hot breakfast, the marchers assembled in the sanctuary to hear one of their better-known members, Senator Hubert H. Humphrey, deliver an impassioned plea for civil rights. Later they were led in singing freedom songs. The emotional service had the marks of a revival meeting, with the saints ready to go marching through Washington proclaiming "Freedom Now." The groups from New York and Washington then boarded buses again to be driven to the Washington Monument, the starting point of the march. There they formed behind a huge banner of the United Church of Christ. Dr. Gibbons believes that at least 2,000 members of that church were among the more than 200,000 who marched for jobs and freedom that warm Sunday in Washington. Churches may have been slow in getting involved in the Civil Rights movements, but on that day it looked as if they intended to atone for their tardiness through sheer numbers.

Dr. Lewis I. Maddocks, Washington secretary for the Christian Social Action Council of the United Church, shares a suite of offices in the Methodist Building with the National Council of Churches. Following the March on Washington, Dr. Maddocks worked at a frantic pace setting up workshops, sending out literature, and answering telephone queries from members asking about up-to-the-minute information on the status of the civil rights legislation.

The church assigned a number of states to each Council staff member for "special cultivation." The staff members also lobbied other churches by urging the executives of the various state Council of Churches to stage a state-wide legislative workshop. The services of Dr. Maddocks were offered for the workshops. Five such workshops were arranged and conducted in August and September in various parts of the country.

Dr. Maddocks mailed information and suggestions for action to social action chairmen across the nation, and provided materials for distribution. The list of mailings sent from his Washington office provides a chronological report on the progress of the bill. Starting with mailings on September 5, 1963, to 300 local social action chairmen in the Midwest, urging them to contact the members of the House Judiciary Committee from their states, Dr. Maddocks made his last mailing on June 3, 1964, a week before the critical cloture vote was taken, urging 500 members in various states to ask their Senators to vote for cloture.

The church also sent letters to all members of the House of Representatives and to fifty-four members of the Senate whose position was in doubt or who were known to be opponents of the Civil Rights Bill, outlining the views of the United Church of Christ's General Synod and the Council for Christian Social Action. Another letter pledging support of civil rights legislation was sent to the forty-six Senators known to favor the bill. Church leaders do not even try to number the letters written by individual church members, or by the three thousand persons who pledged support of civil rights when they joined the Fellowship of the Committed. Never have so many written so much about so important an issue.

*   *   *   *   *

In the summer of 1963, a backlash of white resentment against Negro demands for equality whipped across the country. White House strategists depended heavily on the church lobby for a counterattack. Recognizing the decisive importance of the Midwest, the Council of Churches sponsored a thirteen-state, two-day strategy meeting in September at Lincoln, Nebraska. The Council's newly organized Commission on Religion and Race cooperated with state-wide councils to conduct seminars at Indianapolis, Columbus, Denver, and Evanston, Illinois. And in

Peoria, Illinois, religious and lay leaders met to plan further civil rights moves. Politically sensitive office holders testified to the impact of the churches. "There's still a strong undercurrent of opinion in my district that the Negroes have been pushing too hard, too fast," Democratic Rep. Roush of Indiana was quoted in the *Wall Street Journal,* September 17, 1963. "The Churches without doubt have been the strongest force working to mitigate this resentment."

The same article stated:

> The religious groups often carry more weight than might be expected. One church woman at the Ohio conference told of her efforts to influence GOP Rep. McCulloch of Ohio, a key member of the House Judiciary Committee which handles civil rights bills. The lady lobbyist happens to hold membership on a Republican county committee in Rep. McCulloch's district. So far the Congressman hasn't made clear just how strong a measure he will support.
>
> In Council Bluffs, Iowa, a Presbyterian minister is chairman of the Republican county committee; he thus wields considerable leverage over GOP Rep. Jensen of Iowa.

Violence and death rode in tandem through the South during the spring and summer of 1963. A white Baltimore postman, William L. Moore, was found dead of bullet wounds on a road in northeast Alabama on April 23. He had been walking from Tennessee to Mississippi to protest segregation there carrying a sign saying "Equal Rights for All-Mississippi or Bust." The walk was continued by the Congress of Racial Equality (CORE). Medgar Evers was shot to death June 12 by a sniper as he entered his Jackson, Miss., home. And on September 15 a bomb killed four Negro girls attending Sunday school in Birmingham, touching off street riots by angry Negroes and searing the consciences of decent citizens everywhere. Charles Morgan, Jr., a white thirty-three-year-old Birmingham attorney, went to his office in Birmingham's newest skyscraper and wrote these poignant thoughts on the bombing:

> Four little girls were killed in Birmingham Sunday. A mad, remorseful worried community asks Who did it? Who threw that bomb? Was it a Negro or white?
>
> The answer should be "We all did it." Every last one of us is condemned for the crime and the bombing before it and the ones last month, last year, a decade ago. We all did it.
>
> A short time later, white policemen killed a Negro and wounded

another. A few hours later two young men on a motor bike shoot and kill a Negro child. Fires break out and, in Montgomery, white youths assault Negroes.

And all across Alabama, an angry, guilty people cry out their mocking shouts of indignity and say they wonder, "Why?" "Who?" Everyone then "deplores" the "dastardly" act.

But you know the "who" of "who did it?" It is really rather simple. The "who" is every little individual who talks about the "niggers" and spreads the seeds of his hate to his neighbor and his son.

The jokester, the crude oaf whose racial jokes rock the party with laughter. The "who" is every Governor who ever shouted for lawlessness and became a law violator.

It is every Senator and every Representative who in the halls of Congress stands and with mock humility tells the world that things back home really aren't like they are.

It is courts that move ever so slowly and newspapers that timorously defend the law. It is all the Christians and all the ministers who spoke too late in anguished cries about violence.

It is the coward in each of us who clucks admonition. We are ten years of lawless preachments, ten years of criticism of law, of courts, of our fellowman, a decade of telling school children the opposite of what the civic books say.

* * * * *

The Protestant Episcopal Church was once defined as the Republican Party at prayer. Financier J. P. Morgan used to arrive at the church's annual conventions in a private railroad car. In many American cities, the "society" church has been the Episcopal church downtown. But this has not kept the church in the slum from blending in with its social landscape. Episcopalians early grasped the challenge of the inner city and began devising imaginative methods of ministering to the poor. As the poor in any city always include a large number of Negroes, it should have surprised no one when the Episcopal Church quickly moved to the front of the ranks in the civil rights struggle.

Meeting in Toronto, Ontario, in August of 1962, the House of Bishops adopted the following resolution:

> Resolved: That the House of Bishops of the Protestant Episcopal Church urges the Congress of the United States to pass such civil rights legislation as shall fairly and effectively implement both the established rights and the needs of all minority groups in

education, voting rights, housing employment opportunities and access to places of public accommodation.

The resolution was made part of the *Congressional Record* by Senator Keating of New York on August 14.

In the last week of October, fifty-three Episcopal clergymen and laymen from sixteen states met in Washington to promote what they had promulgated in Toronto. The mass lobbying effort was sponsored by the Adult Division of Christian Citizenship, Department of Christian Social Relations of the Episcopal National Council. The Rev. Arthur Walmsley, secretary of the division, reminded delegates at an orientation meeting that their main purpose was to call on as many Congressmen and Senators as possible to encourage them to pass a civil rights bill "at the earliest possible moment":

"From the standpoint of Christian conscience, it is scandalous that it is necessary to require legislation to give part of the people what all should have," he said. He then added what by now had become a familiar theme and the rationale for the religious lobbyists: "The race issue is fundamentally a moral and religious issue. Congress and the Administration are not taking the crisis in civil rights in the United States seriously enough."

Julian Dugas, representing the Department of Christian Social Relations in the Washington Episcopal diocese, sketched in for the delegates the current civil rights picture in the country, noting that there was a "real ferment" among the Negro community, especially among the younger generation. He emphasized that Negroes are merely seeking what they see others have, nothing more. Their main complaint, he said, is in the area of voting rights, public accommodation, and educational opportunities. Jim Hamilton, of the National Council of Churches' Washington office, outlined the provisions of the Civil Rights Bill and the various changes that were possible under the separate titles of the measure. Delegates then filed into the sanctuary of St. Mark's Episcopal Church to attend a communion service, followed by a breakfast and a greeting by Bishop William F. Creighton of Washington. Then the churchmen immediately moved out to make personal calls on Congressmen. "After a week in Washington," one Midwestern clergyman wrote later, "I felt that our quiet, unpublicized effort has done a lot in reaching many Congressmen and Senators."

But not all of the clergymen were so warmly received. One minister returned visibly shaken from his visit with a Pennsylvania Congressman. Armed with an analysis of the Civil Rights Act, the clergyman outlined to the member why he believed the Congressman should back the bill. The Congressman explained his position on the proposed legislation by grabbing the paper out of the stunned clergyman's hand, tearing it up, and throwing the pieces on the floor.

In the meantime, the "dream bill" that House Judiciary Sub-committee No. 5 reported to the full committee caused division in the ranks of its backers.

"I think we could have gotten the full bill through the com-mittee," Rauh says, "because there was pressure on our side and some of the Southerners felt the best way to kill it was to report a strong bill. And here there was a conflict of theory between the Leadership Conference and the Administration."

Katzenbach, representing the Administration's point of view, urged that the bill be watered down in the full committee. The Administration believed that a "dream" bill could never hurdle the Southern opposition it would inevitably encounter on the floor. Rauh argued that it was better to introduce the strongest bill possible and fight for it than to submit a weaker bill on the premise it would have broader backing. "There were some very bitter battles between Katzenbach and me on this theory," Rauh says, with a wry grin. Attorney General Robert Kennedy also asked for a milder bill in testimony before the full Judiciary Committee on October 15 and 16.

The differences in views were resolved in a compromise bill worked out by representatives of the Administration and Repub-lican leaders McCulloch and Halleck.

*   *   *   *   *

The terse bulletin out of Dallas at 12:41 P.M. on November 22, 1963, read: "President Kennedy and Gov. John B. Connally of Texas were cut down by assassin's bullets as they toured down-town Dallas in an open automobile today." A "flash" saying the President had been fired on had been sent out at 12:34 by Merri-man Smith, of United Press International, who alerted the Dallas UPI bureau over the radio telephone from the press car as it sped toward the hospital. And at 1:33 a White House press aide announced in a crowded nurses' classroom in Parkland Hospital that the President of the United States was dead.

A nation was plunged into mourning, but none felt the loss more keenly than those in the Leadership Conference who knew that civil rights had lost a champion. When Lyndon B. Johnson assumed office, his views on civil rights were unknown. But the saddened, soft-talking new President made it clear on November 27 that he would push as hard as his predecessor for sweeping civil rights legislation. While ranking behind President Kennedy in both eloquence and charm, President Johnson took second place to no one in political persuasion. "President Johnson got the bill moving," recalls ADA's Rauh. "You have to give him credit. The bill had been on dead center but President Johnson was determined to get it moving and he did."

In his first address to Congress following the assassination, President Johnson made it clear he considered civil rights a top priority item for Congressional action. "No memorial oration or eulogy could more eloquently honor President Kennedy's memory than the earliest possible passage of the civil rights bill for which he fought so long," he said.

*   *   *   *   *

Early in December, Father Cronin and the Rev. Robert Spike, from the Council of Churches, met with Burke Marshall, head of the Justice Department's Civil Rights Division. The church leaders wanted to know if the late President Kennedy and Republican Minority Leader Halleck had made any deals to weaken the bill once it reached the floor of the House. "We received private assurances from Burke that the strategy called for no major amendments to be made either by the Republicans or the Democrats on the House Floor," the priest said. "And here's where the religious groups differed with some of the civil rights groups in the Leadership Conference."

Father Cronin said that several civil rights leaders wanted to attempt to strengthen the bill on the House floor to keep the pressure on. But the church representatives of the Leadership Conference objected to trying to strengthen the bill on the floor through political maneuvers. "Those of us less sophisticated in lobbying thought that to make an all-out effort to fight for several amendments on the Floor and then to fail, for tactical reasons, probably would not have worked out too well with our own group," Father Cronin said. "We thought we should accept the bill as it came out of committee — which was a pretty strong bill."

Another split between the religious and civil rights groups developed on whether to push for a discharge petition to get the bill out of the House Rules Committee, headed by staunch segregationist Rep. Howard Smith of Virginia. "We were told Judge Smith was going to report the bill in January, so most of us decided not to go along with the Leadership Conference in the effort to get a petition to discharge the committee," Father Cronin said.

The Rules Committee released the bill January 30 under an open rule calling for ten hours of general debate after which the bill would be read, title by title. Each amendment would be voted on separately. The nine-day debate would begin the next day.

CHAPTER II

Stronger Than an Army

The Civil Rights Bill moved from the House Rules Committee to the House floor on January 31, 1964. The Leadership Conference, in order to keep a tight rope on the bill, transferred its field headquarters from the Mills Building to a first-floor office of the Congressional Hotel, within a block of the Capitol. The Conference, basically satisfied with the bill as reported by the Rules Committee, determined to keep pressure on the Congressmen who favored the bill and to block any damaging amendments proposed by its opponents. How this strategy was initially implemented is described in the *Congressional Quarterly* publication *Revolution in Civil Rights:*

> First it was decided to keep careful tabs on every Member who might reasonably be expected to back the bill. As the public galleries opened before each day's House session, in poured numerous representatives of the various Leadership Conference organizations which had come to Washington for the debate. Each one of these persons had a specific responsibility: to watch a certain number (four or five) of Congressmen, record their attendance and mark down their votes on all proposed amendments. Under this system, suggested by Clarence Mitchell of the NAACP, an effort was made to pair each "watcher" with Congressmen he knew personally, so that he could also call them off the Floor, to ask their support on important votes. Frequently, however, the gallery "spotters" had not previously met the Congressmen they were to cover.

> When a spotter in the gallery saw that one of the Congressmen he was to watch was off the Floor too long, a telephone call would be placed to the central headquarters of the Leadership Conference in the nearby Congressional Hotel. At the hotel, a master chart of office locations in both House office buildings was maintained. The civil rights groups had sought out a friendly Congressman on each Floor and arranged to have two representatives

21

stationed at a telephone in his office. Whenever a useful Member's absence on the Floor was reported, a call would go to the civil rights workers on his Floor. Immediately, a visit would be paid to the truant's office to urge him to be present in the House Chamber.

Persons associated with Negro civil rights groups, labor unions and church groups all participated in the buttonholing of Congressmen. When union agents contacted Members about their attendance or actual votes on the Floor they had a powerful weapon: the record of past or promise of future union help, both in money and manpower, in election campaigns. But union agents were steered clear of the offices of Republicans or Democrats they had opposed in past elections. In large measure the calling on Republicans was done by church representatives.

Leadership Conference lobbyists were briefed daily at the Congressional Hotel headquarters by Joe Rauh of ADA or the NAACP's Mitchell. The Big Four of the Conference — Rauh, Mitchell, churchman Hamilton, and labor's Biemiller — would meet with the House leadership to correlate the overall lobbying activities. Rep. Emmanuel Celler (D., New York), chairman of the Judiciary Committee, acted as the bill's floor manager for the Administration.

Robert Jones, the Washington secretary for the Unitarian Universalist Association, worked as both a gallery spotter and as a member of one of the two-men corridor patrol teams during the ten-day debate and voting on the bill. The peripatetic lobbyist describes his duties:

> The corridor patrol would make a call every hour or two on the offices of friendly Congressmen to make sure they were on the floor and voting.
>
> We didn't care whether those who opposed the bill were on the floor or not.
>
> There was some resentment to our tactics by some Congressmen. Others knew you were doing your job and didn't mind.
>
> When a Congressman was absent we would seek him out and ask: "Why aren't you on the floor? We need your vote. We lost on that last amendment."
>
> It's very hard in the House to know in advance if you have enough votes. Some of those teller votes were very close. You didn't know how they were going to go.

At one point during the voting, Jones called on Rep. Thomas T. (Tip) O'Neill, Jr., from the Eighth Congressional District in

Massachusetts, which includes Cambridge and the north end of Boston. Jones intended to chide the Congressman for having missed several important teller votes.

"I'm doing the best I can, Bob," the Congressman answered, "but right now I'm trying to save some giraffes for the Franklin Park Zoo."

"What in the hell are you talking about, Tip?" Jones asked.

The Congressman explained that a number of giraffes captured in Africa and bound for the city zoo had been quarantined off the coast because U. S. Immigration officials suspected that the animals had hoof and mouth disease. The authorities were threatening to throw the giraffes overboard. Understanding the Congressman's predicament, Jones stopped pressuring until Congressman O'Neill got the giraffes safely ashore.

The friendly lobbyist drew an outright rebuff from Rep. W. R. Poage of Texas, a fourth generation Unitarian who had never voted for civil rights. "I'm sorry," Poage said, "but I'm not going to vote with you." The right of a Unitarian to make up his own mind is a fundamental principle which no other Unitarian would dare violate.

The bill had its enemies off the floor as well as on. The Coordinating Committee for Fundamental American Freedoms, formed in 1963 for the singular purpose of blocking the passage of the bill, spent $133,000 between August, 1963 and December 31, 1963, according to the *Congressional Quarterly's* accounts. Most of the money was used for advertising and publicity opposing the bill. Advertisements were placed in newspapers in the Mountain, Midwestern, and upper New England conservative newspapers. The group assigned two staff men to Rules Committee hearings and kept observers to watch debate on the House floor.

Southern Democrats in the House failed to launch an all-out attack on the bill as expected. Rep. Edwin E. Willis, Democrat of Louisiana and ranking Southerner on the Judiciary Committee, and Rules Committee Chairman Howard D. Smith of Virginia, proposed numerous amendments to weaken the bill, but without success. The new Southern wing of the GOP provided the most effective opposition to the bill in floor debate. Representatives William C. Cramer of Florida and Richard H. Poff of Virginia offered restrictive amendments, a few of which passed.

*   *   *   *   *

On Monday, February 10, 1964, the Reverend J. C. Murphy

of the Community Methodist Episcopal Church in Arlington, Virginia, opened the session of the House with prayer. Four hundred and six members were present.

Democrat Celler and Republican McCulloch had held their coalition together, successfully beating back all major changes in the bill. Although 122 amendments applying to all the bill's titles had been proposed, only 28 were accepted and none of these was opposed by the bill's managers. Of the 94 amendments rejected, many had been submitted by Southerners wanting to wreck or at least weaken the measure. Congressman Thomas G. Abernethy, Democrat of Mississippi, reflecting the extreme viewpoint on the bill, proposed an amendment to create 500 new federal judgeships and authorize $100 million to build jails for the persons he was sure would be found guilty under the new law. The amendment was rejected 130-20 by a standing vote.

Congressman John Bell Williams of Mississippi was not going down to defeat without naming those he believed most responsible for what he considered a reprehensible bill.

"Mr. Chairman," Congressman Williams said, "we have witnessed a sorry spectacle in this chamber since last Monday when we began reading this bill for amendments. From one side, looking over your shoulders, are agents of the Justice Departments, who like shepherds are riding herd over their sheep.

"On the other side, peering from their perch, are the political parasites of our day. They are here to check off members individually as they walk through the tellers on various amendments. I have seen members summoned out of this chamber by these people and called on the carpet for having voted their honest convictions. Members have told me of these pressures being exerted, and the threats that have been thrown at them by these organized political racketeers. The degree of success attained by these pressure activities can be measured by the failure of nearly every amendment that has been opposed by the Judiciary Committee leadership." It was a dramatic tribute to the effective campaign of the church-labor-civil rights coalition.

Another Congressman, Arthur Winstead of Mississippi, took the floor to cast verbal stones at the churches:

"I say to you a great number of liberal church people have flooded Congressmen with letters urging passage of the Civil Rights Bill — probably more than the Negroes themselves — yet they are thinking only in terms of what they believe the Congress should do to right some wrongs which they consider have been placed upon the Negro race. In my opinion, few of them have any idea what this bill contains," he said.

But rhetoric would never stem the tide now beating against the word-dike thrown up by the Southern forces opposing the bill. The Administration, buoyed by its broad-based support, made its decisive move. The House approved the bill by more than a two-to-one majority, casting 290 yeas and 130 nays, with 11 members not voting. The most important piece of civil rights legislation in more than fifty years had cleared its first hurdle and the political battlefront now changed from the House Chamber to the floor of the U. S. Senate.

On February 26, the Senate voted by a roll-call vote 54-37 to place the civil rights bill passed by the House (HR 7152) directly on the Senate calendar. This in itself was a parliamentary victory for the supporters of the bill. Normally, the bill first would have gone to the Senate Judiciary Committee, which under the leadership of Senator James O. Eastland of Mississippi could have used delaying tactics in reporting the bill out on the floor. Senate leaders wanted the bill passed without any major changes, thus avoiding a House-Senate conference. House Republicans had warned that they would not support a watered-down version, and Negroes threatened to take to the streets again unless the bill passed practically intact. A southern filibuster, however, was a political certainty. The Administration hoped to smash or wear down the filibuster without making any major concessions, even though the Senate had never voted to stifle a filibuster.

Majority Whip Hubert H. Humphrey of Minnesota was named bill floor manager by President Johnson. The Southern States bloc turned to Senator Richard B. Russell of Georgia to lead its onslaught against the bill. But the Southern Democrats were not the only hurdle the Administration had to get over. Many Republicans in the Senate protested that the bill was too broad. Senator Dirksen, considered the key to choking off any filibuster, argued that the public accommodations provision of the bill should be voluntary.

The House bill contained language making it illegal for anyone to be discriminated against on grounds of race, color, religion, or national origin in places of public accommodations, such as restaurants, theaters, motels, or hotels. It further permitted anyone denied access to accommodations to sue in court and authorized the Attorney General to file the suit. Senator Dirksen and other reluctant Republicans wanted to omit the enforcement section and substitute a new one allowing the Attorney General to bring suit only where there was reasonable cause to believe that a person, or group of persons, was engaged in a pattern or practice of resistance — such as a group of restaurants practicing discrimination in an area. Republicans also expressed discontent with the Equal Employment Opportunities Title (VII) of the bill. This title would establish a five-member Equal Employment Opportunity Commission with powers to prevent and eliminate in employment any racial discrimination based on race, color, sex, religion, or national origin.

Without the help of the minority members, the Administration forces knew they could not control sixty-seven votes to invoke cloture and squelch the Southern talkathon. The problem was described in *Revolution in Civil Rights:*

> The traditional holdouts on cloture votes had been, in addition to an 18-member Southern bloc, a group of about 24 Northern, Western and border-state Democrats and Republicans, mainly from small states, and states with no civil rights problems. To end the filibuster, a sufficient number of these had to be won over to the cause of cloture — either through a new commitment to the cause of civil rights, or through displeasure at the length of the filibuster. The strategy involved was in two parts: to work inside the Senate through Dirksen, and on the outside through the church groups which joined the civil rights movement in full force for the first time in 1963 and who provided the only possible civil rights constituency for most of the uncommitted Senators.

Father Cronin was one of several religious leaders who visited Senator Dirksen in his office early in January.

"Obviously in January, Senator Dirksen was not going to promise us anything," Father Cronin recalled, "but he was signaling.

"We went out of there feeling we had a bill. He received us very cordially."

The Leadership Conference moved its field headquarters from the Congressional Hotel back again to the Mills Building near the White House. The move was made primarily for tactical reasons: It would be difficult and expensive to direct a four-months-long lobby from a hotel suite.

Joe Rauh of ADA gave the rationale for the Leadership Conference's strategy:

> In the Senate, it's easier to zero in than in the House. Deducting the Southern Senators and total reactionary Republicans that you know you could never change, that leaves you only seventy-five

men to work on. You only need two-thirds for cloture. We had fifty already on our side we didn't have to worry about. So we really were zeroing in on twenty-five people, and when you are giving twenty-five people the works — well, it's not too hard.

This is where the churches played the important part. And we had to rely primarily on the Protestants because the ones we were trying to reach were Wasps — white, Protestant, Anglo-Saxon Americans.

Everybody had bishops talking to them. It worked exceedingly well. It was the best lobbying operation I ever had the good fortune to work with.

* * * * *

Senator Humphrey and Republican Senator Thomas H. Kuchel of California, the Minority Whip, teamed up to keep the liberals from both parties in line. Every morning the Senate leadership met with its staff and with Justice Department representatives to decide on the day's strategy and pinpoint the parliamentary pitfalls. Rauh, Hamilton, Miller, and Mitchell of the Leadership Conference met with the Senate leaders as they had with the House leadership twice a week. Hamilton reported to the NCC Commission on Race and Religion, which disseminated the information to member churches.

Catholic leaders differed with the Protestants on lobbying tactics. The Catholics preferred to work through constituents exerting pressure on their Congressmen rather than through priests buttonholing individual Senators. Certain denominations were more aggressive and quicker to enter the political fray than the slower-moving Council of Churches. Again the United Church of Christ moved fast and early with its troops to do battle with the forces of prejudice and bigotry.

Like the Leadership Conference, the Council for Christian Social Action of the UCC selected the undecided members of the Senate as its targets. The Social Action department hoped to coordinate its action with the NCC in an extra effort at the same time the Senate began its debate on the Civil Rights Act. But the Council could not whip its forces into line until after Easter. The United Church of Christ, however, did go ahead with its "Witness in Washington" for March 16-18, one week after the Senate began its debate.

The planners of the Witness in Washington, unlike those who planned the March on Washington, stressed quality over quantity. Rather than attracting a large number of church members to

Washington, the plan was to bring together influential members from the eighteen states represented by the undecided Senators. Conference staff members and the social action chairman in each of the eighteen states selected one or two personal acquaintances of the Senators who were thought to have influence with the lawmakers. Here again, the church relied more on political power than moral suasion, or perhaps combined the two. Included among those who came to Washington were the chairman of a state Republican Party and a former moderator of the denomination who was a well-known judge in his state. Fifteen of the eighteen selected states responded by sending delegates to Washington.

The effort involved the entire church, from the Executive Council delegation led by President Ben Mohr Herbster, to staff members of the Council for Lay Life and Work, the Church and Ministry, the Stewardship Council, and the Board and Homeland Ministries. The Office of Communication staff showed up en masse. The United Church Board for World Ministries sent a delegation and staff member. In all, more than 100 persons came to Washington for the witness.

During the first afternoon, Dr. Ray Gibbons, director of the Council for Christian Social Action, explained to the assembly the purpose of the gathering. Dr. Lewis I. Maddocks, the Council's Washington secretary, and James Hamilton, conducted the briefing session. Congressman Clark MacGregor of Minnesota spoke at a dinner meeting in the First Congregational Church in Washington.

Fortified by the fellowship with those of like mind and filled in on the facts, the delegates the next day visited with their Senators. Some of the interviews with those Senators who indicated a favorable vote for the Civil Rights Bill were taped for use on radio and television. Releases also were obtained for hometown newspapers.

On their last day in Washington, the delegates met to share experiences, evaluate their interviews and make plans for follow-up action when they got home. A five-minute sound film made in the office of the church's best-known member, Senator Humphrey, was purchased by the church, and free copies were given to a delegate from each state for use on local television stations.

The church's Office of Communication, which handles all press, radio, and television coverage, alerted the Negro press to the

Washington Witness and reaped a rich reward of publicity in Negro newspapers and on radio stations. Dr. Herman F. Reissig, International Relations Secretary, drafted a special statement called "To the Limit of Law's Power," which said, in part:

> In the many-sided struggle to protect the human person in our country — Negro and white alike — we demand the aid of the legislation now before the Congress.
>
> We declare: Let law now be used to the limit of law's power. If stronger legislation than that before the Congress can be devised in support of elemental justice to our citizens, let the legislation be strengthened. Let us not dare to weaken it, giving the people a stone when they cry for bread.
>
> We declare that a solemn moral and patriotic obligation now rests upon every Senator and Congressman of the United States. Old social customs, property rights, Congressional rules are now confronted by clear requirements of human well-being.
>
> Let the word go forth — to all Americans and to all the world — that the Congress of the United States is able to do what justice requires.

In describing the effects of the Witness in Washington, Dr. Gibbons later declared:

> It focused the concern and conscience of the churches at the time and place where these could be most effective. It encouraged other denominations and the National Council of Churches to undertake similar representations. The reports of the delegates indicated the Senators were pleased to have them show such genuine interest, and the testimony of the delegates indicated they felt it had been well worth their time and effort to participate.

Dr. Gibbons indicated that the Washington Witness also passed the pragmatic test of lobbying:

> In view of the fact that the Witness was a form of lobbying, which some church members vigorously disapprove, it was interesting that no protests came to the attention of the Council.
>
> When there is approval of the purpose, there seems to be little objection to using the most effective and appropriate means, even though these [means] are labelled "lobbying."

On April 28, 1964, 6300 churchmen from across the country packed Georgetown University's McDonough Auditorium in Washington for the National Inter-Religious Convocation on Civil Rights. Protestant, Catholic, Jewish, and Eastern Orthodox leaders emphasized the moral issues involved in the civil rights struggle and urged prayer for the passage of the bill. The crowd was so large that it spilled over into an adjoining auditorium, connected with McDonough via closed-circuit television. "The dramatic quality of the meeting was hardly lost on this politically sensitive town," said Father Cronin.

Other signs of the church's commitment to the bill became visible the next day. Daily services sponsored by the Council of Churches' Commission on Race and Religion began at a Lutheran Church on Capitol Hill as a kind of spiritual sequel to the Senate filibuster. Theological students representing more than 100 seminaries — Protestant, Catholic, and Jewish — began an around-the-clock vigil for civil rights at the Lincoln Memorial. President Johnson told the religious leaders:

> It is your job — as men of God — to reawaken the conscience of America, to direct the immense power of religion in shaping the conduct and thoughts of men toward their brothers in a manner consistent with compassion and love.

The churchmen accepted the challenge and the final push for enactment of the Civil Rights Bill of 1964 began.

Within days after the bill passed the House, Attorney James Hamilton of the National Council of Churches hit the campaign trail again in the Great Plains State, while the Rev. Jay Moore, from the Commission on Religion and Race, visited the Mountain States region. They met with groups of twenty or fewer persons — including bank presidents, Red Feather agency leaders, and any other civic leader who knew a Congressman. A power executive in Sioux Falls, South Dakota, told Hamilton he had spoken with Sen. Karl E. Mundt the previous weekend and planned to visit him again in Washington. And a state council of churches leader in Nebraska reported he was keeping pressure on Sen. Roman L. Hruska and Sen. Carl T. Curtis. Clergymen and laymen were encouraged to return to their churches and recruit others in telephone and telegram appeals to their Congressmen, or better still to organize delegations to visit their Congressmen in Washington.

Even as Methodist Hamilton prospected for political gold, the General Conference of his church was holding its quadrennial conference in Pittsburgh's silver-domed Civic Arena. Civil rights was an important issue — but an embarrassing one. The presence of the church's all-Negro Central Jurisdiction made pious pronouncements grate on ears like sounding brass and tinkling cymbals. The church's parliamentary procedure for voluntary integration had resulted in only twenty-seven local Negro churches and no conferences transferring to integrated jurisdictions. Young ministers and theology students picketed the sessions, staging kneel-ins on the Civic Arena steps. In the statement adopted at the quadrennial conference, the delegates confessed with "deep penitence that our performance as a church has not kept pace with our profession." One of the resolutions declared:

> The fact that Methodist churches and churchmen have often failed to work for racial justice in the past does not relieve us from a present obligation to end racial injustice in society as well as in the church. The minimum requirements for justice in the social order include the recognition of equal rights and opportunities for all races in voting, law enforcement, education, employment, housing, public accommodations, and cultural advantages. We support the passage and enforcement of laws appropriate to every level of government for the establishment and maintenance of equal rights in each of these areas of our common life.

Delegates redeemed the hollow-sounding rhetoric of Pittsburgh by voting to abolish the segregated Central Jurisdiction before the Methodist merger with the Evangelical United Brethren in 1968. Their action resulted in large numbers of Negro churches transferring to integrated jurisdictions.

To harassed Congressmen in Washington in the summer of 1964, it must have appeared as if the clergymen of the entire nation had abandoned their pulpits to try their hand at lobbying for civil rights. Nothing could have been further from the truth. Many conservative clergymen refused to do battle for passage of the bill and some even preached against it.

The National Association of Evangelicals, which represents about 2.5 million church members, has long adopted resolutions at its annual conventions emphasizing a non-discriminatory policy in church membership. It avoided participation, however, in the Civil Rights Bill lobby. Floyd Robertson, assistant to the general director of NAE, explained the organization's shyness:

> We felt it was a sociological and political problem as far as government is concerned. A predominant part of our constituency questioned the wisdom of certain parts of the legislation. If we had gotten involved, it would have had a divisive effect on our constituency. So we stayed out.

The Catholics, preferring the indirect method to the direct, turned to its more than fifty-five Catholic interracial councils to build grass-roots support for the bill. "We had a Midwestern

Conference in Omaha, Nebraska, in May to plan strategy for that key state," Father Cronin said. Delegates from fifty dioceses attended. But in Washington, the Roman collar was conspicuously absent in the halls and committee rooms of Congress.

"When the question of cloture came up we did something never done before from our Washington office and probably will never be done again," Father Cronin said. "This was a direct effort to get the church leaders and laity involved in a technical Congressional vote — on cloture. We made calls to key people in communities asking that they telephone or telegraph their Senators to vote for cloture. And most of them did."

By early May, veteran lobbyist Joe Rauh was having some bad moments. "Some of our people wanted to go for cloture a little early," Rauh said. "They were overanxious. If anybody got a little leery and said, 'Don't you think we ought to file our petition for cloture?' we would really clamp down."

At this point all eyes were on Senator Dirksen, who seemed to be taking an inordinate amount of time going over the bill. By May 5, the Minority Leader had suggested over seventy proposed changes to the bill. The Senate leadership and the Justice Department, led by Attorney General Robert Kennedy, began negotiating on Dirksen's proposed amendments.

"Then our job," says Rauh, "was to push our troops in not giving him too much. I don't think they gave him too much. They gave him some we didn't want them to, but on the whole I don't think it was too much." Rep. William M. McCulloch, ranking Republican on the Judiciary Committee, had warned that if the Senate returned a weak bill, he would not support it. Only a few of the Dirksen amendments actually affected the bill as it passed the House. Dirksen, Democratic leaders, and the Justice Department eventually worked out compromises to satisfy everyone. "Dirksen kept saying he re-wrote the bill," Rauh says. "He was a magnificent showman on that. He didn't rewrite the bill at all."

In fact, in an analysis of the bill, the *Congressional Quarterly* states:

> The Mansfield-Dirksen substitute for HR 7152 as passed by the House made numerous changes in House language but only a few substantive revisions.

> The major changes were in the enforcement of Titles II and VI, covering public accommodations and fair employment practices.

Introducing what he termed a "clean bill" Senator Dirksen

said: "We have now reached the point where there must be action; and I trust there will be action. I believe this is a salable piece of work; one that is infinitely better than what came to us from the House. . . . I doubt very much whether in my whole legislative lifetime any measure has received so much meticulous attention."

The cloture petition, signed by twenty-eight Democrats and eleven Republicans, was filed by Senators Dirksen and Mansfield on June 8. Under the rules, the vote on cloture had to be taken one hour after the Senate met two days later.

President Johnson at a press conference June 2 had assured the nation that he was not exerting any pressure to make the Southerners stop talking. "It is a matter for the Senate leadership and not for me," he assured the skeptical reporters.

*   *   *   *   *

Senator Carl Hayden shuffled slowly down the Senate aisle to cast a "nay" vote, keeping intact his record of never having voted in favor of cloture. History, however, had already been made in the U. S. Senate. For seventy-one Senators whose names had already been called had responded with "yeas." By a vote of 71-29, the Senate broke its long-standing record and voted for the first time to cut off a Southern filibuster on civil rights. It was the 75th day on civil rights in general and the 58th on the bill itself. The gallery was packed and silent, although the church lobbyists in the gallery felt like shouting a lusty "hallelujah!" It was a moment of sweet victory and they knew they might never pass that way again — so triumphantly. Of the twenty-six Senators lobbied by the clerical activists, all but four voted for cloture. Even more amazing, eleven of the twenty-six registered the first pro-cloture vote in their careers on a civil rights filibuster. It was a clear-cut victory for the coalition of conscience and power.

On the Senate floor, the mood was different. The Senators, even those who voted against cloture, seemed temporarily confused and perhaps overawed by their history-making action. The speech-making stopped. Silence settled over the floor, and the excited whispering in the gallery ceased.

At 5:15 P.M., Senator John McClellan of Arkansas said "Let's go home" so audibly that it could be heard in the gallery. The weary Senator's suggestion served as the official signal that the Southern bloc's hopes of defeating the Civil Rights Bill were gone with the wind.

Joe Rauh believes that the timing on the filing of the cloture petition was a political bull's-eye. "If we had gone for cloture one month after the filibuster we would have gotten beat," he says. "It took infinite patience and time. When Dirksen came through and said the bill was satisfactory, then we had it."

Senator Humphrey praised the work of the religious leaders in a speech on the Senate floor.

"One of the most refreshing developments in recent years has been the courageous and outspoken position of the religious leaders and laymen of this nation on behalf of racial justice," Senator Humphrey declared. "Their support of the Civil Rights Bill has been acknowledged by both friend and foe of this legislation."

On June 15th the 176th General Assembly of the United Presbyterian Church, U. S. A., met in Oklahoma City. The civil rights issue dominated the meeting — even threatening to result in the censure of Dr. Eugene Carson Blake, the church's highest administrative official. A group from the Presbytery of West Tennessee presented a motion asking that Dr. Blake be censured for some of his aggressive actions in the civil rights struggle. The motion, however, was tabled and the General Assembly voted instead to commend Dr. Blake for his contributions to the cause of civil rights and social justice.

An estimated 800 persons attended the breakfast sponsored by the Presbyterian Interracial Council on the first day of the assembly. The delegates were assured of verbal fireworks. Dr. Blake was to be given an award, along with Negro comedian Dick Gregory, for his civil rights activities. The main breakfast speaker was the Reverend John Lewis, a twenty-four-year-old national chairman of the Student Non-violent Coordinating Committee (SNCC).

In accepting his award (Gregory didn't attend), Dr. Blake began his speech in words to be widely quoted later.

"Fellow jailbirds," he said, "the more I think about the wide publicity I received as a result of my participation in the Baltimore demonstration last year, the more troubled I become about the church of Jesus Christ. It is tragic that the secular press finds so much news when a Christian does what he says."

The Reverend Mr. Lewis, a fiery Baptist orator, had the Council members on their feet cheering at the close of his spirited address.

"Those of us in the Christian Church should be happy, feel

happy, to be called agitators," he stated. "Agitation is a device that is used in washing machines to clean clothes. We are engaged in agitation to cleanse and purify society. This is healthy agitation and costly. Over 5,000 of us have been arrested, mistreated, beaten, illegally jailed, assigned exorbitant bonds.

"But we have a divine mandate to destroy such a false order and to upset such an unreal peace. We must turn this nation upside down in order to set it right side up. It is long past time when all of us must become involved."

The crowd loved it and stood to its feet to cheer. It's a good feeling to know you are obeying divine mandates.

*   *   *   *   *

The U. S. Senate convened at 11:00 A.M. Friday, June 19, 1964. to vote on the passage of the Civil Rights Bill. Much of the excitement surrounding the bill up to this point had subsided. After the chaplain, the Rev. Frederick Brown Harris, gave the invocation, Senator Karl Mundt, Republican of South Dakota, introduced a bill to amend the Communications Act of 1934 in order to prohibit certain broadcasts until after the closing time of polling places in all of the states. Two editorials were inserted into the *Congressional Record,* one from the *Nashville Tennessean,* lauding President Johnson's folksiness and one from the *Louisville Courier Journal,* describing Ladybird's "triumphal tour of Eastern Kentucky." Senator George McGovern, Democrat of South Dakota, reminded the Senate that it was exactly one year ago to the day, June 19, 1963, that the late President Kennedy sent his message to Congress calling for the passage of a comprehensive civil rights law. "One year later that law, which will stand along with the test ban treaty as the greatest achievement of our late President, is about to become the law of the land," he said. President Kennedy had told Congress in June of 1963: "Justice requires us to insure the blessing of liberty for all Americans and their posterity — not merely for reasons of economic efficiency, world diplomacy and domestic tranquility — but above all, because it is right."

The morning business concluded with Senator Thomas J. Dodd, Democrat of Connecticut,.reminding the Senators that the week marked the 100th anniversary of the signing of the order by Secretary of War Stanton permitting the burial of Union soldiers at Arlington National Cemetery.

The final maneuvering on the Civil Rights Act of 1964 began

with a motion by Senator Albert Gore, Democrat of Tennessee, asking that the bill be referred to the Senate Judiciary Committee. Senator Gore wanted an amendment providing financial assistance to public education and to the school lunch programs in school districts not in defiance of a court desegregation order. The motion was defeated 25-74.

Senator Russell B. Long, Democrat of Louisiana, then stood up to deliver a homily on race relations.

"Mr. President," he began with a slight smile on his face, "throughout this debate it has been rather amusing to me to have people suggest that they know more about the race problem in Louisiana than I do.

"When I was a very young boy, I was carried around by a colored woman, who was a servant in our home. She was everything a woman could be in short of actually being the wife in the home and she would carry me in her left arm as she did the housework. My right arm would be around her neck, and my left arm therefore was free. As a result I reached for things with my left arm, and my family always suspected that to be the reason why I am lefthanded today.

"If in those days, perhaps when I was two years old," the Senator continued, "if I had been told that that colored woman was my mother, I would probably have believed it. There have been good colored people in my home from that day to this. I believe I know something about the colored people and about the race problem in my State."

Senator John O. Pastore, Democrat of Rhode Island, gained permission to respond to Senator Long.

"First, Mr. President," he said, "let us remember that we shall be passing this bill today to allow the Negro woman who carried our good friend, the Senator from Louisiana, in her right arm, if ever she is thirsty, to go to a soda fountain in a drug store and get a glass of water, in the way any white person can. That is why we are passing this bill, and fundamentally that is the moral thing we should do."

In speaking in behalf of the bill, Senator Paul Douglas, Democrat of Illinois, was asked a friendly question by Senator McNamara of Michigan. "The churches of this time have gotten solidly behind the civil rights bill which is now pending before the Senate," the Michigan Senator said. "Does the Senator [Douglas] not have faith that the impetus of the religious organizations that are united as a whole will carry over after the legislation has passed and helped to accomplish the very thing that the Senator is now setting out?"

The Senator from Illinois thanked the Senator from Michigan for his question, and replied:

"I believe that the active participation of the church people, which is really a new venture, and the decisive venture in the civil rights struggle, will be of tremendous aid in the years ahead, provided they do not go to sleep, as they did after 1877." Earlier, Senator Douglas had said that beginning around 1877, the provisions of the 14th and 15th Amendments to the Constitution were disregarded throughout wide sections of the country, particularly in the slave-holding Southern states. The North, losing its early enthusiasm for Negro freedom, acquiesced to the South.

"I take great heart in the fact," Senator Douglas continued, "that there is a strong body of opinion in the South which does not agree with the Southern policy of segregation. I was greatly heartened some weeks ago when 335 Presbyterian ministers and laymen from the South presented a petition to some of us asking that the Civil Rights Bill be passed. I conclude that there is an inarticulate but real body of opinion in the South that wants to shake off the evil practice of second-class citizenship and come out in the broad sunlight of human equality, respect and dignity."

But one Southern Presbyterian, Senator Richard B. Russell of Georgia, disagreed with Senator Douglas's interpretation of the churchmen-turned politicians. "There were many ministers who, having failed completely in their effort to establish good will and brotherhood from the pulpit, turned from the pulpit to the powers of the Federal government to coerce the people into accepting their views under threat of dire punishment," the Senator insisted.

Senator John G. Tower, Republican of Texas, expressed both apprehension about the bill and regret over the treatment of Negroes. "As a native Southerner," he said, "I am deeply ashamed of the way that we have treated our Negro citizens in the South. I cannot justify that. . . . We have held them down. . . . [But] we cannot overturn the mores of a whole society overnight, and that is what we are trying to do in this punitive bill."

Ironically, Malcolm X, the Black Muslim leader, used the same words to describe the bill that Republican presidential nominee Barry Goldwater made his theme in the 1964 campaign. "You can't legislate good will," Malcolm said. "The passage of this bill will do nothing but build up the Negro for a big let-down by promising that which cannot be delivered."

Once again the spotlight found Senator Dirksen stage center as the final vote was taken. Taking his theme from the then popular television show "This Was the Week That Was," Senator Dirksen concluded his speech favoring passage in these words:

> But standing on the pinnacle of this night, looking back, looking around, looking forward, as an anniversary occasion requires, "This is the Year That Was" and it will be so recorded by the bone pickers who somehow put together all the items that portray man's journey through time that is history. I am prepared for the vote.

The Senate passed the Civil Rights Act of 1964 on a roll call vote of 73-27, having spent almost four months debating and voting on the bill. Six Republicans joined twenty-one Southern and border-state Democrats in opposing the bill.

Jubilant church leaders gathered in front of the Methodist Building across from the Capitol in a tri-faith thanksgiving service. At the meeting, representatives of the National Council of Churches, the National Catholic Welfare Conference, the Union of American Hebrew Congregations, and the Interfaith Theological Students Vigil for Civil Rights ended a sixty-three-day vigil in behalf of the bill.

It was a hot day in Washington. Unitarian Bob Jones still recalls that Dean Francis Sayre, of the Episcopal Washington Cathedral, was wearing a white suit wet with perspiration. But despite the heat it was a time of praise, joy and good will. As the group later filed through the line to the small, basement cafeteria for non-alcoholic refreshments in the house that temperance built, Father Cronin called out to Methodist minister Jay Moore: "The way ecumenism is progressing, maybe in another five years we can have cocktails in the Methodist Building."

The bill, because of certain amendments, had to go back to the House for final action. Once again Rules Committee Chairman Smith employed a variety of delaying tactics to keep the bill off the floor. President Johnson wanted the bill on his desk before July 4th. The House passed the bill July 2 on a 289-126 roll call vote to approve the bill as amended by the Senate. Six Congressmen changed their minds between February and July. Three who had voted for the bill in February voted against it in July, and three who disapproved of it in February cast votes of approval in July.

Seated before Ladybird and a crowd of legislators and lobby-ists, President Johnson signed the bill into law at 6:45 P.M., in a ceremony televised from the East Room of the White House.

"We believe all men have certain inalienable rights," the President said, "yet many Americans do not enjoy those rights. We believe all men are entitled to the blessings of liberty. Yet millions are being deprived of those blessings — not because of their own failures, but because of the color of their skin.

"The reasons are deeply imbedded in history and tradition and the nature of man. We can understand — without rancor or hatred — how this happened, but it cannot continue.

"Our Constitution, the foundation of our republic, forbids it. The principles of our freedom forbid it. Morality forbids it. And the law I will sign tonight forbids it.

"Let us close the springs of racial poison," he concluded, picking up the first of many pens he would use to sign the historic document. Two persons given these pens were James Hamilton, attorney-lobbyist for the National Council of Churches, and Father Cronin.

*   *   *   *   *

Title I of the 1964 Civil Rights Act bolstered the voting rights provisions of the 1957 and 1960 Acts by making voting registration requirements the same for everyone. The unequal application of requirements had been a device used by Southern registrars to disenfranchise Negro registrants. Title I also authorized the Attorney General to file suits in areas where he had evidence that a pattern of discrimination existed. A three-judge federal court was required to hear the allegations. But local governments still managed to register Negroes at a snail's pace, resulting eventually in voting rights demonstrations in Selma, Alabama, in 1965.

Already in November of 1964, a group of religious leaders and White House staff men had met secretly at Airlie House in Warrenton, Virginia, to discuss how to make the new Civil Rights Bill more effective. Religious leaders wanted to press for a voting rights act. Lee White of the White House staff cautioned the clergymen against pushing for more legislation, arguing that Congress had passed all the civil rights legislation it could digest for a couple of years. The religious leaders were, however, insistent in their demand for a bill. "We made it clear to White that we were going to move ahead," Father Cronin recalls. "It turned out we got one."

On March 17, 1965, President Johnson submitted a comprehensive voting rights bill to Congress "to strike down restrictions to voting in all elections — Federal, state, and local — which have been used to deny Negroes the right to vote." The bill provided for the appointment of federal voting examiners to register persons in any state requiring a literacy test and in which less than 50 percent of the eligible persons voted in the 1964 presidential elections.

Tri-faith testimony was given once again on the Voting Rights Act of 1965. The churches did not, however, become nearly as intensively involved in lobbying as they did for the 1964 Civil Rights Act. "This was largely because we didn't think it was needed," Father Cronin remarked.

Once again the United Church of Christ led the way in follow-through on the 1964 Act. On September 1, 1964, Dr. Ray Gibbons' Council for Christian Social Action proposed a three-pronged program.

The first step called for testing the law in courts and for assuring local and state enforcement. Secondly, the program called for the support of those Congressmen and Senators who voted for the legislation. "The time when Senators will most appreciate such support will be in the fall elections and at such other times as they are running for office," Dr. Gibbons suggested, indicating he thought the church should remain politically active.

Thirdly, the program placed a large share of the responsibility of making the law work squarely on the shoulders of the local churches. "Churches can encourage firms with which they do business to conform to the spirit as well as to the letter of the fair employment section by undertaking vigorous programs of recruitment, training and upgrading of non-white personnel," Dr. Gibbons said. It was one of the first indications that the church later would try wielding its considerable economic power along with whatever political pressure it could apply to bring about social change.

*   *   *   *   *

By the spring of 1967, enthusiasm for civil rights among the church lobbyists began to wane.

"I would say there has been a decline in interreligious cooperation in civil rights for reasons I can't fully pinpoint," Father

Cronin stated in his Washington office. "For example, in 1966 we had a joint interreligious conference with the National Association of Real Estate Dealers. We were hoping to bring out a program between clergy and the real estate people on a local level primarily for voluntary housing.

"Our bishop was going to sign up but the program was scuttled definitely at the Protestant-Jewish ends." He doesn't know why.

Attorney Hamilton, who now heads the National Council of Churches Washington office, agreed that there was a "let-up" in civil rights by religious leaders. "In 1963, the Council set up the Commission on Race and Religion as a crash program to help pass the Civil Rights Act," he says. "We had been passing resolutions long enough. We had to put our money where our mouth was and put ourselves on the map. And we did.

"But in the past year to 18 months (1966 to 1967), it has become more and more apparent to me that we have not as a nation really even begun to write into life what we had written into law. We are not compelling compliances with statutes already on the books, and perhaps this is the larger job we should turn our attention to even though it is not as dramatic as demonstrations." Hamilton at the time was chairman of the Committee on Compliance and Enforcement of the Leadership Conference on Civil Rights.

"I feel that rather than marching up the Hill for a new law every time Congress comes back to town, we ought to give more attention to the enforcement of what we already had fought for," he said.

"Yes, I would say there has been a shift in emphasis on the part of the churches."

Dr. Truman B. Douglass, of the United Church of Christ, declared in March of 1968 that American churches retreated from their initial commitment to civil rights. "We were intimidated by threats of a 'white backlash' which never really developed," the blunt churchman said. "The task of changing attitudes that were more rigid and recalcitrant than the law — a task in which the churches presumably have some competence — we shirked." Dr. Douglass called the churches' failure to follow through a tragedy, pointing out that the local congregation is uniquely fitted to make principles of equal opportunity and human brotherhood a reality. Dr. Douglass may have pinpointed the real cause why the promises of 1964 were not fulfilled by

1968: In his rush to get to Washington, the clerical activist failed to do his homework in the pulpit.

Commenting on an Emergency Conference on the Unitarian Universalist Response to the Black Rebellion, Unitarian Jones made the following statement:

> The lobbying in Washington, the official sponsorship and mass turn-out for the Selma-Montgomery March, the efforts of the Commission on Religion and Race and the Department of Social Responsibility, the work of social action committees in churches — all these efforts have not met the challenge.
>
> Perhaps in our pell-mell rush for results in social action, we have overlooked the simple personal reaching out to each other as human beings. The Black Caucus was plainly telling us that we failed.

In June of 1963 President Kennedy appealed to Americans to "move this problem [of racial injustice] from the streets to the courts and from the courts to the conscience." No other institution was as well equipped for that role as was the church, as Dr. Douglass points out. Ministers, priests, and rabbis are generally regarded as the rightful custodians and interpreters of our deepest spiritual and moral values. Few political issues arose in the Sixties which as clearly involved a moral decision as did the Civil Rights Act of 1964. The pivotal part played by the religious lobbyists in the passage of the bill catapulted the churchmen into the rarefied atmosphere of power politics. It was a heady experience.

The successful political role played by the church activists in the passage of the Civil Rights Act of 1964 was made possible by the mood of the populace at the time. The country's conscience had been pricked. Most Americans really do believe in fair play. They were aghast at the news photos of snarling dogs and electric cattle prods being used on civil rights demonstrators. No thinking, fair-minded person would deny that the Negro had been denied his Constitutional privileges even though some Americans would add — "They're trying to move too fast."

At that point in time, the church lobbyist was, then, in a real sense reflecting the will of the majority of Americans. The clergymen did have the moral weight of the country behind them. Combining prevailing public opinion with his political expertise, the church lobbyist was able to forge this righteous indignation into a political weapon to influence legislators and win votes.

Church lobbyists have not found an issue since, however, that presents such a clear-cut choice of right and wrong. The clerical activists have not permitted moral ambiguity, however, to diminish their fervor. They often move from the position of exerting moral pressure to practicing partisan politics without bothering to make a distinction between the two.

The ecumenical politicians' next major battle was to be fought on a Southern front of the War on Poverty. In the fall of 1966, activists from the same three groups — church, labor, and civil rights — moved into the midst of a controversy swirling around a Head Start program known as the Child Development Group of Mississippi.

A few of the more cautious church lobbyists steered clear of the CDGM controversy. The moral issue was not nearly so clearly drawn as it had been in fighting for passage of the 1964 Civil Rights Act. There were hints of Black Power infiltration, of a political struggle between the regular Democratic Party and the Mississippi Freedom Democratic Party, and even the Office of Economic Opportunity couldn't seem to make up its mind whether to support the Mississippi Head Start program.

Militant church lobbyists refused to be bogged down in moral ambiguities. They were convinced that once again they were in hand-to-hand combat with the forces of evil, and they would give no quarter.

An editorial in the liberal *Christianity and Crisis* magazine (January, 1967) called the clergyman's role in the CDGM confrontation "the second major victory of the 'church lobby' not unlike its success in the passage of the 1964 Civil Rights Act. Although the refunding of CDGM seems a much more modest victory," the article continued, "it may prove in the long run almost as important."

The next two chapters will be a behind-the-lines account of the "second major victory."

CHAPTER III

The Churches War on Shriver

The United States Government declared war on poverty in November of 1964 with the passage of the Economic Opportunity Act. President Johnson named Sargent Shriver, former head of the Peace Corps, to lead the crusade as director of the Office of Economic Opportunity (OEO). The Act states its purpose as "not only to relieve the symptoms of poverty but to cure it; and above all, to prevent it." The scourge of poverty was to be battled in the mountains of Appalachia, in the slums of Harlem, and in the cottonfields of Mississippi. Some wars demand unconditional surrender. Shriver had his marching orders. He would either slay poverty or return slain on his own shield.

A key operating principle of the War on Poverty, couched of course in bureaucratic terms, was that of the "maximum feasible participation of the poor." Simply stated, it meant involving the poor in the administration of their own self-help program. The OEO's front ranks were filled with a platoon of publicists who proudly hailed every skirmish. The emphasis on propaganda drew a salvo of satirical fire from Erwin Kroll and Jules Witcover, who in the Fall, 1966 edition of the *Columbia Journalism Review* wrote an article entitled "Maximum Feasible Publicity." The article stated in part:

> Folklore-building needs professional assistance in modern America, and OEO provides it through its public affairs office. Kramer [Herbert J. Kramer, public affairs director], former vice president in charge of public relations and advertising for Travelers Insurance Company, has brought some fascinating innovations to the long-practiced art of Washington press agentry. His staff of forty-six, supported by a massive Xerox copying machine with a firepower of 2,400 handouts an hour, trumpets the smallest victory in the poverty trenches, conducts seminars for the press, and in general works hard and long to accentuate the positive about

44

Shriver and all phases of his war. Ten telephone lines serve the press during office hours, and Kramer is available around the clock.

Before firing the first shot, Shriver found a firm and fast ally in the nation's churches. The alliance was so strong that it led Shriver to boast in San Francisco in December, 1965, that the OEO had scored a breakthrough in church-state cooperation. "Three or four years ago it was practically impossible for a federal agency to give a direct grant to a religious group," he declared. "Today we have given hundreds without violating the principle of separation of church and state." While there were many who would question the accuracy of the latter part of the statement, no one could gainsay the former. The OEO in the late 1960's funneled an estimated $90,000,000 annually through the churches for community action programs. In the enthusiasm for alleviating human suffering, the churches charitably overlooked any stretching of the separation principle.

If the churches needed a reason for their involvement in OEO projects, they didn't have to wait long. In an article in the December 14, 1965, issue of the *Christian Century*, a liberal Protestant magazine, Shriver spelled out "The Moral Basis of the War on Poverty":

> Both church and state — separate legs supporting one body of effort — are engaged in the economic, political, and moral struggle that we have labeled the War on Poverty. Only a few years ago we all believed that because church and state were separate, they had to be mutually exclusive, that the money of government could not be mixed with the currency of salvation. The War on Poverty has taught us new lessons.

It was to teach Shriver one he had not anticipated nor would soon forget.

The OEO with its billions in anti-poverty gold and the churches with their physical plants and trained personnel, paired off to eradicate the plague of poverty. Church halls, schools, rectories, and settlement houses were converted into manned outposts determined to drive deprivation from the land. But the trumpeting by OEO officials that they were going to help the poor help themselves sounded like a bugle call of warning to certain conservative Congressmen. Persons handling money, even anti-poverty money, automatically accrue political power from allocating funds and hiring personnel to implement the programs. An administrative aide of one Republican senator flatly asserted: "OEO was based on the principle of using federal funds to subvert local political organizations. The Congress caught onto that idea real fast." Entrenched office-holders do not like being threatened by money-wielding autonomous organizations in their own Congressional districts. Thus history may record that OEO had its own built-in, self-defeating system.

OEO-sponsored programs would penetrate into the most remote rural areas of this country, but the names given the federally financed projects were off Madison Avenue. Thus such bouncy titles as Upward Bound and Head Start became a part of the nation's folklore.

The churches responded warmly to Shriver's challenge to eradicate the social cancer of poverty. Someone had to alert the numerous parishes and congregations, however, to the opportunities made available to them through the largess of the Federal government. The Roman Catholic hierarchy turned the assignment over to Thomas Hinton, executive director of the National Catholic Community Service. Hinton is the prototype of the professional without whom the church could not effectively operate in our complex, bureaucratic society.

"After OEO said churches could participate in the War on Poverty, each bishop was asked to appoint local committees to mobilize resources on the local level," Hinton explained in his office in the U. S. Catholic Conference. Hinton maintains unclogged channels of communication with the OEO staff. He made it clear that his relationship with Shriver's poverty warriors permitted him to pick up the telephone or send out a letter to OEO with full confidence he would get a hearing. He said that by 1967, 90 of the 144 Catholic dioceses in the country were participating in OEO community programs with a total of 238,702 persons enrolled in the programs being carried on in 23,029 church buildings, or units, and utilizing 13,799 volunteers — clergy, laity, and nuns.

Hinton prepared a thirty-page booklet called "The War on Poverty" handbook, outlining step by step how churches can qualify for federal funds to operate anti-poverty programs. Appealing to the conscience of his readers, he wrote:

> Anyone who loves his brother can — indeed, must, if he really loves him — contribute to this effort to wipe out deprivation and dependency. New and far-reaching opportunities are available through this legislation. What is required is the willingness, initiative and determination to be concerned about one's neighbor.

Hinton explained the plethora of programs and how parishes could participate. Under Title II of the Community Action Program, he noted, the suggested programs are "in the fields of employment, job training and counseling, health, vocational rehabilitation, housing, home management, welfare, and special remedial and other non-curricular educational assistance. Communities are urged to give special attention to educational problems." The message got through.

Although deeply committed to the principle behind the War on Poverty and joyously serving as the instrument to implement the projects, the churches kept one hand free to chastise the person directing the overall program. Sargent Shriver would soon discover that men of the cloth know how to apply political pressure as well as fight poverty.

The cause célèbre of the church lobbyists was the Child Development Group of Mississippi (CDGM). This ambitious preschool program, designed to prepare underprivileged children to enter school at the same cultural level as their more affluent peers, was not carried out in a church parish but instead extended across twenty-eight counties in the Black Belt of Mississippi. It was given its impetus by a cadre of civil rights workers and clerical activists who believed that Mississippi society needed changing from the grass roots up. They were confident that the change would never occur at the top.

CDGM held an especially warm spot in the hearts of ecumenical churchmen. The staff of the Delta Ministry, an agency of the National Council of Churches of Christ in the U. S. A., organized in Mississippi in response to the civil rights struggle, provided much of the early leadership for CDGM. Mary Holmes Junior College in West Point, Mississippi, served as the conduit (grantee) through which federal funds for CDGM were channeled. The college, operated by the Board of National Missions of the United Presbyterian Church in the U. S. A., with headquarters in New York City, acted as sponsor to bypass a sure-fire veto of the program by Mississippi Governor Paul Johnson. Shriver wisely had persuaded Congress to include in its enabling act the provision that OEO grants to educational institutions would not be subject to the governor's approval.

To understand why the churchmen went the last mile in securing grants for CDGM against bitter political opposition, with Shriver caught in the cross-fire, one must go back to 1963 when Northern churches undertook to change the social structures of Mississippi southern society.

Dr. Robert W. Spike, the boyish-faced United Church of Christ minister who directed the National Council of Churches Commission on Religion and Race from 1963 to 1965, describes the role of the religious activists in Mississippi in his book *The Freedom Revolution and the Churches.*

"In the Mississippi struggle," he wrote, "the role of the churches through volunteers and aid to the civil rights organizations made a significant difference in focusing the concern of the nation there." Militant members of the Student Nonviolent Coordinating Committee (SNCC), he said, were "committed to challenging the awful tyranny of Mississippi. The NAACP, on the other hand, experienced in the travail of Mississippi justice, did not want an open confrontation."

Dr. Spike clearly catalogues the NCC Commission's involvement:

> The commission on Religion and Race decided to support the more aggressive group, within the law, but with the firm conviction that the time for change had come. All the volunteers who went into the state knew full well the great personal danger they faced. Hundreds of ministers also went to Mississippi as chaplains. A full-time, long-range program of community redevelopment known as the Delta Ministry was begun by the National Council of Churches with the Aid of the World Council of Churches.

Dr. Spike asserts that the Federal government relied on the church agents in Mississippi to provide the national government with intelligence on what was really going on in Mississippi:

> At times federal authorities relied heavily on the church bodies for impartial inside information as to what was going on and frequently responded to the urgings of church groups for more federal action there.

This strange cloak-and-dagger partnership of church and state in Mississippi gradually wore thin and then burst asunder under the abrasive pressure of political and ideological differences.

At its inception in September of 1964, the Delta Ministry was looked upon as an agency to distribute food and clothing to the needy. But there was more in the fine print. The Rev. Bruce Hilton, an Evangelical United Brethren minister and journalist who served as a staff member for two years, wrote in the Methodist magazine *Christian Advocate* in January of 1968:

> The General Board of the National Council of Churches, recognizing that true help to the poor involves changing the conditions

which cause poverty, had written into the Delta Ministry's charter a mandate to: "help the people in drawing potential leadership from their midst, and help such leaders acquire the knowledge and skills for competent and responsible leadership within the democratic setting of an American community."

The Rev. Arthur Thomas, a young, mild-spoken, Methodist minister was named the first director of the Delta Ministry. He described the function of the organization as "a long term effort to bring structural changes in the life of Mississippi. The primary start," he said, "would be with the Movement (civil rights oriented) or Negro community." The World Council of Churches also backed the Delta Ministry, and international volunteers came to Mississippi to supplement the staff of about twenty persons.

"We were initially confined to the Delta area but later went to the whole state," Thomas says. "We set up our state office in Greenville where we had a work among the mill people in the city and with the plantation people in the rural areas. Colored women couldn't find employment in the mills and Negro men were used only for maintenance. We tried to negotiate, and failing, we set up picket lines. We finally got them to hire Negro women and upgrade the men's positions."

Thomas says that the Delta Ministry was also directly involved in the strike of twelve Negro families against the A. L. Andrews 1,300-acre plantation. "They were evicted from their homes on the plantation by county jail prisoners who dumped their furniture on the highway," he recalls. "Then they moved into tents. Later they got donations and built their own homes and set up Freedom Crafts Industry in June of 1965." Freedom Crafts products are now sold in shops across the country.

"We began getting our fingers wet in the economy," he says. "We were concerned with education and had been having meetings with people who ran day care centers for children."

During this period, OEO contacted the NCC New York office about the War on Poverty. Thomas describes it this way:

OEO called NCC and said, "Hey, we got a Head Start program. Do you know anyone who might be interested in starting a program?"

The NCC people said, "Yeah, in Mississippi."

Thomas flew back to New York City to meet with the NCC officials and Dr. Thomas Levin, a New York psychologist who later would be named the first director of the Child Development Group in Mississippi.

"We went back to Mississippi and called a meeting of civil rights groups that had been meeting during the winter. We expected about twenty persons and fifty showed up," Thomas said. "Tom Levin started working on the technical aspects of the program. The deadline for the proposal was May 15, 1965. We put together an ad hoc task force and went to work."

The staff worked for six frantic weeks filling out papers, drawing up programs, securing facilities, and recruiting a staff.

"We got up to the last minute and then discovered the whole kit and caboodle had to be approved by the governor," Thomas says ruefully. "We thought we were licked.

"Then we discovered the loophole — a college could get OEO funds without state approval.

"We had two days to find the college."

Thomas chartered a small plane and flew to Tougaloo College in Jackson, Mississippi. He recalled his reception:

> They had an interim president and he hemmed and hawed. Then he said, "I'll bring it up at the next board meeting." That would be too late for us.
>
> The college had just gotten a Ford Foundation grant and our program was extraneous to the main purpose of the college. They didn't want to tackle it.
>
> Then we discovered Mary Holmes Junior College, a Presbyterian college. Presbyterians were active supporters of the Delta Ministry and I chartered a plane again and went up to talk to the president, Dawson Horn.
>
> The United Presbyterians were meeting in General Assembly then and they voted to go along with us.
>
> This gave us the escape valve we needed to bypass the governor.

Dr. Levin was named CDGM director and Thomas was appointed to its board.

Conceived in controversy and born under intense political pressure, CDGM was both hailed and hated. White Mississippi politicians charged at the outset that the organization was a front for civil rights activists and Northern agitators. Ardent supporters acclaimed the program as a grass-roots crusade against poverty, ignorance, and political oppression. A more pragmatic view of CDGM was voiced by Aaron Henry, president of the NAACP Mississippi State Conference. He referred to the project "as the biggest industry in Mississippi." Facts support his frank appraisal. OEO would channel $7,000,000, in two separate grants, through CDGM between May of 1965 and September 15, 1966. By the end of the summer of 1966, CDGM was operating 120 Head Start centers for 9,135 children and employing 2,272 people. The pre-school centers served the youngsters hot lunches, provided medical and dental care, and exposed many of the children to books, blocks and blackboards for the first time.

White Mississippians became doubly suspicious of CDGM when it began operating out of the Mount Beulah Conference Center in Edwards, Mississippi. Mount Beulah, the 35-acre campus of the former Southern Christian Institute, is owned by the Delta Ministry. Local residents regard the campus as a spawning ground for civil rights activists. It also is 180 miles from Mary Holmes Junior College in West Point, Mississippi.

The first CDGM grant of $1,400,000 reached Mississippi in May of 1965 — only a month ahead of two investigators from the Senate Appropriations Committee. Senator John Stennis, the influential Mississippi member of the Appropriations Committee, which controls the purse strings on all OEO projects, requested the committee chairman, Senator Carl Hayden of Arizona, to send the two staff members to Mississippi to make an on-the-scene investigation for alleged fiscal irregularities and improper civil rights activities. Paul J. Cotter, the committee's special counsel, and William J. Miller, an auditor hired by the committee, were given the assignment. Said Arthur Thomas:

> They lived with us there all summer — and so did the FBI. They were checking records and the auditors went around to all the centers.
>
> The Jacksonville paper drew charts on its editorial page showing where all the CDGM centers were.
>
> I never knew I controlled so much of the State of Mississippi until I saw that.
>
> Then they [white supremacists] started shooting at us and burning a few centers. They tried to run Levin off the road — in his car — and kill him one night.
>
> OEO knew what it had gotten into and were pleased — at first.

OEO's pleasure was short-lived. Senator Stennis is well liked and highly respected by his colleagues in the Club. But he makes a formidable enemy, and he had declared an all-out war on CDGM.

The political overtones of CDGM were enough to strike fear in the heart of any Mississippi politician. Most CDGM staff members belonged to the renegade Mississippi Freedom Democratic Party (MFDP). Freedom Democrats are a constant thorn in the political flesh of loyalist Democrats. MFDP members showed up at the 1964 Democratic National Convention to challenge the credentials of the regular Democratic Mississippi delegation. This nationally televised confrontation was the only flaw in the well-oiled convention which otherwise went all the way with LBJ. Freedom Democrats also unsuccessfully sought in 1965 to block the seating of Mississippi Congressmen on the grounds that the officials were not legally elected because many Mississippi Negroes were denied the right to vote. This attempt also proved to be a futile exercise.

Attorney Cotter and auditor Miller of the Appropriations Committee staff made their first inspection tour of CDGM centers on June 29, 1965. "The headquarters offices at Mount Beulah campus were totally inadequate, were in disorder, and dirty," they reported. "The employees in some cases slept on the floor, and in other cases on the cots in the office. A large percentage of the personnel seemed rather unkempt, giving a general beatnik atmosphere to the whole place." OEO immediately demanded that CDGM move its headquarters back to the campus of Mary Holmes Junior College.

Cotter and Miller returned to Mississippi two months later to see whether the recommendations made by OEO had been put into effect. Six days later the Washington investigators faced a baffling problem — the CDGM records had disappeared over the weekend, along with the three accountants from the New York City firm of Spokny-Gersten retained by OEO to set CDGM's bookkeeping in order.

The proprietor of the Stonewall Jackson Motor Lodge in Jackson told the government agents that the three accountants had rented rooms for the weekend but that their beds had not been slept in. He said that the last he had seen of the trio was Friday, August 27, when they stopped for a short time at the motel and then left in a car loaded with cardboard boxes.

The two investigators later learned that OEO had taken exception to the firm's accounting fee of $35,000. CDGM was ordered by OEO to recover all but $10,000 of the $26,500 already advanced to the accounting firm.

The attempt to recover the fees sparked a heated debate between the New York accountants and CDGM officials. Neal Gersten and M. J. Spokny flew down from New York City to confront CDGM directors at a board meeting August 7, 1965. The accountants charged that they were being made scapegoats for CDGM's problems and then began cataloguing the reasons why CDGM workers were not receiving their paychecks on time. According to Gersten and Spokny, many CDGM employees never filled out W-4 forms, the positions of teachers were incorrectly listed, and workers failed to list their addresses and Social Security numbers. Many employees didn't or couldn't even sign their forms. The two men also said that officials had never prepared an actual list of all CDGM personnel.

As Cotter and Miller combed the Delta for the missing records, Marion Wright, a Mississippi attorney and CDGM board member who was in New York, called CDGM headquarters and said that the records and the missing accountants were in New York City. The board demanded that the records be returned immediately — with an accountant to put them in order.

The records were returned by air express in two large cartons on Monday night and were available for examination on Tuesday, August 31. But they were not accompanied by an accountant from Spokny-Gersten, and the firm was subsequently discharged. Cotter and Miller never did learn why the Spokny-Gersten accountants whisked the documents from Mississippi to New York City. A careful examination of the records revealed that they were still in a chaotic state. But although Cotter and Miller had difficulty deciphering the much-traveled records, they did come across an item that attracted their attention.

The records showed that on June 16, CDGM paid $30,710 to the Mount Beulah Delta Ministry as an advance payment for board and rooms for personnel attending a planned CDGM orientation session. The money, however, was paid two weeks in advance — at the same time that the Mount Beulah Center was being used as a staging ground and lodging place for Mississippi Freedom Democratic Party members and other civil rights activists planning a demonstration in Jackson.

The government investigators also said OEO findings indicated that the $30,710 paid to the Mount Beulah Center was "overstated" by $20,810. Miller said this was done by charging CDGM personnel $8 per person for room and board in contrast to the $2 per person charged civil rights demonstrators. The Committee staff members believed that the advance payment raised the question as to the possible subsidization of civil rights activities with federal funds. These findings of course were reported in detail to Senator Stennis and the Appropriations Committee.

Reacting to Senator Stennis' charges of fiscal irregularities and illegal civil rights activities on the part of CDGM personnel, Shriver decided to make his own investigation. The field general of the War on Poverty sent South one of the largest armies of bureaucrats since the days of Reconstruction. During June, July, and August of 1965, CDGM was under continual surveillance. Shriver even asked former Congressman Gillis Long of Louisiana, who was in the South attending the funeral of a Congressman killed in an accident, to drive out of his way to attend an orientation session for CDGM teachers at Mount Beulah on July 5-6, and to report on any unusual activity. Mr. Long complied with the request. CDGM's long hot summer of audits and inspections culminated with a center-by-center checkout of the Head Start project in all twenty-eight counties August 8-16.

Senator Stennis went for CDGM's jugular vein, by attempting to cut off its flow of life-sustaining federal funds. By October he believed he had enough damaging evidence to convince the Senate's Committee on Appropriations that CDGM was perverting the purpose for which it was created. Armed with reports, audits, and on-the-spot interviews from his own staff and those of the field men of the Committee itself, Senator Stennis petitioned for thirty minutes to present testimony at the OEO appropriations hearing. He believed he had an air-tight case against CDGM — and indirectly against Shriver.

The battle then moved from the Mississippi Delta to a hearing room in the Senate office building. Concerned clergymen and civil rights activists waited anxiously in the wings.

At 10:07 a.m., October 14, 1965, the Subcommittee on Deficiencies and Supplementals of the Committee on Appropriations was rapped to order by its chairman, Senator John O. Pastore, the diminutive but dynamic Democratic Senator from Rhode Island, who was somewhat apprehensive because he felt he hadn't been given all the facts he should have before conducting the hearing. A former prosecuting attorney, Senator Pastore knows a case in court can be lost by lack of attention to detail.

"I will read a letter directed to me from our distinguished colleague Senator Stennis," the chairman began. Sitting with Pastore on the subcommittee, in addition to Senator Stennis, were Democratic Senators Allen J. Ellender of Louisiana, Robert C. Byrd of West Virginia, William Proxmire of Wisconsin, Ralph Yarborough of Texas, and Carl Hayden of Arizona. Republican members included Senators Leverett Saltonstall of Massachusetts, Margaret Chase Smith of Maine, and Gordon Allott of Colorado.

The first three paragraphs of Senator Stennis' letter to Senator Pastore were as follows:

> Dear John: Several weeks ago I made the public statement that my own investigation, and that of the staff of the Senate Appropriations Committee, had revealed irregularities in the use of Federal funds granted to one of the largest Head Start projects under the poverty program. The investigation also revealed that personnel employed by the Head Start program were engaged in activities entirely outside the program.
>
> Since that time, I have continued to investigate this matter and have discovered additional evidence of improper, if not unlawful, expenditures of appropriated money.
>
> In order that the Subcommittee on Deficiencies and Supplementals of the Senate Appropriations Committee can have these facts available as a basis for examining witnesses who will appear on behalf of the appropriation for the Office of Economic Opportunity, I request 30 minutes to present testimony on these facts as soon as possible after the hearings are started.

Senator Pastore peered up through his glasses. "I understand at this point that it may take more than 30 minutes. I don't care how long it takes. I am paid to be here and I will stay here."

Senator Pastore turned to Senator Stennis. "In view of your allegations made in your letter, Senator," he said, "I should tell you that I invited Mr. Sargent Shriver, together with whom else he wanted to come here, to rebut anything or explain his side of the situation."

Senator Stennis' Southern courtesy covered any irritation he may have felt. "I am certainly glad you did, Mr. Chairman," he replied. "We also supplied Mr. Shriver and his group with written copies of most of our testimony, all that we had up to that point, in advance, several days ago, so that he would be informed. I am certainly glad that he is here. He will be heard later, of course."

Senator Stennis then told the committee why he had asked for time to present testimony.

"Let me say that my presentation here is not to be a general attack on the Head Start program, as such," he began. "We have some mighty good ones in Mississippi. They have done good work.

"Coming down to the project about which this testimony

relates, I learned, members of the committee, that this project was gotten out as an educational project in the name of Mary Holmes Junior College, an institution for colored students at West Point, Mississippi, one that I was fully familiar with. I had the honor once of being judge in that county, and I knew where it was, of course, and its activities.

"But they said the activity would center and it would operate from Mount Beulah Center down below between Jackson and Vicksburg, which is 180 miles or more from West Point. I knew Mary Holmes Junior College had never been connected with the Mount Beulah Operation Center. It was a different kind of project. That was to be a red flag to me that trouble was coming on a racial basis if something wasn't done, because that had been a center of — civil rights activities had centered there. It had been a hotbed for racial zealots."

Warming to his subject, Senator Stennis began to sound like a prosecutor out to get a conviction. He said the investigation by the Committee staff members revealed that numerous Head Start checks on federal funds had been issued to CDGM personnel in the amount of $100 each and charged to petty cash without supporting vouchers. He charged that thousands of dollars were spent for equipping churches and other buildings to be used as centers without adequate control records. This made the recovery of property improbable if not impossible.

"Employment application for Mississippi Head Start projects required applicants to list civil rights and political activities in which they had been engaged," Stennis continued; "further, thirty of the central and administrative resources staff who operate the program, of thirty, twenty-one of them had extensive civil rights backgrounds in SNCC or CORE and twenty-five of the thirty were out-of-State residents.

"Two of the Head Start employees were arrested by the Washington police on the U. S. Capitol grounds in connection with the march of August 9, protesting U. S. involvement in Vietnam at a time when the payroll records of CDGM indicated, that is, the project, that these two persons were employees in the central headquarters group of Child Development Group of Mississippi, and whose post of duty was 1000 miles from the jail to which they were taken after their arrest."

Senator Stennis closed his opening statement with a charge of misuse of federal funds by CDGM personnel. He then got down to specifics.

"I believe this is the first time that the proof will show that federal money was used to pay for a march to picket the Congress, here on Capitol Hill, against the proposition of supporting our flag and our boys who are fighting a shooting war. I don't believe that has ever happened before in the history of the nation. That proof will be developed later."

The Mississippi Senator asked that a letter to Dr. D. I. Horn, president of Mary Holmes Junior College, from Jules Sugarman, deputy program director for Project Head Start, be introduced into the record. The letter, dated July 31, 1965, included the following:

> We have just had an opportunity to evaluate information developed by the OEO personnel who recently visited the Child Development Group of Mississippi at Mount Beulah, Mississippi.
>
> While we are pleased with the reports of the significant success of the program at the centers, we are also greatly concerned about the central management and financial practices of CDGM. The audit discloses information which could have far-reaching financial and program implications to the detriment of the Mary Holmes-CDGM program and the Project Head Start as a whole.
>
> We have concluded that effective action must be taken immediately to correct the deficiencies noted in the attached audit report findings.

The letter requested Dr. Horn to arrange for the immediate transfer of CDGM's central headquarters from Mount Beulah back to Mary Holmes Junior College. It asked for a more effective "exercise of your management responsibility." It ordered that the program's medical program be intensified. The letter closed with the exhortation that all corrective action "can and must be accomplished within seven days from receipt of this letter."

Cotter, the Appropriations Committee special counsel, was the first witness called to testify by Senator Stennis. He told the subcommittee that Dr. Levin, the New York psychologist, dominated the project. Cotter said that Dr. Levin, along with the Rev. Arthur Thomas, director of the Delta Ministry, "had been the moving force in the creation, planning, submission of the budget, and even the selection of most if not all of the directors of the CDGM board of directors.

"The project, which was state-wide," Cotter continued, "relied almost entirely on operating outside the regular Mississippi school system. Churches, houses and other buildings were rented for the teaching centers. The community groups which would be responsible for the various teaching centers consisted of Negro residents of the various communities. It was expected that the enrollments would be almost entirely Negro children."

Cotter also said that of the central administrative staff of thirty-one people, twenty-five were from out of state, ten were colored, and twenty-one white. He said that their applications indicated that twenty-one of the staff had been active in civil rights activities such as SNCC and CORE sponsor.

"The central staff, composed for the most part of young people, had little training for the undertaking involving the expenditures of $1,400,000 over a period of fourteen months," Cotter said.

In his testimony, William Miller referred to the $30,710 paid by CDGM to the Delta Ministry as an advance payment for room and board for the one-week CDGM orientation session for teachers at Mount Beulah Center. He said that OEO said the charge was not properly supported by documentation and recommended that CDGM obtain a refund of $20,810.

"From whom?" Senator Pastore asked.

"From the Delta Ministry, which is a branch of the National Council of Churches," Miller replied. He added that the $30,710 check went to the National Council of Churches in New York.

"Was there any element of fraud that you could see in it?" Pastore then asked Miller.

The auditor thought a moment. "I wouldn't say there was an element of fraud," he replied. "The thing that impressed us was that this $30,000 was paid two weeks in advance at the same time the Delta Ministry was housing demonstrators [at Mount Beulah] that were going to march in Jackson thirty miles away. They were providing board and room for demonstrators coming down from — I don't know where they came from. Some came from Chicago. I don't know where they all came from. But they were being housed at this conference center.

"There was just a question that arose in our mind as to why they should be paid $30,000 in advance when they didn't even know how many were coming."

Senator Pastore looked down at the witness table where Cotter and Miller were sitting.

"I hope we are not being misunderstood here," he said, "but the way this record is being developed it is as though a grandiose crime was committed. I am trying to establish whether these things are inefficiencies, whether they are the result of fraud.

I think this is quite important. We have two witnesses sworn
and there has been mention that maybe we will have to go to
the Justice Department. I want a bill of particulars on all of the
violations of the law that you found in your investigation."

"It is in the report, Senator," Cotter pointed out.

"Nobody ever gave me a report," Senator Pastore said curtly.
"Don't give it to me now. I want you to read from the report."

Senator Stennis cut in.

"I think we have to present the facts piece by piece, Mr. Chairman, and then hear from the Office of Economic Opportunity,
and then determine what, if anything was irregular; what, if
anything was overpaid; and what, if anything was unlawful,
illegal or what, if anything was crime. I didn't say there was
any. I don't know."

Senator Pastore then explained his line of questioning.

"Before we can begin to ask witnesses on the other side what
their reasons were or what explanation they can give, we must
know the violations," he insisted.

"I have some major items here," Senator Stennis said, "that I
think raise questions of concern to you and other members of
the committee.

"For instance," he continued, "one of the points is that of
$35,000 — there was an allowance of a $35,400 accounting fee,
and $27,000 of that was actually paid. Wasn't some of that dis-
allowed or challenged?"

Miller, still at the witness table, said that it had been.

"How much of that was challenged?" Senator Stennis asked.

"That is what I want to get at," Senator Pastore said, with a
note of impatience.

"I am coming to it as fast as I can," Senator Stennis replied.

"Item by item, and I would like to list them all," the persistent
subcommittee chairman directed. "There must be a lot of other
abuses besides these."

"I am just trying to develop the high points," Senator Stennis
explained.

"Are you going to ask what they were?" asked Senator Pastore.

The Senator from Mississippi said he would.

"You bring them out," Senator Pastore said. "Go ahead. But
what I want, what I would like to have for the record, is all of
the things that these gentlemen found wrong."

Senator Ellender told the chairman he could find that out in
the report.

"But I haven't seen the report," Senator Pastore retorted, "and I am sitting here now."

"Why don't we let the Senator from Mississippi proceed?" Senator Byrd suggested. "He said he could bring this out."

"This is what I am asking for," Senator Pastore said.

"Let him proceed," Senator Byrd said. "I have a previous engagement for noon and I will have to leave in a few minutes, but I would like to hear as much of the testimony as possible before going."

"The chairman has been generous with me on the time," Senator Stennis admitted.

"Absolutely," agreed Senator Pastore, "This started out as a half-hour meeting and I said I would stay here until the cows came home. I want this developed in systematic form. I don't know how I can explain to the committee except that I haven't seen the report. I don't care how long the gentleman from West Virginia stays here. I am the chairman of this committee, and this will be presented in a regular and routine form."

"I understand that, and I am a member of the committee," the gentleman from West Virginia said. "The Senator from Mississippi stated that he wanted to develop these points. Why not let him proceed?"

"He was interrupted by the Senator from Louisiana, claiming it is in the report," Senator Pastore replied.

"And previously interrupted by the chairman," Senator Byrd added.

"Who has a perfect right to interrupt any time he feels like it," the chairman, obviously piqued, said testily.

"Of course he does," Senator Byrd agreed. "But why not let the Senator from Mississippi proceed?"

Senator Stennis, turning to auditor Miller still in the witness chair, continued:

"I believe it would be helpful to the chairman and the other members if we list now those demands that were made by OEO on this group and then follow up in these gentlemen's testimony as to what was done or what was not done. Do you have a copy of the demands that were made?"

"I have a summary of the most important ones," Miller said.

Senator Pastore interrupted. "We are not joining minds here. You are talking about the reforms that were made. I want to know the abuses."

"This is what shows, Mr. Chairman," Senator Stennis explained. "These are alleged abuses by OEO. I want to show what OEO alleged and then show what was done to follow it up."

"Go ahead. Do it your way," Senator Pastore said, slumping back in his chair.

"I would do it your way but I don't know — "

"When I present a case in court I present it word by word by word as to what they found and what happened," Senator Pastore said as if he were lecturing on law. "I want to know first what the abuses were before I know what the corrections were."

"This is exactly what I am trying to do, of course, within a limited way," Senator Stennis said, his Southern courtesy wearing thin. "I spent twenty years in a trial courtroom, in a very limited fashion," he added.

Senator Pastore wasn't impressed. "Well, I spent thirty-five years there."

Senator Saltonstall, playing the role of the peacemaker, interceded: "I have the highest regard for the gentleman from Mississippi and the highest regard for the Senator from Rhode Island. They are both good lawyers. Now let's go ahead."

At 12:15 A.M., Senator Stennis finally finished presenting his testimony. Now it was the turn of Sargent Shriver to take the stand. The articulate anti-poverty warrior would need all the words in his command to extricate the embattled Head Start program.

*   *   *   *   *

Sargent Shriver, the urbane director of the Office of Economic Opportunity, moved into the witness chair. He was flanked by Donald Baker, OEO general counsel; Dr. Julius Richmond, Project Head Start director; William P. Kelly, director of the office of management; Robert Cassidy, deputy director of the management office, and Nathan Cutler, office for management audit section.

"I would like to begin," Shriver said after being sworn in, "by expressing my appreciation to Senator Stennis for the courtesy he has shown to our office and making available to us the information he has from time to time given us.

"As far as I am concerned, the subject matter of this discussion would be best confined to the facts and not allegations or emotional implications drawn from facts. I am delighted to have the opportunity to appear before this committee to present the facts and set the record straight."

Shriver then gave a detailed account, including the dates, of how his office conducted extensive audits and investigations of CDGM during the preceding summer months. He submitted for the record a summary of every action taken, including the grants, the disallowances and the issues still under question. He admitted CDGM's accounting system had been weak and that one accounting firm was dismissed and a new firm employed to get the project's records into shape. He conceded that the $8 fee charged the CDGM staff by the Mount Beulah Center instead of the usual $2 per person charge was questionable.

"I'm not saying they were wrong, but they were questionable," Shriver told the Senators. "In view of the fact that this involves the National Council of Churches of Christ in America, I would like to point out that I don't think the National Council of Churches of Christ needs $30,000 advanced from us to pay the bills.

"The implication that the money we advanced was used to pay for the cost of civil right workers is not substantiated by facts," Shriver added. "It is merely an impression that people have, but it is not proven."

Shriver also explained that the $8 which the CDGM Head Start personnel were charged for room and board by the Mount Beulah Center was far below the $16 per diem national average.

The anti-poverty chief then turned his attention to the two Head Start employees arrested in Washington while picketing in protest to the Viet Nam war. Shriver said that as a matter of fact there were four young persons rather than two from the Head Start program who were arrested.

"The unfortunate thing is that the newspaper accounts failed to mention that they were in the Capital of the United States at their own expense and they were not paid for the days they were away from their work," Shriver said.

Senator Pastore interjected that he didn't question a citizen's right to participate in a lawful peaceful assembly but he told Shriver he would have been happier if the OEO chief could say, "After we found this out we fired four of them."

"Perhaps this was a mistake in judgment," Shriver admitted. "Maybe we should have fired them. All I am saying is that we have not taken the position that anybody who participates in a political or civic action on their own time automatically gets fired by the Federal government."

Shriver also denied the charges that CDGM was run by out-

siders. He testified that of the 3000 professional people, volunteers and poor people employed as aides in the program, 2,850,
or 95 per cent, were native Mississippians. He also said that his
office made it clear that civil rights work or political activity
would not be permitted during working hours.

The witness then inserted in the record a summary of a report
by Dr. Robert Coles, research scientist at Harvard University,
who visited the CDGM centers. He read two paragraphs:

> By means of repeated interviews with the children and their
> parents . . . I tried to evaluate clinically, in some depth, the
> impact of the program on their minds, their attitudes, their feel-
> ings, their habits. It is my opinion that the Head Start programs
> I saw throughout Mississippi achieved a truly extraordinary de-
> gree of success in reaching and significantly improving the physical
> and mental health as well as the future educational competence
> of many children involved in them.

> I saw children grow a bit, gain a bit of respect for themselves,
> feel that, after all, there is a lot more possible than they and
> their parents ever thought to be the case. . . . I simply want to
> thank you all for helping a rather impoverished group of Ameri-
> can boys and girls achieve some real start toward a healthy and
> literate life.

Shriver handed the letter to a recorder to be entered into the
record and then concluded with a defense of the CDGM program:

"I am well aware of the fact," he said, "that in the day-to-day
operation of a program of this nature, mistakes will be made.
We have made our shares of mistakes, and they haven't been
confined, I might add, to Mississippi. The Mary Holmes Junior
College and the subcontractors down there did make administrative errors. However, these errors, I believe, were discovered
in a timely manner by my own office. Many of them have been
corrected and the remainder will be. The public money and the
public interest will be safeguarded."

Shriver's vigorous defense of CDGM caused churchmen to rise
up and call him blessed among men. But the praise was pre-
mature. In another year, almost to the day, Shriver would be
back before the same subcommittee arguing equally as eloquently
why CDGM should NOT be refunded. And clergymen again
would rise up — this time to picket.

CHAPTER IV

Where the Action Is

On February 23, 1966, OEO gave CDGM a $5.6 million grant. Again the funds were channeled through Mary Holmes Junior College as the grantee. The new grant would allow CDGM to operate a Head Start program for 9,135 children in 121 centers. The program was to extend through August 31.

Buoyed by the grant, CDGM officials filed an application on July 7, 1966, for $41 million to be used in a mammoth Head Start program enrolling 30,000 children. The application was returned by the Atlanta OEO regional office because it was incomplete.

OEO continued to receive reports during the summer that CDGM was still having serious administrative problems. OEO's Regional Director Sloan in Atlanta sent a series of questions on civil rights, expenditures, and program administration to the CDGM board, and asked that the answers be forthcoming in two weeks. He received the information on August 8. The information was submitted to the OEO Office of Inspection for review. Sloan wired CDGM not to plan on extending its program beyond September. CDGM replied ten days later with an application for a new full-year program.

CDGM seemed to have a penchant for making enemies among Negroes as well as whites. Even NAACP officials complained they were discriminated against. The minutes of the Board of Directors Meeting of the Mississippi State Conference in Natchez on September 25, 1966, reveals the following:

> The president [Aaron Henry] reported on a situation involving the Child Development Group of Mississippi. He reported that he had talked with several NAACP presidents concerning information that he had from OEO that the Child Development Group would have difficulty getting refunded and the total program of

CDGM was in danger of being curtailed. He reported that he had been asked by OEO to help to put together a group that OEO could depend upon to run this program in a business-like manner and in accord with OEO guidelines. Several members reported that the NAACP had been discriminated against by the CDGM group and had no NAACP representation on its board and central staff and very limited employment in the field. Only Loake County and the Gulf Coast were the two areas where NAACP people had been employed in any meaningful amount. The president reported that several branch presidents had previously complained to him about the way they were treated by CDGM. The president said that in response to the reaction of the NAACP members on the CDGM crisis, the position that he and the field director [Charles Evers] had taken was to support the CDGM group if it was possible for the group to get refunded because the program sponsored by CDGM was of great assistance to the Negro people of Mississippi. If in the event CDGM could not be refunded then the position should be to help put together another group that could be funded in order to guarantee the salvation of the program. It was moved by Attorney Jack Young and seconded that this become the position of the State Conference of the NAACP, the motion was unanimously carried.

The battle lines were being drawn and it looked as if CDGM might have to retire from the field.

On September 27, Donald M. Baker, OEO's chief attorney, filed a memorandum with Shriver —

to confirm and amplify my oral opinion of August 31, 1966. I advised you that in the light of the information then available it appeared it would be extremely difficult to make a determination that Mary Holmes Junior College and its operating delegate, CDGM, were qualified to administer the funds and the programs which they had applied for to this agency.

Baker said, based on the experience OEO had with CDGM on the other two grants, he saw no basis for improvement:

They have shown themselves unable to benefit either from experience or assistance. Indeed, there is substantial evidence that they are actually unwilling to take such steps as are necessary to improve their operation.

Baker told Shriver that he was basing his conclusions on the points that CDGM had become oriented toward the economic needs of adults rather than the educational and development needs of children, that CDGM was not disposed toward bi-racial community action agencies and that the organization had shown "pervasive and almost unremitting hostility toward any direction from this agency [OEO]."

On September 27, Shriver issued his bulky "CDGM Situation Report." The first two paragraphs stated:

> OEO audit, inspection and program personnel have conducted reviews of the Child Development Group of Mississippi. In each of these areas they have found serious deficiencies and irregularities to the extent that it has been deemed imprudent for the CDGM-administered program to be refunded.

> As a result of an interim audit by OEO, it has been determined that approximately $654,000 could not be approved at this time as valid grant expenditures. . . . These expenditures, which are discussed in greater details in this report, reflect lack of proper supporting documents, inadequate information, and activities unrelated to the Head Start objectives.

The Situation Report included eight pages of accusations charging CDGM with nepotism, sloppy record keeping, excessive staff salary, inadequate controls of automobiles, poor administration, and a go-it-alone policy which excluded cooperating with existing community groups. It looked as if Senator Stennis had won his battle against CDGM.

Reaction to the report would reach all the way to the White House. CDGM supporters were outraged. Shriver was depicted as a cross between Judas and Benedict Arnold who sold out CDGM because of political pressure from Senator Stennis — or perhaps even President Johnson himself. But the OEO's field general was not one to back away from a fight. Supported by his well-equipped publicists, he launched his war of words with CDGM supporters. Shriver was willing to fight it out in lines if it took all winter.

His first missive was fired October 2, in reaction to charges by critics he was scuttling CDGM. Alert observers noticed that sharp tactician Shriver included in it a path of retreat. The release stated, in part:

> Sargent Shriver, Director of OEO, has made no assurances to any senator in correspondence or otherwise, that the Child Development Group in Mississippi would be terminated, as indicated in the press last week.

> CDGM has been extensively audited and inspected by the Office of Economic Opportunity. The results of OEO's investigations and audits became available on September 15, and a decision was reached by OEO on September 27th that CDGM in its *present*

[italics mine] organizational form, with its *present* administrative and operating personnel, and a record of management, cannot lawfully be refinanced by OEO.

The release pointed out that OEO had been reviewing applications from Mississippi from other groups to fill the gap left by CDGM.

One such application is expected from an outstanding bi-racial group in Mississippi which has committed itself to one-third representation of the poor on its board of directors. In its desire to preserve Head Start and the community action programs in Mississippi, OEO hopes to act on this application as soon as possible.

The name of the new "outstanding bi-racial group" was the Mississippi Action for Progress (MAP). The new organization was administered by an eighteen-member bi-racial board of directors headed by Owen Cooper, prominent businessman and Baptist lay leader of Yazoo City. The Rev. Merrill W. Lindsey of West Point, Mississippi, district superintendent of the Methodist Church, was vice president. Other board members included Aaron Henry of the NAACP; Hodding Carter, III, editor of the *Greenville Delta Democrat Times*; Wilson Evans, president of the Gulfport Local, International Longshoremen's Union, and LeRoy Percy, Episcopal lay leader and board chairman of the Mississippi Chemical Company.

A few days later, on October 11, OEO announced that it had awarded a $3,020,906 grant to MAP to conduct a full year Head Start program for 1500 children in Mississippi. Shriver said that $10 million in all had been reserved to finance the MAP child development programs, which could ultimately reach between 4500 and 5000 children.

Few Head Start programs have been started with such high praise from OEO. "No federal program in Mississippi has ever been under the direction of such an outstanding board of white and Negro leaders," Shriver said. "Two years ago, it was the unanimous opinion that this could not be done in Mississippi. But it has been done." MAP also received the blessing of Governor Paul Johnson, who signed its charter.

But the *New Republic* magazine thought it spotted a political conspiracy. In a "we-told-you-so" editorial of October 13th, 1966, the magazine charged:

Sargent Shriver last week officially announced termination of the Child Development Group of Mississippi, the controversial Head

Start program. In September, this journal predicted he would do so. In part Shriver's decision was in response to pressures from Senator Stennis and represents the desire of the White House.

The Head Start program is to be stripped of its community action functions which had involved many poor Negroes, and handed over to an 18-man biracial board of "moderate" Mississippi Democrats. The White House was instrumental in setting up the board. The president is anxious to paste together a loyalist Democratic party in Mississippi in time for next year's gubernatorial elections, and the CDGM program has been sacrificed to this end.

The magazine then purported to give the names and dates involved in what it considered an underhanded political plot:

Harry McPherson Jr., special counsel of the president, negotiated the deal. About a month ago, he called Douglass Winn, a Greenville, Mississippi lawyer, who is a personal friend of the president's. Following this conversation, Winn got two "moderate" Democrats to agree to be members of a new board. Owen Cooper, president of the Mississippi Chemical Corp., agreed to be co-chairman. LeRoy Percy, chairman of the Mississippi Chemical, would be a board member. Both Winn and Cooper are members of the President's Club. Cooper is considered to be a possible "moderate" candidate for governor of Mississippi next year. The White House called Roy Wilkins, head of the NAACP, who in turn got in touch with Aaron Henry, a one-time Mississippi Negro radical turned moderate; Henry agreed to be the other co-chairman.

Early in September, Henry, Cooper and Percy met with Shriver in Washington, where future plans were discussed. Representatives from the Mississippi NAACP are also understood to have met in secrecy with Senator Stennis.

Hodding Carter, III, editor of the *Greenville Delta Democrat-Times,* was enraged by the *New Republic* article. In letters to the editors of the *New York Times, Washington Evening Star* and *Washington Post,* he wrote:

It's a lie to assert or imply that State NAACP members met secretly with Senator John Stennis prior to or after the MAP's formation. They have never done so. It is a lie to assert that the White House contacted Roy Wilkins who in turn contacted Aaron Henry to serve on the new board. The only contact was made between MAP's board members and OEO representatives. It is a lie to say that any White House assistance or Douglass Winn had any part in putting the MAP Board together. They did not. Winn played absolutely no role in contacting or convincing anyone on MAP's board to serve.

In a letter of protest to the *New Republic,* Dr. John A. Morsell, NAACP assistant executive director, said that the article stating the White House prevailed upon Wilkins to intervene in the controversy was a "plain, unvarnished lie. Mr. Wilkins," Dr. Morsell insisted, "has not discussed CDGM either with Aaron Henry or anyone in the administration."

Rebuking the magazine's snide description of Aaron Henry as "a one time Mississippi Negro radical turned moderate," Dr. Morsell said:

> Short of losing his life, no Negro in Mississippi can surpass Aaron Henry's credentials as a militant leader in the fight for racial justice. How many bombings, beatings and jailings does your writer require?

Aaron Henry confirmed Carter's rebuttal, in a telephone interview with the author in March of 1967.

"I am sure the White House was not involved in what we were trying to do unless it was with those who made a request of me to help," he said. "Ted Berry [director of OEO's Community Action Program] was my contact and Berry is a man of complete integrity.

"Berry called down and said he did not think OEO was going to refund CDGM. We certainly couldn't let a program die that benefitted 10,000 Negro kids and employed nearly 2000 persons. This was perhaps the greatest industry in the state.

"Berry said it could be refunded outside the present structure. He asked me to supply him with some names of persons who could operate the program within the OEO guidelines. I didn't care who ran the show. My prime interest was to keep it in the state.

"After I finished talking to Ted I tried to get in contact with Wilkins to tell him my position, but I never did get to talk to him. I never was in contact with Senator Stennis on this matter.

"The next thing I saw was the press giving Wilkins credit for setting up the whole damn thing.

"I later found out Berry had called Hodding Carter and asked him to put together a list of names. I submitted about forty names and Carter did, too. We both have pretty much the same friends in regard to liberals in politics and business."

What about the charge that he had changed into a moderate from a radical and was cooperating with the White Power Structure?

"I think the issues that we have won for the Negro community,"

Henry said, and then hesitated — "that there are some members
of the white community who are acquiescing to that position.
We have won some battles and some changes. We certainly are
not going to throw this away.

"Either we were seeking bi-racial support or we were lying
about it. It is foolish to say now that some whites are willing
to come to the conference table that we [Negroes] won't come."

*   *   *   *   *

"Nowhere, other than in its efforts on behalf of civil rights
legislation, has the leadership of Protestant agencies more fully
committed itself to battle than in the case of CDGM," wrote
Larold K. Schulz, executive coordinator of the Anti-Poverty Task
Force of the National Council of Churches. He credits major
commitment of staff and financial resources of the Board of
National Missions of the United Presbyterian Church, the National Council of Churches and other church bodies as the crucial
effort in winning the war with Shriver.

Church leaders once again joined with liberal unions and
social service agencies under the umbrella of the Washington-
based Citizens Crusade Against Poverty (CCAP) to do battle with
Shriver. CCAP is a private action group financed by national
foundations. Ironically, the executive director, Richard Boone,
is a former deputy director of OEO's Community Action Program.
The United Automobile Workers and Ford Foundation are
major contributors to CCAP's support.

The CCAP executive committee consisted of Dr. Jon L. Regier,
associate general secretary, Division of Christian Life and Mission of the National Council of Churches; Philip Bernstein,
director of the Council of Jewish Federations and Welfare Funds;
the Most Rev. Raymond J. Gallagher, Bishop of the Diocese of
Lafayette, Indiana; and a nonecclesiastical member, A. Philip
Randolph, president of the Brotherhood of Sleeping Car Porters.
Aaron Henry also was a CCAP board member at the time. This
kind of entangling alliances is not unusual in Washington,
although an outsider may find them difficult to understand.

CCAP personnel were convinced that the Administration was
using anti-poverty funds in Mississippi to promote its own
political fortunes in that politically fragmented state. Schulz in
his article in *Christianity and Crisis* wrote:

> Although there never has been an administrative relationship
> between CDGM and MFDP [Mississippi Freedom Democratic

Party] many persons are involved in both. Members of the CDGM Board of Directors involved in MFDP were under heavy fire, and OEO negotiators called for the head of the Rev. James O. McRee, the chairman of the board. The action is most understandable when one recognizes that Mr. McRee is a possible threat to the political ambitions of Mr. Henry, the former running on an MFDP ticket and the latter possibly on the ticket of the Mississippi Democratic Conference.

CCAP thus set up its own Board of Inquiry to get at the facts about CDGM and its problem in getting refunded. The inquiry board was headed by A. Philip Randolph and the Rev. Robert Spike, now Professor of Ministry at the University of Chicago's Divinity School but just as actively involved in social matters as when he directed the NCC Commission on Religion and Race. (With Dr. Spike's early involvement and interest in the Delta Ministry and CDGM, it might be argued that he could hardly be objective in conducting an inquiry into a program which he so obviously approved.)

Other board members included Paul Anthony, executive director of Southern Regional Council, Inc.; Philip Bernstein; Dr. Kenneth B. Clark, Professor of Psychology at the City College of New York; Frances Coe, member of the Board of Education in Memphis; Eli E. Cohen, executive secretary of the National Committee on Employment of Youth in New York City; Clarence Coleman, director of the Southern Regional Office of the National Urban League, Inc., in Atlanta; Robert Coles, research psychiatrist to the University Health Services of Harvard University; Ralph Helstein, president of United Packinghouse, Food, and Allied workers in Chicago; Dr. Vivian W. Henderson, president of Clark College in Atlanta; John P. Nelson, Jr., New Orleans attorney; and Judge Justine Wise Polier of the Family Court in New York City.

Not too surprisingly the Board of Inquiry came back from Mississippi with a glowing report on CDGM activities.

"The CDGM is a well administered, carefully organized, creatively run organization demonstrating integrity, fiscal responsibility and managerial competence," the report stated.

The board said it was

> unable to avoid the conclusion that the charges levied [against CDGM] are a thin mask for a politically dictated decision — a decision which is all the more tragic in that it represents a yielding to those forces which have stood in historical opposition to prog-

ress for the poor and underprivileged in Mississippi — including Senators Stennis and Eastland who have opposed all civil rights, labor and anti-poverty legislation.

The board further noted that at least $100,000 was spent by the OEO Office of Inspection and the General Accounting Office in investigating CDGM.

The CCAP investigators also accused Shriver of CIA tactics, charging that statements by Dean Clyde Ferguson of Howard University's law school indicated that Howard law students were hired by the OEO to infiltrate CDGM. According to the report, students were instructed to dress in clothes typically worn by civil rights workers in the South, to win the confidence of CDGM personnel, and then collect whatever inside information they could with regard to accumulating a list of charges against CDGM.

"There is now under way a thorough-going attempt by OEO to dismember CDGM, to turn its programs over to other groups, and to insure that a hearing on the merits, if held, will be nothing more than an exercise in futility," the report concluded.

With these verbal barrages bursting all around him, Sargent Shriver assumed the stance of Stonewall Jackson at the first battle of Manassas. He would not be moved. And he quickly moved onto the offense by employing the most-used weapon in his arsenal — the public relations release.

"The Board's review of the Mississippi situation adds nothing new," Shriver said in his public statement. "The information available to the government was collected many months by professional auditors, inspectors, and analysts. Therefore, OEO does not forsee any change in its position."

Shriver added that he planned to "move as fast as possible away from de facto racially segregated programs, such as CDGM, to racially integrated programs." He said he planned to diversify the Head Start program in Mississippi to prevent a monopoly by CDGM.

Shriver made good on his promise to diversify. On October 7, OEO awarded a $1.2 million grant to Rust College in Holly Springs, Mississippi, to administer a Head Start program for 600 pre-school children. The MAP award of a promised $10 million was announced four days later. A $713,000 grant was given the Southwest Mississippi Opportunity, Inc., of Woodville, Mississippi, for a program enrolling 935 children, over the veto of Governor Paul B. Johnson. The governor objected to the program because members of the board were formerly involved with CDGM. But Shriver said since CDGM was not exercising any control over the project, he would fund the program.

Concerned churchmen became more militant both in their support of CDGM and in their criticism of Shriver. On October 14, seventy-five church specialists from the United Church of Christ, the United Presbyterian Church of the U.S.A., and the Protestant Episcopal Church met in Chicago. CDGM loomed so large in their discussions that they adjourned their joint planning session to fly to Washington, D.C., to picket OEO headquarters in protest over its refusal to refund CDGM. The seventy-five churchmen circled in front of the OEO offices for three hours. They were joined by local religious leaders and by board members of CDGM who were in Washington. The anti-poverty specialists in the churches threatened to halt cooperation between themselves and OEO unless CDGM's grants were continued. The church officials brought all the pressure they could, knowing that OEO depended heavily on church-sponsored organizations to translate federal funds into actual poverty-fighting programs on the community level.

Shriver refused to change his public position, stating that OEO would not refinance CDGM in its present form. He reiterated the argument four days later in his appearance before the Appropriations Committee in Senate Room 128. Shriver, once again surrounded by his assistant directors and deputies, came before the committee to plead his case for OEO.

The hearing started on a humorous note. Shriver began his opening statement with an appeal for $1.75 billion for the overall budget to fight the War on Poverty during fiscal 1967. To bolster his argument, he quoted Senate Minority Leader Everett Dirksen as having said, "I want to vote for the anti-poverty bill. I am still willing to put $1,750 million more on the nose."

Senator Saltonstall interrupted. "Mr. Shriver, most respectfully, if I read correctly he didn't say 'more.' He used the words '$1,750 million on the nose.' "

"Yes," Shriver agreed.

"You said, 'More on the nose,' " Senator Saltonstall insisted.

"I was talking about more being considered in addition to what we have had in the past," Shriver explained.

"But what is significant is that he quoted a Republican," Senator Pastore interjected.

Senator Saltonstall played along. "I refuse to answer that. Mr. Shriver has got to answer that one."

The unflappable OEO director followed the lead of the Senators. "I was delighted to have the support of Senator Dirksen for the $1,750 million."

"I was just a little disturbed that you used the word 'more' in connection with this statement," Senator Saltonstall said.

"Excuse me. You are correct," Shriver admitted. "I should not have used the word 'more.' I was using it to imply that this was over and above what the Congress has already appropriated in the past."

"What you are asking is to have us put back $187 million?" Saltonstall asked.

"That is correct — and to support Senator Dirksen in doing so," Shriver replied, obviously convinced that a little humor in a hearing can go a long way.

"He is in the hospital," the Senior Senator from Massachusetts informed Shriver.

"Well, it would be good news, maybe, for him," Shriver replied. Laughter filled the committee room.

Lengthy statements by Shriver on the need for funds for his plethora of antipoverty projects — the Job Corps, the Neighborhood Youth Corps, VISTA, the Green Thumb Program, rural loans and programs to help migrants and the Menominee Indians — were all heard before CDGM was brought up. (The delay may have been caused by the absence of Senator Stennis.)

"Mr. Shriver," Senator Pastore said, "I would like to ask you about that Head Start Program. There has been some indication or there has been some rumor or gossip to the effect that the department (OEO) knuckled under, under pressure on the part of some members of Congress, and there were politics injected in this action."

Shriver was quick to respond.

"I categorically deny that allegation here on the record," Shriver practically hissed in protest. "I have denied it elsewhere.

"In the first place the decision about this was made within our agency by a dozen or more of the top officials of the agency operating so far as I know without any duress, influence, or otherwise from members of Congress or other political personalities. They were operating on the basis of information which had come to their attention as a result of our work in following up this particular grant and from other sources."

Shriver then went into a long chronological account of how CDGM had received two grants from OEO over the protests of many. He said OEO people first felt, however, that with the proper assistance CDGM could overcome its deficiencies. But despite all the direction and assistance OEO could provide, CDGM failed to improve.

The OEO chief then launched into an item-by-item account of the failures of CDGM. If it hadn't been for the accent, it would have sounded almost like Senator Stennis of a year ago.

"We found that people were paid and time and attendance sheets were certified by supervisors for employees who were not even in the State of Mississippi," Shriver charged. "We found that at least five of the fifteen administrators of various areas under this program had certified that certain employees were on the job when in fact they were not on the job. We found a variety of conflict of interest matters that included people on the board of directors as well as staff members. We found cases of nepotism. We found that property paid for by the Government was used for nongovernmental purposes. Automobiles, for example, were used on weekends and at night times for activities that clearly were not connected with the program."

When asked by Senator Pastore what the status of CDGM was, Shriver replied: "The matter now stands that we have told this particular agency, Mr. Chairman, about three or four weeks ago that we could not refinance it in its *present* form, with its *present* personnel, with its *present* procedures.

"We have indicated," Shriver continued, "that we are always ready, to the extent of our ability and the money that you give us, to finance programs and institutions which appear to have the integrity and the competence to carry on the programs which the Congress authorizes. Consequently, if this agency were able to make the kind of basic, fundamental, and I think massive changes in its personnel and procedures which could bring it into line with other agencies that we finance nationally, we could certainly take another look at it."

Senator Pastore then asked permission of the committee for the Rev. Joseph W. Merchant, executive of the United Church of Christ, to testify in behalf of CDGM. Mr. Merchant said he was speaking in behalf of seventy-three urban specialists from three denominations — the Protestant Episcopal Church and the United Presbyterian Church in addition to his own.

He told the committee that three clergymen had met with Shriver and had had a two-hour discussion on CDGM. Shriver, he said, had promised to meet with the CDGM board on October

24. "We feel this is an accomplishment because we have been trying to secure such an opportunity and up until now the charges that have been made have not been reviewed by them," Mr. Merchant continued. "They [CDGM] have not had the opportunity to examine them in some detail and to do anything about it." Mr. Merchant said he thought the matter could be reopened and the CDGM contract renegotiated along the lines Shriver had testified.

"I do ask the privilege of saying that I have no desire to get into any controversy which seems to have hit the press on the credibility of Mr. Shriver," the minister said. "We gave public apologies for any implication of this in our statement yesterday afternoon." Mr. Merchant referred to the twenty-one-page clean bill of health given CDGM by the CCAP Board of Inquiry.

"Now the thing that we are concerned about is that the people have a right to determine and govern their own institution, and under certain conditions in Mississippi this is just not true," Mr. Merchant said. "Under CDGM this is an integrated program, it is a program that is the people's choice."

Feeling he had used a phrase that the Senators could understand, Mr. Merchant continued: "In the case of the new institution, MAP, there is no justification that we can see for claiming that Aaron Henry is the people's choice in Mississippi, and . . . [it] has to be said that there are other voices and other forces that are not represented in MAP."

Shriver asked for and was granted a rebuttal period. "It is a little bit deceptive, I think, to describe any of these programs at this stage of the game as 'the people's choice,'" he said. "Sad to say — in my judgment it is sad to say — for the most part in Mississippi there wasn't any choice and perhaps you might say there never has been any choice.

"We chose to fund CDGM at the beginning because it was a group that was willing to work with us, whereas it was also at the same time a fact that there were not other groups, at least not many other groups, in Mississippi who were ready to operate or willing to operate this new agency of the U. S. Government."

Shriver added that OEO's intent was to move CDGM — a multi-county operation — closer to the communities it served. He also explained that the new Head Start agencies in operation would diversify the program and prevent any one group of having a monopoly.

Senator Pastore interrupted Shriver's testimony to insert in the record a letter from Senator Clifford Case (R., N. J.) supporting CDGM. A couple of paragraphs must have made Shriver wince. Case wrote:

> In a most arbitrary fashion, however, the Office of Economic Opportunity on October 2 announced that it would not continue to fund the CDGM. Whatever its real reasons, those it gave the public related to the administration of CDGM.
>
> The OEO charges, however, do not square with reputable reports that the Mississippi group is regarded as one of the most successful in the country.
>
> A spokesman for Ernst & Ernst, Mississippi auditors of CDGM, has been quoted as saying this about the administration of the program:
>
> "CDGM accounting procedures are a model for poverty programs throughout the United States and have been recognized by OEO representatives as the most efficient and best run program in the country."
>
> It is hard not to agree with CCAP's conclusion that the charges "levied are a thin mask for a politically dictated decision — a decision which is all the more tragic in that it represents a yielding to those forces which have stood in historical opposition to progress for the poor and underprivileged in Mississippi."

Shriver's explanation of how CDGM could have a superior auditing system and still be poorly administered provides an insight into the semantics one faces in getting at the facts of the CDGM program. "There is no question," Shriver admitted, "about the fact that the auditing system that was established is a good auditing system. It is also a fact that there are deficiencies that come into any organization even though you have a good auditing service." Shriver then called on Nathan Cutler, OEO's chief auditor, to expound on this thesis.

"While the system that was installed was adequate in our opinion," Cutler interpreted, "both the public accountants and ourselves found many instances, as Mr. Shriver pointed out, where there were deviations from the system, and these were beyond the responsibility of the public accounting firm. These were management judgments.

"I do want to say the accounting system was good. It was so good it permitted us to disclose these instances without too much difficulty, which was unlike last year when the records were in disarray."

All references to CDGM ended on an optimistic note with Mr.

Merchant telling the committee, "It seems to me that this is still in a condition susceptible to negotiation."

Senator Ellender of Louisiana then began questioning Shriver about Head Start programs in his state. With Senator Stennis absent, CDGM didn't seem to be such a burning issue.

The day after Shriver appeared before the Appropriations Committee in Washington, the *New York Times* ran a full-page advertisement with a bold headline pleading: "Say It Isn't So, Sargent Shriver." The advertisement was paid for by an ad hoc committee called the National Citizens Committee for the Child Development Program in Mississippi. Dr. Truman Douglass, the aggressive United Church of Christ official, headed the committee. The advertisement, signed by 150 churchmen and other "friends" — including Dr. Martin Luther King, Jr., and Walter Reuther — stated:

> Of all the battles Sargent Shriver has fought to keep politics out of the poverty program, none is more crucial than the campaign to save the Child Development Group of Mississippi.
>
> At the moment it looks as if Sargent Shriver has given up.
>
> CDGM was what Sargent Shriver had in mind when he spoke about the maximum feasible extent to which the poor may participate in the solutions of their own problems. It is, in fact, what Sargent Shriver and his poverty warriors have been battling for all along.
>
> Unfortunately, the prospect of a self-emancipated Negro community isn't welcome everywhere in Mississippi. Some political leaders see it, with clarity, as a threat. So they want Sargent Shriver to drop CDGM and then channel the funds through a group of directors they'll approve.
>
> They've accused the CDGM of everything from nepotism to using a school kitchen to prepare food for the Meredith marchers. And with their charges in one hand, and a collection of political threats in the other, they have made Sargent Shriver knuckle under. All he has to do, they say, is replace CDGM with another board. They will allow a grant to go through.
>
> The issue is clear: Politics and the Poverty Program don't mix. Nobody knows it better than Sargent Shriver. Unless it's those 35,000 Mississippians who are waiting now, to hear that they can continue the work they started.

Readers of the *New York Times* who turned to the editorial page could read Shriver's reply to the advertisement on the day it was printed.

Shriver insisted that for over two weeks he had been saying that "it wasn't so, that it hasn't been so, and that it will not be so.

"It is shocking to me that any American, and especially members of the clergy, should rush into public print impugning the motives of a public official before ascertaining the facts."

Many churchmen, incidentally, agreed with Shriver, feeling that CDGM supporters were so emotionally involved that they failed to see some black militants were using CDGM for their own purposes. CDGM officials of course denied the charge.

Shriver then repeated his previous statements that CDGM could not be refunded because of payroll padding, nepotism, conflict of interest, and misuse of property. He would not be moved.

*   *   *   *   *

The Reverend Merchant's expressed hope that Shriver and the CDGM could reach an agreement through negotiations failed to materialize immediately. The next meeting between the concerned parties, in Atlanta in late October, was more of a confrontation than any kind of give-and-take session. Joe Rauh, vice president of Americans for Democratic Action (ADA) who was acting as attorney for CDGM, describes the battle of Atlanta:

> The tenor of that meeting was so hot you could have fried an egg on the forehead of every participant. Shriver caught a plane out of there before we came to any kind of a decision. We debated with Kramer and a couple of others hoping for a settlement.
>
> We waited so long that Shriver had landed in Washington and was consulted on whether he would accept our offer — which was pretty good — and he turned it down. We sat there for hours and I kept missing plane after plane for Washington. It was 2 o'clock in the morning when I got back.

When the discussion became locked-in with no apparent agreement in sight, Rauh dictated the following statement to be given the newsmen outside the door:

> We express keen disappointment at the failure of today's negotiations with Mr. Shriver. We expressly regret OEO's misinformation, intransigence and lack of understanding of Mississippi's problems. We have, in good faith, been willing and remain willing to discuss with OEO appropriate steps to be taken by CDGM towards refunding on a continuing and substantial basis. Towards this end, additional meetings will be held in the very near future between OEO and CDGM officials. We will, however, continue to put before the public all of the facts surrounding OEO's ac-

tions regarding CDGM and to use every available means to insure funding.

Kramer was at an adjoining typewriter writing out a reply while Rauh dictated his. He contacted Shriver and was given authority to issue the following statement:

> I am astonished at the statement issued by the board of CDGM following my meeting with them today — that the meeting ended in failure. When I left to return to Washington I felt that it was being conducted on an amicable basis and that solid ground-work had been laid for future productive meetings.
>
> OEO had agreed to work closely with representatives of CDGM to attempt to overcome the serious deficiencies which we found in their program and which led to our decision that it could not be refunded as presently organized.
>
> CDGM has asked me to make a commitment to refinance their program on a continuing basis, something this agency has not been asked to do by any other program of any kind administered by OEO. This would be completely beyond the authority which Congress has given me to administer programs on a year-to-year authorization. In any case, the application which CDGM had submitted to OEO exceeds by more than one-third the financial guideline given to them.
>
> I authorized a statement to be made to the CDGM board that OEO would continue to meet with CDGM to attempt to work out deficiencies of program, personnel, management capability and fiscal responsibility. If such matters could be resolved I said I was "very hopeful that OEO could refinance their program."

By this time, church lobbyists were convinced that Shriver was dancing to a tune piped by the White House. They then decided to appeal their case to a man who had the ear of the President — Vice President Hubert H. Humphrey.

Vice President Humphrey, chatting animatedly with a dozen church officials in his suite in Miami Beach's Hotel Fontaine-bleau, was in an expansive mood. Only a few minutes earlier his speech to the General Assembly of the National Council of Churches had been interrupted several times by 5,000 cheering delegates. Obviously buoyed by the enthusiastic reaction of the audience, Mr. Humphrey continued in his room to expand his theme of churches seizing initiatives in areas where the government is legally unable to enter.

"We are now in stage two of this wave of social reform — the tough working stage of the follow-through," he had told the audience, "when we find out how hard the job is, how long it will take, how much money it will cost, how many of our efforts need to be revised and improved. It is a time when all too many crusaders are inclined to leave the march."

An articulate idealist, the genial Vice President was enjoying the company of men who shared his views of reshaping the nation's social structures. He also knew most of the men in his room by their first names. They had worked closely with him when he, as Senate Majority Whip, led the bipartisan effort to pass the 1964 Civil Rights Act. Mr. Humphrey again expressed the Administration's appreciation.

"Now how about some of your current programs?" he asked. "If there are ways we can be of help to you, we want to be."

Dr. Truman Douglass quickly filled the verbal gap. "Mr. Vice President," he said, "we need your help right now in getting the Child Development Group of Mississippi refunded."

Dr. Kenneth Neigh, General Secretary of the Board of National Missions of the United Presbyterian Church, could understand the Vice President's somewhat quizzical attitude. "It was difficult for anyone to have a grasp of the situation at that time," Dr. Neigh explained. "But the Vice President was sympathetic and listened. It was not a matter of having to change a point of view."

Larold Schulz recalls that the Vice President "hadn't been very well briefed on the matter. Mr. Humphrey had, he said, "been a long-time friend of those of us in the church group engaged in social justice — to use that term broadly. We had worked with him on civil rights when he was Senator, and this was a continuation of that relationship. We were disenchanted with his stand on Vietnam but we didn't let that stand in our way for CDGM. He told us he would check in and do all he could."

At a breakfast news conference the next morning, Vice President Humphrey repeated to the press the promise he had made to the church officials. "We do not operate the program, but if we can't find a solution to this sticky question, then I think we should close shop," he said.

The Vice President quickly made good on his promise to produce results. In only two days he had the emotional issue off dead-center and the opposing factions negotiating.

Dr. Douglass was having lunch at the National Arts Club in New York City on December 10 when he got a call from the Vice President. "He told me that OEO had made an offer of an $8.5 million grant for ten months for CDGM, and he hoped we would accept it," Dr. Douglass said. "I knew then he had talked to Shriver."

Dr. Douglass was not as definite as some of his colleagues on the question of the President's personal involvement in the knotty refund-or-not-to-refund CDGM question.

"Either he [the Vice President] or Mr. Welch [Humphrey's administrative assistant] said they had been in touch with the White House," Dr. Douglass said. "President Johnson was in Texas at the time recovering from his operation. They may have just talked to one of the President's assistants. Mr. Humphrey may have persuaded the President to change his mind — I have no knowledge of that. But it is pretty evident that Humphrey doesn't go counter to the President. This is my own deduction from the way things developed."

CDGM board members came up from Mississippi to negotiate with OEO officials. But before that they held an intensive two-day caucus with officials of the CCAP. "We met in the Statler-Hilton hotel," recalls Dr. Douglass. "OEO at the time was demanding the resignation of John Mudd [who had succeeded Dr. Levin as CDGM director] and we didn't want to see him fired."

Final negotiations with OEO officials took place in the agency's offices at 1200 19th Street, N.W. CDGM officials included Director Mudd; the Rev. James McRee, board chairman; Marion Wright, a Mississippi attorney; and Edgar Carroll, vice president for development of Mary Holmes Junior College and grant administrator.

Dr. Neigh and Bryant George, associate director of church strategy and development for the United Presbyterian Church, represented their communion at the conference table. Donald Baker, chief counsel, and Jules Sugarman, deputy director of the Head Start project, did most of the negotiating for OEO. Shriver and Vice President Humphrey did not attend the meetings.

Dr. Neigh got an urgent call in his New York office December 16 from CCAP urging him to return to Washington immediately. He hopped a plane for the Capital. When he walked into the CCAP office, he was told the Vice President wanted him to call him right away. "The Vice President told me a settlement was in the offing — and it was announced that night by Shriver," Dr. Neigh says. "Something had to happen at the top to get it settled that quickly."

James Hamilton, Washington representative for the NCC who served as a liaison man with Humphrey's staff, believes that it was the Vice President's pressure on Shriver that released the grant.

"I'm sure the White House was involved," Hamilton says. "There certainly were political considerations in the decision to refund CDGM."

Dr. Douglass said that one of the problems during the negotiations was created by the inaccessibility of Shriver. "We had been getting the run around," he says. "We would think we had reached an agreement when the OEO staff would run back to check with Shriver. I talked to the Vice President about keeping Shriver in contact with negotiations at all times. Apparently, he did."

The long struggle ended December 16, 1966. Shriver, in what appeared to many as a face-saving statement, emphasized that CDGM was being refunded only because it agreed to comply with OEO conditions. In a letter to Dr. Neigh, he listed the terms of the agreement:

> Specifically, the board of CDGM has been enlarged, the biracial character of the board has been strengthened, new qualified staff members have been assured for key managerial roles, guidelines of financial responsibility should eliminate discrepancies in last year's program, the mechanism for controlling management and financial procedures has been significantly strengthened, and procedural discrepancies in the previous grants are being corrected.

The Board of National Missions of the United Presbyterian Church had to agree to maintain "continuous surveillance" over the operation of the grant. Edgar Carroll of Mary Holmes Junior College was given authority to suspend any activity of the program he considered in violation of OEO guidelines within forty-eight hours. The Board of National Missions also assumed full financial responsibility for any disallowance of expenditures discovered by public auditors. Shriver said that this would serve as a safeguard of the taxpayers' money. CDGM's scope of operations was reduced from twenty-eight counties to fourteen. But CDGM Director Mudd kept his job.

Dr. Neigh says Shriver's public statement was an attempt to prove that the refunding was not a victory for the church lobby.

"It was a real slick public relations job," Dr. Neigh says. "They said the church agreed to be more active in administration. There is no change at all in our responsibility. This over-emphasis on our part makes it look like we are violating the church-state separation principle. And we would be if we directed the program.

"We certainly have tightened the nuts and bolts in our machinery so questions cannot be raised in the future about fiscal irresponsibility, but we are not interfering with the programs."

*   *   *   *   *

Theodore Berry, director of OEO's Community Action Commission (CAC), discussed the church's role in CDGM in his fifth floor office.

"The churches came in a little late," he said, tamping the tobacco in his pipe. "The church got emotionally swept into the matter. But the church owed a responsibility to be more involved before the fact than after.

"Personally, I think CDGM would have been refunded even if the churches had not been involved.

"Head Start funds come out of this office," he continued. "We want the program continued in Mississippi, but we did not want CDGM to have a monopoly. They thought they could strong arm us and bulldoze their way through.We showed them they couldn't.

"We were at one point demanding that Mudd be replaced. But we agreed he could stay on as long as he got a good deputy director and strong personnel.

"I think it is to our credit that we funded CDGM in the first place when there was so much opposition.

"I personally have felt no pressure. But if the churches feel they have won a victory, and this will in any way strengthen their support in the War on Poverty, then let them enjoy the luxury of their boast."

Richard Boone, a former assistant to Berry, who became CCAP'S executive secretary, disagrees with Berry.

"This certainly was not a victory for OEO — they fought tooth and nail to kill the program," he said, with a scornful chuckle. "They used a full variety of weapons to try to prevent making a grant.

"The crucial forces in the determination of policy were not at OEO — they were in the White House and in Congress. My guess is that after the last go-around with Stennis, OEO made a determination not to refund CDGM.

"But the White House had poor intelligence — it underestimated the strength of CDGM supporters. There were over $200,000 spent to keep CDGM alive.

"I think the intervention of the Vice President and the conclusions reached by the White House, the Hill, and OEO that the coalition supporting CDGM could not be bought off, lulled off, or bulldozed out of the way, made Shriver decide to award the grant."

* * * * *

CDGM Board Chairman James F. McRee is a forty-eight-year-old Methodist minister who pastors the Asbury Methodist Church in Canton, Mississippi.

"I think the church made a big impact in getting us funds," he says. "If it hadn't been for the churches, maybe the full story never would have been told. I think some of the things OEO accused us of, they believed because they had not made a thorough investigation. I think they were trying to rush things."

McRee admitted that CDGM had been attacked internally as well as externally. "The Mississippi Freedom Democratic Party fought CDGM like all other groups. And I'm the Madison County chairman for MFDP." He chuckled. "That's one of the complexities of Mississippi politics. Some in the MFDP thought CDGM was a sell-out. SNCC thought it was a sell-out. We had some SNCC workers earlier, but most are out now. The Black Nationalists also attacked us. They felt we had become too satisfied.

"The White Power structure feels like CDGM is a threat. When you have thousands of people who never voted before, and then they make more money than they ever had in their lives, you might consider it a threat.

"I belong to the NAACP, but I support all civil rights groups. CDGM is not a civil rights organization. It is a federal program to help the poor. We don't care what people belong to, as long as they play by the rules of OEO and the CDGM board.

"I am opposed to the black structure and I'm opposed to the white structure. My belief is black and white together.

"We have tried to get whites involved, but many of them refuse to work with us. The Supreme Court ordered schools desegregated in 1954 but the Federal government with all its powers still hasn't desegregated all the schools. How then did they expect us to integrate our program in such a short time?"

The fog of suspicion hovering over CDGM was not dispelled by the OEO's announcement that the Head Start project would be refinanced. Rowland Evans and Robert Novak, investigative reporters, wrote the following in their January 30, 1967, column:

> The bitter internal power struggle for control of the Federal poverty program in Mississippi has entered a new phase with black power radicals waging tenacious guerilla warfare against biracial moderates.

Moreover, this warfare has pointed up what many Northern Liberals have refused to see. The Child Development Group of Mississippi (CDGM), which runs Head Start nursery schools throughout the state, has become an instrument of the black separatist movement.

The present war over the Head Start Program is symptomatic of how fuzzy the Northern liberals are in their opaque view of what is happening here. It began in late August when Sargent Shriver's OEO, the chief poverty agency, urged the biracial moderates to form MAP as a successor to CDGM. What followed was an OEO decision not to refund CDGM, and the war was on.

Church lobbyist David Maguire believes that two major lessons for the church emerged from the CDGM struggle. The first lesson is that although the President is consummately powerful, his political judgment is not infallible. Maguire holds that Vice President Humphrey interceded with President Johnson, calling to his attention the questionableness of recapturing Mississippi, even with a core of loyalist Democrats dispensing anti-poverty funds through MAP.

The second lesson is that effective protest requires in addition to persistence, the coalescing of powerful groups and their steady application of political pressure. "The church clearly is one such group, and a far more potent force than most churchmen realize," says Maguire.

But while the church lobby won the CDGM battle, it may have helped to lose the War on Poverty. As Albert C. Saunders, Secretary for National Affairs for the United Presbyterian Church U.S.A., pointed out to readers in his "Washington Special Report" newsletter of January 31, 1967:

The net result has been reduced support for OEO by religious and secular anti-poverty organizations. This factor, combined with the status of OEO appropriations and directly-run programs, made the outlook for the anti-poverty war bleak in January.

Saunders said that educators were calling for the transfer of the Head Start program to the Office of Education. Senator Abraham Ribicoff (D., Conn.) suggested shifting the community action programs under OEO to the Department of Housing and Urban Development, and the Job Corps to the Labor Department. The Ninetieth Congress was much more conservative than the free-spending Eighty-ninth. The war in Vietnam, rather than domestic needs, received the greatest attention and the most sympathetic treatment when it came to appropriations. Concerned over the diminishing support on the part of religious groups, OEO officials called on church leaders to reassert their backing of OEO programs on a local level in order to prod Congress into providing funds. Most of these predicted changes did take place two years later under President Richard M. Nixon.

The church's deep involvement in CDGM from the outset weakened its posture as social critic and gadfly of the government in relation to the value of CDGM. As Rabbi Richard G. Hirsch, director of the Religious Action Center of the Union of American Hebrew Congregations and secretary of the Civil Crusade Against Poverty, pointed out: "You can't accept money with one hand and slap the giver with the other."

The church lobby tried taking and slapping simultaneously. Theoretically, the value judgments made by the church should not depend on issues. But churchmen do run the risk of weakening their judgmental, or prophetic, role by serving as an agent for government as they did, and do, in CDGM.

Rabbi Hirsch, who is more interested than many of his clerical colleagues in making a distinction between the role of the church and that of government, explained his reasoning for supporting CDGM: "The issue was complex but there comes a time when you have to make a decision," he said. "In this instance, I thought some poor people who had been getting federal funds were now being sacrificed for political reasons — and for political reasons with which I didn't agree."

Rabbi Hirsch's statement pinpoints the issue: Should the church be galvanized into action for political reasons or moral principles? If the same people could have been helped through MAP rather than CDGM was it really the church's duty to select the agency? Or were the church activists so emotionally and economically involved they acted from the wrong reasons even for a good cause? This makes churchmen vulnerable to the charge they too often act more like political power brokers than prophets speaking out for justice.

The prevailing attitude that if the government has money which the church can use, then damn the theology and the constitution and full speed ahead, is a religious shortcut with long-run implications. The idiom of Utopia is not the language of the church. And church leaders should be wary of politicians espousing noble but unrealizable goals. Confusing the Great Society with the millennium was both poor theology and poor politics.

The church is not above its Master and certainly Christ identified with the "abused and humiliated members of society." He did not, however, take governmental grants from Pontius Pilate. As Congressman Walter H. Moeller, a Lutheran minister who served in Congress, so aptly stated: "There should be cooperation between Church and State in a manner which will neither destroy the distinction between the two nor obliterate the purpose for which both exist."

CHAPTER V

Scaling the Church-State Wall of Separation

The former country schoolteacher who became President of the United States obviously was in his element. Lyndon Baines Johnson was back home in Texas, surrounded by admirers and about to sign into law the first bill providing general federal aid for elementary and secondary schools. The frosting on the cake was the setting in which the historic occasion would take place — outside the former one-room schoolhouse at Stonewall, Texas, where he first attended classes.

"I predict that all of those of both parties of Congress who supported the enactment of the legislation will be remembered as men and women who began a new day of greatness in American society," President Johnson intoned. The President was in an expansive mood — and not without good reason. Congress had passed the Administration's Elementary and Secondary Education Act of 1965 in less than ninety days. The bill, HR 2362, was approved by the members of the House 263 to 153, and the Senate passed the bill 73-18 on Friday, April 9 — two days before the President was whisked by plane to Texas for the sentimental journey to Stonewall.

The Administration forces achieved a legislative breakthrough in getting the Senate to approve the bill in the exact form it had been passed by the House. The skillful floor action of the Senate sponsors eliminated a House-Senate conference, where so many education bills had been scuttled in the past.

The genius of HR 2362 was its subtle — some say ambiguous — church-state compromise. Strict separatists and religious pressure groups had successfully blocked for more than a generation any bill containing federal assistance to church-related schools. HR 2362 knocked these traditional opponents off the wall of separation in one fell swoop with its ingenious child-benefit theory. This theory, as formulated by the Johnson Administration, states that public aid may be given to economically deprived children — some of whom may be attending religious schools — as long as the funds are not directly channeled into the coffers of the church schools. This argument maintains there is a constitutional distinction between giving public aid to parochial *students* and giving public aid to parochial *schools*. Opponents disagreed, insisting that any aid to private students has built-in benefits for the school.

Both the timing and the wording of the bill had been carefully planned. The age of ecumenicity was in full bloom. Catholics and Protestants were meeting across the nation in "living room dialogues," and preacher and priest had linked arms to fight the common foes of poverty and human injustice. Anyone even daring to suggest in such an atmosphere that HR 2362 was fudging on the constitutional question of providing public aid to church-related schools took the risk of being branded a religious bigot. It was a risk that only a few of the most stout-hearted would take.

While paying some lip-service to the safeguards of the Constitution, the majority of church bureaucrats joined in a paean of praise for HR 2362. Dr. Arthur S. Flemming, the first vice president of the National Council of Churches of Christ and the lead-off church witness before the committee holding hearings on the bill, continually referred to HR 2362 as "an instrument of reconciliation": "I believe that President Johnson and his associates should be commended for providing us with this opportunity of approaching an old unsolved problem with a new spirit," he stated.

The warm praise given HR 2362 as an "instrument of reconciliation" was exceeded by the testimony of H. B. Sissel, Secretary for National Affairs of the United Presbyterian Church, who sounded as if he thought the bill had been forged somewhere near the summit of Mount Sinai. "I think that this bill — and I stand in awe of those who drafted it — represents a fantastically skillful breakthrough, or at least a possibility of a breakthrough, in the stalemate which has been hung up on the church-state dilemma for many years," Mr. Sissel told the committee.

The proponents of the bill pointed out they had precedent for the child-benefit theory in the dual enrollment, or shared time, concept contained in previous legislation. Under dual enrollment, parochial students take their religious studies in the private school and secular subjects in the public school. This arrangement permits the parochial school to eliminate certain secular subjects or services at a considerable savings.

President Johnson's strategists drew up the general aid to education bill fully aware that the Democrats commanded an overwhelming majority in Congress who were ready and able to roll over any opposition. The political pressure applied in gaining the bill's unparalleled swift passage caused cynical critics to refer to the bill as "the railroad act of 1965."

President Johnson, preferring to base his leadership on consensus rather than pure political clout, wanted to avoid bulldozing his way through any opposition based on church-state separation principles. Two traditional hurdles already had been removed. Barry Goldwater's crushing defeat in the previous November presidential election delivered a knockout blow to conservatives who had long protested that federal aid to schools would be followed by federal control. And the Civil Rights Act of 1964 ended the protracted struggle between segregationists and civil rights groups over aid to "separate but equal" schools in the South. Title VI of the Civil Rights Act states:

> No person in the United States shall, on the ground of race, color, or national origin, be excluded from participation in, be denied the benefits of, or be subjected to discrimination under any program of activity receiving federal assistance.

That meant if Southern school districts wanted federal funds, they would have to prove that their students were attending integrated schools—or that plans were being made for them to do so.

The only remaining obstacle to passage of the first federal aid to education bill was the church-state issue. President Johnson's advisers came up with a simple but effective plan: Peg the bill on the poverty program and then rush it through Congress so opponents would not have enough time to analyze it and mount an attack. The swift success of the strategy must have surprised even the most optimistic proponents of the plan.

By building his educational program around the needs of poor pupils and the schools which served them, the President struck a sensitive chord in a guilt-ridden society uneasy with its affluence. "Poverty did for the Elementary and Secondary Education Act what Sputnik did for the National Defense Education Act," quipped Congressman Albert H. Quie, a conservative Republican who made an unsuccessful attempt in 1967 to revise the ESEA.

One must back up 185 years to gain a historical perspective of the Federal government's role in education in order to appreciate fully the political skill of the Administration in blunting the thorny church-state issue on which so many education bills had been impaled.

In 1785, the Congress of the Confederation adopted the Survey Ordinance, which reserved one section of every township in the Western Territory for the endowment of schools within that township. Two years later, the Northwest Ordinance, adopted by Congress, declared: " . . . religion, morality and knowledge being necessary to government and the happiness of mankind, schools and the means of education shall forever be encouraged."

In 1862, the Morrill Act established land-grant colleges. But the states ran into difficulty supporting these colleges, causing Congress in the second Morrill Act of 1890 to authorize annual federal grants to pay for the operation. The land-grant colleges were designed to provide working classes the opportunity for both liberal and practical education.

The U. S. Office of Education, founded in 1867, is one of the oldest government agencies. It was part of the Interior Department from 1869 to 1939, then transferred to the Federal Security Agency. And in 1953, the FSA became the Department of Health, Education and Welfare.

The government began giving grants for vocational education in 1917 under the Smith-Hughes Act. During the Depression years of the 1930's, the government made educational activity part of its relief program.

The Lanham Act of 1940 was the forerunner of emergency educational aid and the "impacted" areas aid of the late 1940's and early 1950's. The Act gave federal aid to build, maintain, and operate schools in communities with populations swollen by an increased number of defense workers and military personnel.

The GI Bill of Rights enacted in 1944 provided unprecedented aid to millions of returning servicemen. (Veterans of the Korean War and Vietnam got more limited benefits.) Following World War II, the Federal government's contributions to education skyrocketed. The National Defense Education Act of 1958 got its biggest boost October 4, 1957, when the Russians launched the first earth satellite (Sputnik).

The NDEA, calling for $1.6 billion for federal-state education programs, emphasized science, mathematics, and foreign languages. It was an emergency measure to fill a technological gap created by the lack of engineers and scientists. A report by the Joint Atomic Energy Committee in March of 1956 said that the

U. S. was permitting 80 percent of its potential scientific and engineering manpower go down the drain because of the failure of qualified high school students to go on to college and of college students to finish their education. The bill, with an appeal to national pride, had comparatively smooth sailing through Congress.

In 1961, President John F. Kennedy, the nation's first Catholic President, tasted the bitterness of "church power" politics. He was handed a severe legislative defeat on a general school aid bill because of stiff opposition by the Catholic bishops.

In his education message, President Kennedy asked for $2.3 billion in grants over a three-year period to be used by the states for the construction of elementary and high school classrooms and for boosting teachers' salaries. The President, who had convinced the electorate in 1960 that he would not favor his church over others, emphasized that no general school aid funds were allocated for private schools "in accordance with the clear prohibition of the Constitution." The Catholic bishops took the traditional stance that the public school bill should include aid for parochial schools or it should be defeated. The President replied in a press conference that "across-the-board" loans as well as grants to private schools were unconstitutional. The religious school aid controversy became so heated during the Congressional debate that the bill was defeated.

The outlook for expanded general aid to education looked dim indeed. As late as 1962, some experts were saying that it would be impossible to reconcile the church-state conflict and therefore it was highly unlikely any federal aid to education legislation could get through Congress.

But in 1963, Congress did a turnabout — proving that even politicians can rise above their principles — and passed a flurry of bills totaling more than $2 billion for education. Ironically, the bills reflected in the main the broad education program suggested in January by President Kennedy — who did not live to see them enacted. The new attitude toward education caused President Johnson to dub his former colleagues on the Hill as the "Education Congress of 1963."

"The Federal Role in Education" booklet, published in 1965 by the *Congressional Quarterly* Service in Washington, includes this passage:

> From nursery schools to university campuses, it would be hard to find a single pupil, teacher or classroom in the nation not in

some way affected by the government's expanding interest and assistance.

Congress authorized the government to buy lunches, to supply funds to improve the teaching of science, mathematics and foreign languages, to lend colleges money to build dormitories, to educate veterans and to grant funds for school construction, operation and teachers' salaries in areas "impacted" by taxfree federal property. BUT UNTIL 1965 NO AID PROGRAM WAS ENACTED WHICH COULD BE CONSIDERED A GENERAL SUBSIDY FOR EDUCATION.

The historic argument for a broad program of federal aid to public elementary and secondary schools maintains that American students constitute a national asset too valuable to be trusted wholly to the states. Opponents counter that education is strictly the concern of the state and local districts and that to accept federal funds would mean accepting federal control. The intrusion of the religious issue into the debate made it even more intense.

As early as 1948, Senator Robert A. Taft, Mr. Republican from Ohio, saw what he thought was a glimmer of light penetrating the church-state separation wall. "The Supreme Court has in effect said that we cannot appropriate money for education in sectarian schools," he observed in a Senate debate. "The court has not ruled so clearly, however, on incidental services." The Ohio Senator then made the observation that at that point in history, nineteen states were providing bus service for parochial students, five states were helping to furnish free books, and several states were providing health services for both private and public school children. "We should not interfere with states which do not want to give these services and which have disapproved of them in many cases," he concluded. "We should no more force states to give them than we should prevent the states that want to give them from so doing."

Senator Brian McMahon, Democrat from Connecticut, presented the viewpoint of millions of Catholics: "Under the Constitution and under the decision of the Supreme Court, Congress could not, if it would, devote a single penny of tax money for the purpose of promoting the religious training of the child," he said. "But under the same decision of the Supreme Court it is entirely permissible, as I read them, to cover . . . bus transportation, nonreligious school books . . . recreational facilities, and health services.

"The little ones who are in the nonpublic schools are not

there of their own choice," he asserted. "In 99 cases out of 100 they are there because their parents have sent them there, and under the law, they are entitled to attend these schools."

Senator McMahon's views were clearly the wave of the future. But the waves were a long time getting ashore. When it looked as if even a ripple bearing assistance to parochial schools was headed toward the beach, it would be dashed broadside against Thomas Jefferson's seemingly impregnable wall of separation between church and state.

Another aspect of federal aid to education revolved around the system of "separate but equal" schools embedded in the South. Until 1954, the Supreme Court has held that federal aid to states with segregated, dual systems was Constitutional. School bill provisions aimed at withholding federal funds to segregated schools were always defeated by the Southern-led bloc of con-servative Congressmen.

The U. S. Supreme Court in its ruling on Brown vs. the Board of Education of Topeka, Kansas, in 1954, finally made the nation's conscience square with the Constitution by saying that segregated schools were after all unconstitutional. Liberals and civil rights workers were overjoyed — and misled into believing that the battle has been won. It had not. Key committees in Congress, controlled by Southern Representatives and Senators, were always able to muster enough strength to block the passage of any bills which prohibited aid to segregated schools.

The impasse produced a strange situation. Amendments aimed at cutting off aid to segregated schools became a legislative device employed by those opposed to ALL federal aid to education. The anti-federal assistance advocates knew that a bill with such provisions could never hurdle the Southern Democrat-conserva-tive Republican bloc. As a result, many liberal Congressmen found themselves in the awkward position of opposing civil rights amendments knowing that such amendments spelled certain defeat for the entire bill.

The doctrinaire liberal, however, did back the civil rights amendments. He felt compelled to vote his conscience rather than compromise his principles even though the definition of politics is "the art of the possible." It wasn't until 1964, with the passage of the Civil Rights Act, that the Federal government was given enough leverage to start cracking down on the separate but equal school systems.

By the late 1950's, the Catholic constituency of the country was clamoring for what it considered its rightful share of the federal tax dollar for parochial schools. The authors of "The Federal Role in Education" describe the tenor of the times:

> The [religious] issue remained very quiet during most of the 1950's, exploding again at the very end of the decade. This time it was because the proposals omitted federal aid to private schools. The Catholic Bishops insisted that this constituted discrimination. The clergy was generally supported by Congressmen from predominantly Catholic districts, but opposed by almost all other religious groups, and in Congress particularly by Southerners from Fundamentalist areas.
>
> The Catholic position was prompted by the economic problems their parochial school system was encountering. This system, which educated approximately 13 percent of the nation's school children, was having trouble raising money for construction and — as religious orders could not supply the needed teaching power — attracting lay teachers. Federal aid for public schools only would aggravate these economic problems. In addition, the fact that Catholic parents with children in private schools paid both their tuition and taxes supporting public schools was a major argument of the bishops.

The ranks of religious lobbyists supporting federal aid for private schools before 1965 were rather thin. The National Catholic Welfare Council, based in Washington and later reorganized as the U. S. Catholic Conference, the Council of Catholic Men, and the Catholic-dominated Citizens for Educational Freedom were the three major lobbies urging public support of private schools.

The religious organizations supporting general aid to education but opposed to funds for private schools included the National Council of Churches, the Baptist Joint Committee on Public Affairs, the American Jewish Congress, the Unitarian Universalist Association, the National Lutheran Council, the National Association of Evangelicals, and the contentious Protestants and Other Americans United for Separation of Church and State (POAU).

Lobbyists representing mainstream Protestant denominations lined up with Roman Catholic clergy and Orthodox Jewish rabbis to support HR 2362. Those arrayed in a futile attempt to block the bill came from the most disparate of theological backgrounds. The small minority providing the stiffest opposition included the Union of American Hebrew Congregations (Reform), the American Jewish Congress, the conservative Protestant National

Association of Evangelicals (2.5 million members) and the theologically liberal but Constitutionally strict Unitarian-Universalist Association of 100,000 members. The American Civil Liberties Union provided some of the most articulate arguments against the bill. The Protestants and Other Americans United for Separation of Church and State took the traditional stance suggested by its laborious title.

* * * * *

President Johnson, speaking above the roar of the big guns deployed for the War on Poverty, submitted his message on education to Congress on January 12, 1965. The tack taken by the President to convince Congress to pass his education bill became clear at the outset.

"Poverty has many roots but the tap root is ignorance," he explained. Building on the ignorance-breeds-poverty theme, the President continued:

> Poverty is the lot of two-thirds of the families in which the family head has had eight years or less of schooling.

> Twenty percent of the youth aged 18-24 with an eighth grade education or less are unemployed — four times the national average.

> Just as ignorance breeds poverty, poverty all too often breeds ignorance in the next generation.

> Nearly half the youths rejected by Selective Service for educational deficiency have fathers who are unemployed or else working in unskilled and low-income jobs.

> Fathers of more than one-half of the draft rejectees did not complete the eighth grade.

The President pointed out that low-income families are heavily concentrated in particular urban neighborhoods or rural areas, and went on to emphasize that education is the key to this country's greatness:

> Nothing matters more to the future of our country; not our military preparedness — for armed might is worthless if we lack the brain power to build a world of peace; not our productive economy — for we cannot sustain growth without trained manpower; not our democratic system of government — for freedom is fragile if citizens are ignorant.

> Elementary and secondary schools are the foundation of our educational system.

Forty-eight million students are now in our grade and high schools.

71 percent of the nation's expenditures for education are spent on elementary and secondary schooling.

If these schools are to do their job properly, they need help and they need it now.

His fiscal year 1966 budget would, he said, request $1 billion for the new program, and the federal grants to states would be made available to the children in both public and "private non-profit elementary and secondary schools" — the latter a euphemism for church-related schools and the wording that would be used in the actual bill. (The modifier "non-profit" later would be stricken from certain sections of the bill.)

"We are now embarked on another venture to put the American dream to work in meeting the new demands of a new day," President Johnson concluded. "Once again we must start where men who would improve their society have always known they must begin — with an educational system restudied, reinforced and revitalized."

The Administration's draft of the bill was introduced the same day — in the House by Rep. Carl D. Perkins, a Democrat from the Appalachian regions of Kentucky and chairman of the General Education Subcommittee, and in the Senate by Wayne Morse, Democrat from Oregon and chairman of the Labor and Public Welfare Education Subcommittee. This review will focus only on the legislative history of the bill in the House, since the Senate passed the House bill with hardly a change. "The Senate bill even included the typographical errors contained in the House bill," Congressman Quie stated.

The Elementary and Secondary Education Act of 1965 contained five major titles, each authorizing a major program.

Title I proposed over $1 billion for public school districts on the basis of the number of children from families with annual incomes of less than $2000 — the line of demarcation set by the Administration to identify low-income families. The Administration boasted that 90 percent of the nation's 33,000 public school districts would benefit from Title I. The formula for allocating funds to school districts consisted of multiplying the number of students from families with incomes of $2000 or less (including those on welfare) by 50 percent of each state's average expenditure per school child. Public school boards, for the first time in their history, were required to consider the needs of private school students when applying for federal grants. The child-benefit concept contained in Section 205 (a) 2 in Title I, stipulated that public school boards applying for federal funds had to give assurance

> that, to the extent consistent with the number of educationally deprived children in the school district of the local educational agency who are enrolled in private elementary and secondary schools, such agency has made provision for including special educational services and arrangements (such as dual enrollment, educational radio and television, and mobile educational services) in which such children can participate without full-time public school attendance.

Title II authorized $100 million in fiscal 1966 for grants for the purchase of library resources, textbooks, and other printed instructional materials "for the use of children and teachers in public and nonprofit elementary and secondary schools in the State."

Title II contained a by-pass section that would permit the U. S. Office of Education to provide library resources and instructional materials for use by children and teachers in states with constitutions forbidding the furnishing of any materials to parochial schools. More than thirty state constitutions had such prohibitions.

Title III provided $100 million in grants to the states for supplementary educational centers and services for "vitally needed" educational services not otherwise available. The Office of Education said that the centers, designed to enrich the educational resources of local communities, should be administered by a "consortium" of several educational and cultural institutions in the community. The original language of the bill in effect set up a federally financed school board which would include both ecclesiastical and public officials and which would operate alongside the public school board. Among the services to be provided under this title would be counseling, remedial instruction, and health, recreation, and social work services to help persons enter, remain in, or re-enter educational programs.

Title IV broadened a 1954 law by providing grants for educational research on the university level, and Title V authorized funds to stimulate and assist states to strengthen their state educational agencies.

In their definitive article "The Church-State Settlement in the Federal Aid to Education Act," Dean M. Kelley, Director of the Commission on Religious Liberty of the National Council of

Churches, and George R. LaNoue, Assistant Professor of Government and Education at Columbia University, made these incisive comments shortly after the passage of ESEA:

> The Elementary and Secondary Education Act of 1965 is the beginning of a stream of legislative enactments that will have more impact on the future of education than any previous legislation in the history of the country. That the Act will produce great educational change is hardly debatable. First, there will be the stimulus of the Act's $1.3 billion on current school programs. This amount, not insignificant in itself, is only the beginning. President Johnson has made it perfectly clear that he intends to increase the amount dramatically in the future and he is likely to succeed. Once a federal channel of aid is opened, it is a comparatively simple matter to expand the aperture so the great volume can flow through it. It is more difficult to make any very substantial alteration in the delicate pattern of political compromises that determine how the flow comes out and where it goes — at least until there is a major shift in political power.
>
> Since the Act is the first step toward a basic program of federal aid to elementary and secondary education, its effect on church-state relations is enormously significant. Although the church-state provisions in the Act have been vigorously denounced on one hand and stoutly defended on the other, the essential concepts, much less the details and subtlety of the settlement have rarely been understood. Until one looks at this settlement in the context of its legislative history, it is difficult to judge whether it is a peace treaty that will strengthen education without undermining the First Amendment, as the defenders claim, or whether it is an invitation to sectarian conflict that will endanger the public school system and destroy separation of church and state, as its attackers insist.

Thus the stage was set. The drama would be played out, not under the floodlights, but behind the scenes where religious lobbyists caught unprepared could only watch the inexorable chain of events march past and in most cases were forced to fall in line and march to the tune called by the White House. It was not the lobbyists' greatest hour.

CHAPTER VI

A Split in the Ranks

At what point DID the religious lobbyists learn the details of the President's proposed federal aid to education bill?

It was difficult to get an answer to that question even two years later. Dean Kelley told me informally in April of 1967 that "the government didn't seek us out. They did contact, to some extent, a few groups such as the National Education Association and the National Catholic Welfare Conference. Monsignor Hurley and Bud Consedine lobbied heavily on ESEA. [Msgr. Francis J. Hurley was associate director of the NCWC Department of Education and William R. (Bud) Consedine was chief legal counsel for the NCWC.]

"When we criticized some of the Administration staff for not attempting to work out anything in advance with the religious groups," Kelley continued, "one guy in the Office of Education penciled on an early copy of the bill 'My Lord! Why were we meeting with Hurley and Consedine all these months?'"

Kelley arranged a meeting between Douglas Cater, a White House legislative assistant, and a church-state consortium which he, Kelley, headed. The meeting took place on January 4, 1965, in the Executive Building adjacent to the White House — eight days before the bill would be introduced in Congress.

"Cater outlined the shape of the President's educational message to go to Congress a few days later," Kelley said. "Cater explained [that] the bill would be based on the child-benefit concept.

"After the meeting with Cater, we went back to the National Council of Churches office [in the Methodist Building across the street from the Capitol] to report to the other members of the consortium.

"The group divided down the middle on the bill. The main

Protestant bodies had the feeling the President's proposal was constructive. While we had misgivings about some of the language of the bill, we felt that could be ironed out. The Jewish Organizations, the National Association of Evangelicals, the Seventh Day Adventists, and the American Civil Liberties Union representatives were all opposed. The Baptists, Methodists, Episcopalians, Lutheran Council, United Church of Christ and the National Council of Churches were for the bill.

"The schism has remained," Kelley stated, somewhat sadly.

Traditionally, the most politically potent religious agency in the nation's Capital is the Roman Catholic Church's National Catholic Welfare Council, later changed to the U. S. Catholic Conference. The Conference, the administrative arm of the American bishops, operates out of an imposing ten-story building at 13th Street and Massachusetts Avenue.

Msgr. James C. Donohue, director of the Department of Education of the U. S. Catholic Conference, occupies a first-floor paneled office covered with nonreligious paintings depicting sea scenes, a covered bridge, and a weather-beaten barn. Affable and debonair, Msgr. Donohue described in March of 1967 the role of the Catholic Department of Education vis-à-vis the government. He had not been the director in 1965.

"We are the civil arm of the National Conference of Catholic Bishops," he explained, ignoring six pipes in a holder to light a cigar. "We are concerned with the whole picture of Catholic Education in the United States. We represent Catholic education to government and work to coordinate efforts of Catholic educators out in the field.

"The Church's position — if there has been one — is one of neutrality on the question of federal aid to education as a theoretical question. We hold no specific brief for the desirability of government involvement pro or con.

"BUT if the government is going to get involved in American Education in any substantial way — given the court-backed parental right of choice of education for the good of the total American educational effort — we believe the private school should be helped the same as the public school. We believe this because we are performing a public service in education to over six million future citizens. One of every seven students is going to a Catholic school.

"Some Catholic educators say we would be priced out of the market if aid were given to public schools but not private schools because we must compete for the services of the lay teacher. I'm not so sure of that argument. I'm more concerned with the fairness and rightness of the thing. I personally feel there are things that can be done to aid religious-oriented education that is constitutional."

Msgr. Donohue credited Francis Keppel, U.S. Commissioner of Education, with being the peacemaker for the 1965 Secondary and Elementary Education Act. "Frank was the first commissioner to get together the various factions which had been contributing to an impasse at the elementary-secondary level and work out a compromise. He set up a meeting with various groups and got them to sit down and reason together," the Catholic educator said with a wide grin, using the catch-phrase of President Johnson.

Msgr. Donohue made it clear that his relationship with the U. S. Commissioner of Education was informal — and close. He said he kept continual contact with the U. S. Office of Education and lunched regularly with the education commissioner. "We work on the premise the Hill is no place for a clergyman," he said, in answer to the question whether he considered himself a lobbyist. "That is definitely the role of the layman in the church. There is something about the Roman Catholic collar — it is more felt than expressed," he said, without completing the sentence. "This business of going up and cornering a Congressman is unfitting — that is not our role. I got my Ph. D. in Education. I was the superintendent of Catholic schools in Baltimore. I'm an educator. I would not even attempt to deal with Congress but with the Office of Education.

"One of our jobs here in Washington is to present the Church's case to the government. Our legal department talks to people in government about our need. The legal department would do the lobbying. The government, knowing we represent the Church, turns to us when they want to know the Church's position — and they always want to know," he concluded.

William (Bud) Consedine, chief legal counsel for the U. S. Catholic Conference, occupies a small space on a floor above Msgr. Donohue's more comfortable paneled office. The white-haired, ruddy-faced attorney who clenches his fists when emphasizing a point became upset when asked whether he lobbied, and quickly denied any attempts to do so. He also refused to permit the interview to be taped and said he did not want to be quoted.

Consedine compared his role with that of a corporation attorney — the corporation in this case being the U. S. Catholic Conference — who keeps his eye on legislation to protect his client. His staff of five lawyers, two of whom are largely concerned with the research and analysis of legislation, assist in keeping an eye on legislation. Upon further questioning, Consedine conceded that a Congressman "might" contact his office to get the reaction of the bishops on proposed legislation.

Consedine was being far too modest about his part in helping to shape the embryonic legislation destined to become the Elementary and Secondary Education Act of 1965. Dr. Wilbur J. Cohen, who was an assistant secretary of legislation for the Department of Health, Education, and Welfare from 1961 to 1965 and subsequently named HEW secretary, made it clear in an interview in December of 1969 that Consedine represented the official Catholic position from the outset.

Dr. Cohen himself was the principal architect of the church-state settlement. The loquacious educator put the following perspective on the consultations leading up to passage:

"I spent a great deal of my time from 1961 to 1965 trying to find the solution to these problems, and although a lot of people worked from a lot of different points of view, it was my assignment of responsibility, first from President Kennedy, in working with Ted Sorenson, and subsequently with President Johnson, to put all the pieces together that made that a viable piece of legislation.

"During the course of the 1961-62 acts which failed, and which I handled intimately in relation to Delaney's [Rep. James J. Delaney of New York] opposition and that of the other members on the Rules Committee, I came to realize that no matter what you did, if you used the concept of that time based on the average daily attendance in public schools [as the formula for funds], the Catholics were opposed because that took in only the public school attendance.

"If you used the concept of all children, the Catholics still were opposed because that lumped the Catholic children with the rest and you were not giving any special recognition to Catholic children.

"It was out of this concern of reconciling differing points of view that I met, mostly with Consedine — I dealt a great deal with him — and some of the other lawyers for the National Catholic Welfare Conference."

Rep. Delaney, normally a supporter of the Kennedy Administration, was a thorn in the flesh in the school legislative battles of 1961, Dr. Cohen recalled. President Kennedy came under criticism from the Catholic Church hierarchy for failing to make provisions for private school loans in his education requests of $2.3 billion in 1961. Thus to the bill's natural enemies in the House — conservative Republicans and Southern Democrats — was added a potential of eighty-eight Democratic Catholic members. In an attempt to salvage the bill, the Administration sent up to the Hill proposals for extending and expanding the National Defense Education Act. That Act already authorized loans to private schools (and grants to public schools) for equipment for teaching science, mathematics, and foreign languages. The strategy called for Congress to provide an amendment permitting private schools to get loans for the construction of classrooms in which science, mathematics, foreign languages, English, and physical fitness could be taught. The rationale was that the funds would be for special "defense" purposes and not direct aid to the school.

Catholics in Congress feared that a public school bill would be passed but that the private school provisions in the NDEA would be defeated. Two Catholic members of the Rules Committee, Delaney and Thomas P. O'Neill of Massachusetts, voted with the five Republicans and two Southern Democrats on the Committee, to hold up the public school bill until the NDEA was reported to it.

The parochial school aid issue became such a divisive factor in the committee — the Catholics arguing that unless they got assistance for parochial schools they would oppose the public school bill and the Republicans and Southern Democrats insisting just as strongly that they would oppose federal aid to parochial schools — that it scuttled all school legislation. The five Republicans, two Southern Democrats, and Delaney voted to table both the public school bill, the NDEA, and a college aid bill. The summer of 1961 was dry indeed from an educational point of view. And it left its imprint on the memory of Dr. Cohen. "We had the votes in 1961 — except for Delaney and the Rules Committee," Dr. Cohen said. "President Kennedy used to say to me, 'Why don't you get one more Republican to vote for it?' It was because of that imbroglio that it was largely my idea to go to the low-income family concept — to change the allotment formula from the child or the per pupil to the number of children whose parents have incomes of $2000 or less."

Dr. Cohen explained that the child-benefit theory acted as

the legal wheels for the bill to roll on while the allotment formula was the spearhead shattering the hardened religious attitude
which had blocked all previous bills for the past generation.

"My job was to deal primarily with the legislative people
while Dr. Keppel [U. S. Commissioner of Education] was the man
who was on the extremely high level of conversations with the
various educational groups," he said. "My dealings were more
with the staff of the committees — with people like Consedine and
others who were working out the nitty-gritty of the bill.

"It's one thing to talk about the child-benefit theory in the
legal sense and it's another thing to talk about church and state.
When you get right down to it [at this point Dr. Cohen grabbed
a pencil and a piece of paper to simulate writing] — when you're
drafting a piece of legislation with pen and pencil and you're
trying to figure out how to say the words that (A) will be constitutional and (B) won't get people excited, that is difficult. I
would be working at home and my son, who was in law school,
would say to me 'That's illegal' or 'That's undesirable.' There
was a very careful line to be trod.

"I worked very closely with Senator Morse and his legislative
assistant, Charles Lee. They were more important in the development of this legislation than any two other people," Dr. Cohen
said. "The Senate didn't touch the bill because of Senator
Morse. Congressman Perkins was not an intellectual leader, but
he was committed to getting the bill through. But the hard work
was done with Morse and Lee, Consedine, Keppel, and Sam
Halpern, who was my assistant at the time."

Doesn't the ESEA of 1965 actually provide benefits to private
schools?

"We didn't give money to the schools," Dr. Cohen insisted.
"We worked on the child benefit theory to provide services to
children in private schools. As long as the title to the book
remains in the hands of the public authority and can be withdrawn at any time and is under public control, the argument was
made that this still was consistent with the child-benefit theory.
That remains to be seen," admitted Dr. Cohen. "That still hasn't
been tested yet. It may or it may not be legal, but the idea behind
it was to try to find something that would merit the support of
all segments."

With that as the criterion, one would have to admit Dr. Cohen
succeeded in his mission.

*   *   *   *   *

Rabbi Richard G. Hirsch, director of the Religious Action Center of the Union of American Hebrew Congregations (Reform), was still convinced in 1967 that "in terms of religious problems for the bill, the key participants were the Catholics. They were on the inside track. Then," he continued, "come the Protestants. The Jews were way down the line.

"The Protestants said 'We're in favor of the bill but — ' and they came out looking as if they were in favor of the whole bill. We said we're opposed to it if you have these things in it ['these things' being provisions for aid to private school students], but the things we were opposed to were the same provisions the key Protestants were saying 'but' about.

"The Catholics always had taken the position that they opposed any bill that did not include aid to private schools. Then suddenly in 1965 they were saying they would support Johnson's education bill. So obviously if they were going to support it, the bill must include federal aid to private schools. I opposed it on the basis of principle — not as anti-Catholic," the young Rabbi stated.

(Rabbi Hirsch came under sharp criticism by certain subcommittee members for his testimony, which included the line, "In the guise of aiding the child, this bill does aid the school.")

There were others concerned about the ramifications of the Education Act of 1965. Rabbi Hirsch attended a White House conference for educators in March 1967 at which President Johnson told the following story.

During the debate on the proposed ESEA, an influential Southerner called the White House demanding to talk to President Johnson right away. Bill Moyers, press secretary, said that the President was inaccessible. The caller said he had learned that Catholic schools were going to get federal monies from the education bill and he wanted to protest. Moyers informed the persistent caller that the President was in the White House pool with evangelist Billy Graham. The caller heaved a long-distance sigh of relief.

"Oh, if he's with our Billy, don't bother him," he said, apparently assured the conservative Protestant point of view was getting a full, albeit wet, hearing.

* * * * *

Dr. C. Emanuel Carlson, executive director of the Baptist Joint Committee on Public Affairs, is the acknowledged expert on

church-state relations among the Washington-based church lobbyists. A dignified, silver-haired man of slight build and slow
speech, Dr. Carlson oversees the operation of the Joint Committee (representing eight Baptist conventions of twenty-four
million members) in a third-floor suite office in the $2 million
marble Veterans of Foreign Wars Building at 2nd and Maryland
Streets.

Dr. Carlson has been in Washington since 1953. His office staff
consists of three men on the executive level and five women
assistants. His staff supplies news from the Capital directly to
the Baptist Press in Nashville, Tennessee. His Office of Information has direct TWX connections with the Baptist Press and
a number of Baptist state convention offices. Dr. Carlson taught
at Bethel College in St. Paul, Minnesota, for twenty-five years,
where he also was dean of the faculty. He has emphasized that
he considers his role as one of educating his constituents rather
than exerting political pressure.

"The Baptist conventions agreed on a mandate that focuses on
church-state relations and religious liberty," he explained, lean-
ing back in his high-back swivel chair. "We really don't want
to get involved in the other issues the way other churches do.
We make a distinction between lobbying and the right of petition.
We look on a lobbyist as one out to get some advantage through
a direct contact with a legislator. The right of petition includes
the right of a corporate petition or resolutions by church bodies.
But we have no mandate to try to get special consideration for
Baptist churches or conventions."

Dr. Carlson communicates with his constituents through a
"Report from the Capital" bulletin published ten times a year,
through special staff reports, and through the Baptist Press.

"We are aware of the impact of communication on legislation,"
Dr. Carlson admitted. "Folks who talk about indirect lobbying
as being more effective than direct lobbying are correct.

"We analyze and report on public affairs to a sizable religious
movement — it is altogether possible there is some influence on
legislation but through the democratic processes," he emphasized.

Denying that he ever had any private conferences with any one
of the White House staff, Dr. Carlson released a staff report on
January 4, 1965, which sounded as if the author had been meeting with Administration aides — or at least had been looking
over their shoulders.

The report pointed out the expanding role of the national government in education:

> The government's provisions for the general welfare of the people may include those who are enrolled in church-related schools and activities. Thus a housing loan was made to assist colleges in providing dormitory rooms and dining facilities, and an act on agricultural surpluses made these available to church-school lunch rooms and to summer Bible camps. Health services, transportation, and other asserted welfare services are being given.

Dr. Carlson thought that the President gave "leading hints" in his policy statement of November 1, 1964, on what he planned to propose in 1965. At that time, President Johnson urged the nation to meet its needs for 400,000 new public classrooms and for 800,000 new public school teachers over a five-year period. He called for concentrated efforts against city slums and rural poverty, and in behalf of expanded and improved colleges, more adult education, and stronger local education systems — all of which later would be incorporated into his 1965 Education Bill.

"In due time the current speculation will give way to firm recommendations from the Administration," Dr. Carlson predicted. ("Due time" proved to be eight days after the staff report was released.) Dr. Carlson told his readers that the Congressional elections of November of 1964 improved the prospects of legislation providing federal support for educational programs:

> Not only did the Democratic party gain additional seats, but it consolidated its forces and greatly reduced the blocking power of the voting combinations of conservatives. Without waiting to see the reorganization procedures, it is safe to guess that the House Rules Committee will be more responsive to the House majority, and that committee leaders will be more team-minded. In the past, education bills have usually required bi-partisan support in order to have a chance because of the two parties within the Democratic party. This situation may have passed. Even the economy-minded in Congress may view the election results as a "mandate" on this subject.

The Baptist staff report explained that the enactment of the Civil Rights Act in 1964 probably eliminated "riders" to education bills formerly tagged on by those requiring equal rights on any bill offering federal aid to schools or by those resisting federal funds in defense of "states rights."

"Another problem which has made federal educational aids difficult to pass has been the parochial school issue," Dr. Carlson wrote:

Fifty or sixty Congressmen, or even more, have had sufficient pressure for the inclusion of parochial schools so they have been unwilling to support any education bill that does not provide aid for those as well.

The vast amount of publicity given to the Vatican Council's struggle for religious liberty has had a variety of consequences which are hard to measure. For the world to watch this effort in behalf of a new policy, if not a new theology, may have reduced the apprehensions of some voters. . . . The net impact on American voters can be guesswork only.

Leaders in the Roman Catholic educational program are frankly and openly in search of new paths to the future. A few bishops have enunciated their concern for the independence of the church programs, whether these be large or small, and one or two have declared against the acceptance of public funds should such funds be available. Yet, on the large the pressure of the Roman Catholic demand for participation in federal funds, if such are voted for educational needs, stands unchanged.

In the light of all these situations, one can judge that no Congress has ever approached the question of federal support for education in a more fluid situation.

Dr. Carlson zeroed in on what he called the "available components" which the Eighty-ninth Congress could utilize to pass a federal aid to education bill:

Categorical aids is a concept that has emerged in the American public mind in recent years. It is likely to be an important piece in the making of future designs. [It certainly has become such. "Categorical aids" in contrast to "block grants" specify what the federal money may be used for and by whom.]

Personal aid is a second major component for future educational legislation. Having begun in the depression, then been used for transportation and lunches, and more recently as loans to students and summer session stipends for teachers receiving in-service training, this idea is no obviously available for almost any use. It could give assistance to low-income pupils or it could provide general family aid for all education. How far will the American nation go in the use of educational aids to the person?

Dr. Carlson is very adroit in leaving a door open by asking a question just when the reader thinks he is getting ready to settle down to a firm position.

Dr. Carlson then touched on the legislative device employed in the Economic Opportunity Act, which later would become the pivot of the Elementary and Secondary Education Act:

One use which is already provided by legislation is that of educational aids designed to relieve poverty. The statistics are quite clear that lack of schooling and lack of school proficiency are major causes of unemployment and poverty. In the attack on poverty it is good economy to give "educational aid" so as to move people from the welfare rolls to a self-supporting status. Even the less socially-minded may be hard pressed to defend perpetual relief as preferable to educational aid. In short, as our affluent economy goes through a revolution in productive skills, special educational efforts cannot be avoided for those of employable skills.

For this purpose the Economic Opportunity Act will use personal aids in many forms and through many institutions. But how far will the nation go? If this becomes the device for broad federal assistance, it will go far toward *shifting educational financing to a welfare approach.* [Italics mine.]

The "shared time" idea continues to linger on the horizon as a device which might help toward the solution of the parochial school issue. Under the preferable label "dual enrollment" this idea has had some attention by the U. S. Commissioner of Education.

The idea was first launched by some Protestant leaders, and has been generally well received by many Catholic leaders. The proposal suggests that pupils be allowed to take some school work in the public school while they are also enrolled for instruction in "value subjects" in a church school. By this device costly instruction in the sciences, in manual arts, and in physical education could be taken in the public schools as the normal right of all pupils even though they received instruction in religion, music, art, literature, and the social studies in a church school.

Dr. Carlson may not have helped to write the Administration's script but he at least was looking at the same scenario. Emphasizing that "predictions are not merited," he ignored his own advice and went on to take this carefully worded prediction:

Leadership in non-governmental organizations [not only] reflect the prevailing opinion in their groups, but they also assist in the adjustment processes that make up democratic procedures. [Translated, that means lobbying.]

If the American public mind can resolve its inner tensions regarding educational support, there can be little doubt of the readiness of the Administration to recommend it, and of Congress to enact it. [He was right on both counts.] The nation has apparently reached a determination to break through its blockade and to project educational opportunities that are suited to the new day in which the nation finds itself. A half-dozen areas of change now point with some clarity to new formulations which could become the basis for a decade, or a century, of federal assistance to education.

The "inner tensions" and the "new formulations" would be threshed out in ten days of hearings before the General Subcommittee on Education of the Committee on Education and Labor of the House of Representatives. The new day in education — and church-state relations — was about to dawn. But first there must be the twilight zone of committee hearings.

CHAPTER VII

A New Concept in Education

The General Subcommittee on Education of the Committee on Education and Labor was called to order at 10 a.m., Friday, January 22, 1965, by its chairman, the Honorable Carl D. Perkins, Democrat of Kentucky. Congressman Perkins' self-deprecating demeanor camouflages the native intelligence and dedication of the soft-spoken Kentuckian who regarded President Johnson's aid to education bill "as one of the most significant recommendations ever made by a President to the Congress on this subject." Ignorance and poverty for too long had produced slag heaps of helpless humanity in eastern Kentucky. Chairman Perkins was not going to permit religious controversy stifle an education bill containing so many welfare benefits. He would ramrod the committee relentlessly until it had done its job and the bill was approved.

The fact that the members of the Tuesday-to-Thursday Club — as cynical newsmen call Congressmen — began hearings on Friday was an obvious indication of the priority given the bill by the Administration.

The majority members of the subcommittee included John Brademas of Indiana, Ralph J. Scott of North Carolina, Hugh L. Carey of New York, Frank Thompson, Jr., of New Jersey, and William D. Ford of Michigan. The minority members consisted of Charles E. Goodell of New York, John M. Ashbrook of Ohio, and Alphonze Bell of California.

Overwhelmingly outnumbered, the Republican conservatives nevertheless found a hard-charging champion for their point of view in Representative Goodell of New York. (Goodell did not try winning a reputation as a liberal until 1968 when he was appointed to the Senate to fill the vacancy caused by the assassination of Senator Robert F. Kennedy.) Aggressive and articulate, the lawyer skillfully hemmed the majority members into verbal cul-de-sacs where they were forced to stew in their own inconsistencies. Representative Goodell's prime concern centered on trying to define the limits of federal control over federal funds used by local school districts – a goal he was unable to reach. The committee gadfly took advantage of all opportunities to needle witnesses, however, as well as majority committee members, on apparent church-state conflicts in the bill. It all was good clean political fun, but it never influenced the eventual outcome of the bill, which was predestined for passage from the beginning.

Staff members present at the hearings included Dr. Deborah Wolfe, education chief; H. D. (Jack) Reed, Jr., subcommittee general counsel, and Charles Radcliffe, a special education counsel for the minority.

The hearings opened with Anthony J. Celebrezze, Secretary of Health, Education, and Welfare and Francis Keppel, Commissioner of the Office of Education, presenting the bill and providing the rationale for its passage.

Lacing his arguments with quotations from President Johnson's speech on education to Congress on January 12, Secretary Celebrezze made this eloquent appeal in behalf of HR 2362:

> The President's request to this Congress was not for more of the same but for something new and different in magnitude, in concept, and in direction.
>
> The transmittal of the President's education message to this Congress, then, signaled a new beginning and called for a new era in education.
>
> It is a major innovation from Federal proposals and policies in recent decades, particularly with respect to elementary and secondary education.
>
> It is a key to significant and far-reaching improvements in the quality of elementary and secondary education, upon which our total educational progress ultimately depends.
>
> It directs special and notable attention to the education of the children of the poor and, at the same time, enhances the quality of the whole of education.
>
> It is unprecedented in size and scope.
>
> It is imaginative and eminently practical, seeing first things first and focusing funds where the needs are greatest.
>
> For these reasons, the President's program can provide a foundation on which we can build a Great Society, a society we can create

not in a day, nor in a week, but in the deliberate, purposeful steps we take beginning now.

The rationale followed:

> Education's deficiencies, we have come to recognize, are nowhere more marked than in the poverty of the schools that serve the children of the poor — in the heart of our great cities and in many rural communities. In the core of these cities and communities, poverty reduces local resources to the peril point. Because the tax base is low, funds for education are inadequate and the schools and the children suffer.

Conceding that there were obstacles to be overcome in enacting the proposed legislation, Secretary Celebrezze made clear that they were not insurmountable and indeed already may have been hurdled:

> In the past, various proposals for federal assistance to our educational system have met with resistance because of concern federal help may result in federal control.
>
> The Congressional consideration of educational legislation in 1963 and 1964 resulted in weighing that issue carefully and recognized that the federal role in education is that of a partner with the States and localities and that in this responsible partnership the control of education rests where it always has — at the state and local level.

He paused for the benefit of the conservatives of the committee to make sure they had heard him correctly.

Secretary Celebrezze said that any objective analysis of the bill would show that it was designed to strengthen the hand of the states and communities. The role of the Federal government was that of a "necessary stimulant of funds and purpose."

The secretary then patiently explained to the committee, title by title, how the bill would stimulate funds and purpose on the local level:

> As a matter of first priority, the President is requesting, for the fiscal year 1966, $1.4 billion for elementary and secondary education. Of this sum, $1 billion is to aid elementary and secondary education at the point of greatest need; that is, to assist school systems with children of poor families — families with incomes of less than $2000 a year. Thereby it is aimed specifically at giving these children and their school districts a chance to provide the best education for those who assuredly need it most.
>
> This proposal is incorporated in Title I — [and here the government witness made a generous gesture for the benefit of the Committee Chairman] — "of Mr. Perkins' bill."

The second element of the President's program to improve elementary and secondary education authorizes $100 million in the fiscal year 1966 for better textbooks, teaching materials and library books for both public and private nonprofit schools. This is provided in Title II of the bill.

The third portion of the program, contained in Title III of the bill, authorizes $100 million in the fiscal year 1966 for supplementary educational centers and secondary schools and to encourage collaborative efforts among public and private schools.

The fourth part of the program, included in Title IV of the bill, authorizes $45 million in the fiscal year 1966 to establish new educational research laboratories to develop and disseminate new techniques and ideas which can effectively improve education for all school children.

The fifth provision in the program, included in Title V of the bill, authorizes $100 million in the fiscal year 1966 to begin a program for the essential strengthening of our State departments of education. Upon these departments, we must depend if we really mean to keep American education both strong and decentralized.

Secretary Celebrezze then bolstered his argument with charts filled with statistics depicting the "enrollment explosion" (48,-000,000 children ages five to seventeen) and the number of families living in poverty (5,000,000 children are in families earning less than $2,000). One chart showed that in inner-city high schools, as many as 60 percent who enroll in the tenth grade may drop out before graduation. Following his visual presentations, Secretary Celebrezze rested his case.

Then Congressman Goodell, arriving late for the first hearing, gained permission from Chairman Perkins to read a prepared statement revealing his attitude toward the bill.

"All Americans share the goal of having the best attainable education available to all our children," he began. "This year federal education expenditures will total nearly $5 billion. According to the publication of your Department [HEW], that is $1 for every $6.5 spent for all education, public and private, from kindergarten through the university.

"If these proposals are enacted that you have described here today," he said, looking at Secretary Celebrezze, "federal expenditures will have soared to about $7 billion, or $1 for every $5 spent for education in America. This massive federal effort is scattered throughout scores of programs in over forty federal bureaus and agencies and affects all levels of education.

"These new administration proposals involve, in my opinion, some fundamental and extremely difficult issues of public policy," he warned. "These are such things as the degree of federal involvement in private education, the nature and extent of federal educational activities carried on outside our regular schools and school systems.

"Federal intrusions in education may well be becoming so extensive and complicated that some forms of stifling federal controls are virtually inevitable," he capped off his statement.

With the battle lines drawn and the tone of the opposing argument set by the Congressman from New York, the U. S. Commissioner of Education, Dr. Francis Keppel, took the witness chair. Submitting a lengthy written statement for the record, Commissioner Keppel turned his persuasive verbal powers on the committee.

"Perhaps here I am a little more emotional than I usually am," admitted the commissioner. "Our educational system — and I deeply mean this, and the Secretary does, too — our educational system must simply shine as a bright spot in the life of a disadvantaged child. It cannot be permitted to exist, this system, as simply another version of the cultural-economic blight these children find at home," he said, with feeling. "And it does sometimes. This I think is the core of what the Secretary and the President are putting before you."

He concluded with this clincher: "I think Wendell Wilkie said, 'Only the strong can afford to be free.' I would like to argue, sir, that this bill is designed to that end."

Chairman Perkins said he wanted to ask some questions before other members of the committee began their interrogation of the government witnesses. One point he wanted to make clear at the outset: "Does this bill," he asked Secretary Celebrezze, "prohibit the expenditure of funds for religious activities or instruction?"

"Yes, the last provision of the bill does," Secretary Celebrezze replied.

"Would you read that particular provision into the record?" he requested Secretary Celebrezze.

The secretary complied: "Page 68, Section 605, under 'Limitation of Payments under this Title':

> Nothing contained in this Act shall be construed to authorize the making of any payment under this Act, or under any Act amended by this Act, for religious worship or instruction.

"I may also add that the preceding section, Section 604, is also an important section because that section reads:

> Nothing contained in this Act shall be construed to authorize any department, agency, officer, or employee of the United States to exercise any direction, supervision, or control over the curriculum, program of instruction, administration, or personnel of any educational institution or school system, or over the selection of library resources or printed or published instructional materials by any educational institution or school system. .

"This is, of course, to prevent the Federal government from interfering with the internal affairs in trying to strengthen education and keep the responsibility for education in the States," Mr. Celebrezze said.

If the Secretary thought he had disposed of the church-state and federal-funds-beget-federal-control twin issues, he did not have to harbor that illusion long. "Mr. Secretary, what limitations, if any, do you recognize on federal involvement in education?" Congressman Goodell asked as soon as he could gain recognition from the Chair.

The Secretary went into a lengthy answer on the history of federal involvement, the shift from an agricultural to an urban society, to the responsibility of the government to assist those school districts with a weak tax base.

But Mr. Goodell was not satisfied with that rambling reply. "Mr. Secretary, I agree with you as to the importance of education and there is a federal role," he said, not without some exasperation, "but I do not believe you named any limitations on the federal involvement. I am interested where we are headed here. How far do you believe we should go with federal involvement in education? Are we simply trying to stimulate, to try to change the direction of education at various levels? What are the limitations of federal involvement here?"

Secretary Celebrezze was not easily intimidated.

"The only limitation I can see is that the Federal government has a responsibility to see that every young man and every young woman and every illiterate person has an opportunity to get a decent education in this country. . . . I think it is a national duty to do something about this.

"By whatever means is necessary?" Congressman Goodell shot back.

"No, I do not say that," Secretary Celebrezze replied. "I am talking from the monetary point always. I emphasize that. I have said it now a half dozen times. Always leaving the control of the education on the state and local level."

"Complete control?" insisted Goodell.

"Complete control of it," Celebrezze said.

Lawyer Goodell had learned well the art of persistent interrogation.

"One hundred percent control on the state and local level? The federal responsibility is to provide the monetary resources?"

Secretary Celebrezze commented that when Congress appropriates money, its specifies how the money is to be used.

"This is the whole point," Goodell interjected, believing he had found the opening for which he had been probing. He then gave the committee the benefit of his views:

"It seems to me in these debates we often are kidding ourselves, we are looking at an illusion that if you get federal involvement to the degree that you are discussing monetarily, we as public officials must see to it that the money is directed properly and used and focused to meet the needs as we conceive them at the federal level. . . . If all you wanted to do was to help the locality in a monetary sense, you could pass the tax resources back to the localities, but you obviously want to do more than just give them more monetary support. You want to direct and guide them in certain ways."

Congressman Goodell then asked Secretary Celebrezze how many states permit aid to private schools?

"That varies a great deal," Secretary Celebrezze said, "whether by state constitution or state statute; the last count I saw, I think there were something like thirty-four. Our summary was that states having relatively absolute prohibitions against the use of public funds to aid sectarian schools, prohibited by the Constitution, were twenty-eight, prohibited by statute were four."

Without asking Secretary Celebrezze to explain the phrase "relatively absolute," Congressman Goodell turned to what would become known later as the "bypass clause." "In Title II," he noted, "the $100 million for library resources and instructional materials, textbooks, and things of that nature, you have a provision which says, if I interpret it correctly, that you may give the aid directly if the state is not permitted to give it?"

"The Commissioner of Education," corrected Secretary Celebrezze.

"The Commissioner may give it directly if the state does not authorize it?" repeated Congressman Goodell.

"Yes, that is on textbooks and library resources," the Secretary said.

(At this point of the legislative history, it is obvious that government witnesses were reflecting the reality of the bill — the money would go directly to the schools. Secretary Celebrezze and Dr. Cohen both conceded that grants would go to parochial schools rather than to students, as their colloquy with Mr. Goodell indicates.)

"In other words," the New York Congressman continued, turning to Dr. Keppel, "in these thirty-two states, if there is one which will not permit state funds to go to a private school, you, the Commissioner, would make the grant directly to the private school for textbooks that are approved by the public school authority? Is that a correct statement of what would happen?"

Before Dr. Keppel could answer, his staff man, Dr. Cohen, assured Congressman Goodell: "That is correct; that is one possibility, but I don't think you should go back to the thirty-two-state figure."

"Well, whatever it is," mumbled the Congressman, not wanting to play the numbers game.

Concerned about the direction the answers were taking, Mr. Perkins interrupted to ask a question of the Administration's witnesses: "Isn't it true that the aid goes to the pupil and not to the school?"

Dr. Cohen's answer would be used by Congressman Goodell throughout the hearings to embarrass the Administration.

"We have to be sure we are talking about the correct title," Dr. Cohen said. "In Title I, we are talking about federal funds that go to public educational bodies. . . .

"Now, the other question Mr. Goodell then developed had to do with Title II in the library resources, in which there is a somewhat separate situation in which if the state law, the [state] constitution and the law and the practice and the policy prohibit the use of federal funds to the state for this particular purpose or purposes, then the Commissioner can purchase directly for them, as in the testing program under the National Defense Education Act."

"To the school or to the library?" asked Mr. Goodell.

"To or for the school or the library; yes sir," Dr. Cohen said.

"Then it is not to the student, it is to the school," Congressman Goodell said, seizing upon the damaging admission.

Representative Thompson of New Jersey said he considered HR 2362 "a particularly delightful concept. Of course," he continued, "I am not one who shares, to the extent Mr. Goodell apparently does, the fear that the Federal government is going to control education. I am less afraid of it than I am on the judgment of some of the locally elected school boards with respect to the administration of education programs."

Congressman Thompson then informed the committee that Congressman Hugh Carey of New York had had to leave earlier but had left some questions behind for Commissioner Keppel. The questions and their answers provide an interesting explanation of how Commissioner Keppel believed the bill would apply to parochial schools:

Q. Is it mandatory that every school district receiving funds under this legislation provides programs for the benefit of the private, nonprofit schoolchildren who come from low-income families?

Mr. Keppel: Yes, Mr. Thompson. That is assuming, of course, that there are low-income nonpublic schoolchildren in the area served by the program.

Q. What if the state law prohibits such programs?

Mr. Keppel: Well, sir, in every state some type of special educational program or arrangement can be devised for the benefit of all children. . . . We don't believe such programs as the preschool and afterschool — and all of this makes sense for the particular types of schools we are speaking of — violate any state law. We know some states would not permit shared or dual enrollment, but we believe most states would. If shared time isn't legally permitted, then, for example, educational TV, radio, and so forth, are possible.

Q. Will the public school districts be able to send educational specialists, speech therapists, and so forth, into nonpublic schools to provide services directly to the children of low-income families?

Mr. Keppel: The legislation before you would permit such services if the local school district wanted to establish them. . . . We estimate that such programs would be probable in eighteen states, possible in twenty-five, and possibly precluded in seven states.

Q. Could a child participating under an arrangement in which the child would have no attendance in the public school — in other words, does the phrase "full-time attendance" imply there must be some [public school] attendance to qualify?

Mr. Keppel: The answer is No.

Mr. Thompson turned to a touchy question of his own on the delicate issue of providing on-site services to parochial schools. "The services authorized under Title I can be either by bringing the child to the public school or if this isn't practical, by sending the service to the nonpublic school child where he is. The former arrangement would be shared time and the latter shared services," he said, leading into his question: "You see no impediment to this?"

Mr. Keppel said that he did not, but with qualifications: "Again, subject to local or state limitations in which we said there were variations, that is right."

The question was explored further by Congressman Goodell the next day with another government witness, Dr. Adron Doran, president of Morehead State College in Morehead, Kentucky. Dr. Doran, a constituent of Chairman Perkins' Seventh Kentucky District and a member of the Legislative Commission of the National Education Association (NEA), testified as part of the NEA panel favoring the legislation.

Congressman Goodell tried to get Dr. Doran to define the limitations on how far a public school teacher could go to give service to a parochial school student. "The question is," the tenacious Congressman asked, "can the public school teacher go and teach one class a day in the private school?"

"There would be no difference between her going in and spending some time in teaching the children a subject than taking a lunch and serving it to children that are hungry," Dr. Doran said.

Interrogator Goodell found it incredible that the college president saw no difference between learning and eating.

"You say there is no difference?" he asked again, as if he had not heard the answer correctly.

"I see no difference," Dr. Doran insisted.

"This would be proper under this legislation?"

"Yes, and you would not be supporting the private school in doing that," Dr. Doran said, sticking to his guns.

The New York Republican then led the Kentucky educator into a constitutional prickly patch. "The next question is, if there are enough children there to justify it in that private school, the public school teacher could teach full time to help those children in the private school?"

"I have no hesitancy, personally, to say Yes," replied Dr. Doran, giving a very liberal construction to the proposed bill.

Congressman Goodell changed his line of questioning to the

constitutionality of using public funds to remodel private schools.

"What about remodeling?" Goodell asked.

"I think so," Dr. Doran answered — hesitating. "Just ordinary decorating or the changing of a lighting system, I think you could use funds for that."

Goodell closed in for the kill.

"Is this where the constitutional line is drawn — between MAJOR and MINOR alterations?"

"I am talking about the bill before us," Dr. Doran said.

Congressman Brademas of Indiana, one of the staunch supporters of public funds for private schools, interrupted to extricate Dr. Doran.

"Mr. Chairman, I know we are short of time," the Indiana Democrat addressed the Chair, "but I do hope the Democrats will have a chance to ask a few questions."

Chairman Perkins said he had a few questions himself, and took off on another tack.

The NEA found itself in a dilemma on HR 2362. Dean Kelley and George R. LaNoue described the organization's quandary:

> For the National Education Association, representing more than 900,000 public school teachers and administrators, the bill presented some difficult tactical problems. In its original form the bill met almost none of NEA's traditional federal aid requirements. For example, the bill's aid was categorical rather than general, provided little or nothing for teachers' salaries, bypassed the states in Titles II and III, and set significant new procedents for aid to parochial schools. Yet the bill was certain to pass, and NEA could not afford to antagonize further the Office of Education, which has regarded it in recent years as a negative force and which has excluded it from the inner circle of policy-making. Furthermore, one of the principal objectives of NEA's activity has been to achieve general federal aid to education. The organization's failure to secure this goal has been loudly pointed out to teachers across the country by its growing and aggressive rival, the American Federation of Teachers (AFT). Consequently, despite some internal dissension, NEA decided to take a "see-no-evil, hear-no-evil, speak-no-evil" stance on the bill.

Robert McKay, chairman of the NEA Legislative Commission, began his testimony by reaffirming NEA's position on aid to education.

> Basic to the NEA's policy is an unalterable insistence that federal funds be allocated to the states and school districts without federal control.

General federal support funds, the NEA policy suggests, should be
commingled with state public education funds and their distribution within states should permit the same administrative discretion as for state public education funds. [At this point he sounded
as if he had not read the bill.]

Central to the association's policy on federal support is the position that expenditure of the federal funds be only for the purpose
for which the states and localities, under their constitutions and
statutes, may expend their own public education funds.

NEA policy likewise insists that legislation providing general or
specific aids be consistent with the constitutional provision re-
specting an establishment of religion and with the tradition of
separation of church and state.

Having paid verbal tribute to tradition, McKay then faced up
to the political realities of 1965:

The President's proposals do not, in my opinion, violate these
principles. In its approach and emphasis the program has the
wholehearted support of the NEA.

We believe that Mr. Johnson's message constituted one of the
strongest commitments to meeting the urgent needs of education
ever to come from the White House. We believe the President has
forthrightly faced up to the practical problems of getting a school
support bill enacted and has offered a proposal which should have
the backing of all individuals and groups interested in the educational welfare of the nation.

Before retiring from the hearing room, McKay would also have
to do verbal battle with Congressman Goodell.

Chairman Perkins, in an attempt to bolster the legislative history showing that the bill would not infringe on the Constitution, inadvertently opened the gate for Goodell to come charging
out again with customary vigor.

"We have been talking here about dual enrollment," the
chairman reminded the NEA panel. "Do you consider the dual
enrollment as contemplated in Title I or any other provisions
in this bill in violation of the constitutional provision of separation of church and state?"

"Mr. Chairman," McKay responded, "on behalf of the NEA
may I express the firm conviction that this program in no way
violates the principles of separation of church and state. If it
did, I would not be here testifying in favor of the bill."

When Goodell complained that the Republicans weren't getting enough time, McKay facetiously noted, "The answer you
heard was from a Republican, Mr. Goodell."

Goodell did not share McKay's frivolous attitude. "That's fine," he said. "You made the point, but I am not sure you have read the bill. Have you read Title II?" (That section provided funds for the purchase of library resources and other instructional materials for use by teachers and children in nonpublic schools.)

"I have read the bill from cover to cover," McKay assured a skeptical Goodell.

The New York Congressman said he wanted to make sure McKay understood that in states barring aid to private schools, the U. S. Office of Education would give the aid directly.

"That is not the way I read that provision, Mr. Goodell," McKay rejoined.

"How do you read it?"

"I read it that the instructional materials, the library books, the other materials will go to the child," McKay said.

Goodell disagreed.

"We had testimony just the other day from the Administration that it is not to the child, but it is to the school or to the library," he said. "How do you give a library book to the child? It goes to the library in the school." Congressman Goodell would refer continually to the testimony of Dr. Cohen throughout the entire proceedings.

For five days, the Administration witnesses came before the subcommittee to voice endorsement of the bill. And for five days, Congressman Goodell played the role of Defender of the Constitution, Guardian of the First Amendment and Watcher of the Wall between church and state. He continually forced Administration witnesses to seek refuge in subterfuge — while the bill marched inexorably toward passage and becoming the law of the land.

Then came the time for the religious lobbyists to appear before the subcommittee. Most were called because the Administration knew that it had their qualified approval at least. A few would make a vain attempt to bring about major changes in the bill. All would have their day in court — although the decision was a foregone conclusion. But even a democracy has to have its share of rituals. The lobbyists would say their pieces — but few were listening. Some of the testimony, however, proved revealing, perhaps more so than the lobbyists themselves realized at the time. A fundamental change in church and state relationships was taking place and the church lobbyists were more spectators than participants in the historic event.

CHAPTER VIII

HR 2362: An Instrument of Reconciliation

Dr. Arthur S. Flemming, former secretary of Health, Education, and Welfare and president of the University of Oregon and first vice president of the National Council of Churches of Christ, had a problem. As the "heavyweight" church witness to appear before the General Subcommittee on Education, he was woefully lacking in clear-cut directives from the religious organization he was representing. But this little detail was either unknown, or ignored, by Chairman Perkins in his warm welcome.

"I personally feel you need no introduction before this committee because we are well aware of your great contributions to the country when you were Secretary of the Department of Health, Education, and Welfare," the chairman told Dr. Flemming. "It goes without saying you are going to make another great contribution in your testimony here today."

Dr. Flemming's testimony would result in some changes in the proposed bill — the changes were later called the "Flemming amendments" by the church lobbyists. But the contributions stemmed more from Dr. Flemming's expertise and experience as an educator than from any position papers of the NCC. The swiftness of the hearings and the new child-benefit concept contained in HR 2362 caught the NCC off balance. The conciliar organization consists of thirty-three member communions with more than forty million Protestant and Orthodox constituents. The NCC legislative machinery is not geared to react to fast-breaking political power plays as utilized by the Administration in the passage of ESEA. As a result, Dr. Flemming had to quote from four-year-old NCC resolutions in parts of his testimony.

One should never underestimate the National Council of Churches, however. The Council did approve the child-benefit theory at its general board meeting in Portland, Oregon, on February 26 — a month after Dr. Flemming had testified in its behalf before the subcommittee.

Perhaps Dr. Flemming was speaking with an eye toward retro-active approval when he told the subcommittee: "It is my re-sponsibility this morning to represent and explain the position of the National Council of Churches on the important issues being considered by this committee." (Dr. Flemming had several hours of briefing from Dean M. Kelley, the Council's Director of the Commission on Religious Liberty, before going up to the Hill to testify.)

In his written testimony, which Kelley helped to prepare, Dr. Flemming said that the Council:

1. Approved of federal aid to public elementary and secondary schools.

2. Opposed government grants for parochial schools.

3. Supported "exploring" dual school enrollment.

4. Favored supplying "distinctly welfare services" to all chil-dren — whether enrolled in private or public schools.

Dr. Flemming concluded his testimony with an appeal for action and a prediction that HR 2362 would become "an instru-ment of reconciliation":

> The church and state issue as related to education has been one of the principal roadblocks standing in the way of constructive federal legislation in the areas of elementary and secondary edu-cation. It has likewise been a divisive factor in the life of our nation.
>
> I hope that all concerned, both inside and outside of the Con-gress, will analyze HR 2362 with the end in view of doing every-thing possible to make it an instrument of reconciliation. I be-lieve that it can be.
>
> I believe that President Johnson and his associates should be com-mended for providing us with this opportunity of approaching an old unsolved problem with a new spirit.
>
> If HR 2362 does become an instrument of reconciliation, it will at the same time become the instrument which will provide sound educational opportunities for millions of our young people who otherwise will not have them, opportunities which they must have if they are to move in the direction of achieving their highest potential.

The eloquent churchman then promised: "The National Council of Churches is prepared to do anything it can to make HR 2362 such an instrument of reconciliation."

Dr. Flemming in both his written and oral testimony made two major suggestions: that "public" ownership of school library resources and instructional materials be adequately spelled out in Title II, and that the educational community centers called for in Title III be administered by public authorities "responsible to the electorate."

Dr. Flemming hedged a bit, however, under interrogation from the indefatigable Mr. Goodell. Referring to the NCC policy statement of favoring "distinctly welfare services to all children" such as dental or medical services and lunches, Congressman Goodell asked Dr. Flemming if he considered textbooks as falling in the category of "distinctly welfare services?"

"You can have an interesting discussion on that as to whether the word 'welfare' is broad enough to include it," admitted Dr. Flemming. "As I have indicated a little later in my testimony, I believe definitely that the two principal provisions that have been included in this bill, including instructional material, do fall within the category of assistance to students," Dr. Flemming said. "And if these safeguards I have recommended are included, safeguards similar to those urged by the board in its 1961 statement, I see no problem."

The New York Congressman did see a problem. "As a practical matter, Mr. Flemming," he told the witness, "we have had testimony from the Administration which would indicate they take a somewhat contrary view as to how Title II would be administered." Mr. Goodell was determined to exploit Mr. Cohen's earlier statements to the fullest. "In the testimony, Mr. Celebrezze was here with Mr. Keppel and Mr. Cohen, and they specifically stated in Title II, as distinct from Title I, the textbooks and instructional materials would be a direct grant to the school, or library. This is on pages 129 and 130 of the testimony last Friday. I can read it to you if you are interested in having it. It was in response to a question following up my question. Mr. Perkins said 'Is it not true that the aid goes to the pupil and not the school?' Mr. Cohen came back and said —"

Chairman Perkins made a determined attempt to undo the damage. "Since I mentioned that," he interrupted, "let me make this observation: I think clearly what Mr. Cohen stated, who was not the regular witness, was a slip of the tongue."

This was a pivotal point in the ten-day hearing. Slip of the tongue or not on the part of Dr. Cohen, Chairman Perkins, Secretary Celebrezze and Commissioner Keppel did not attempt to correct Cohen when he made the original interpretation. And under Mr. Goodell's incessant goading, the statement had become a major source of embarrassment to the Administration. The bill eventually would be written to make it clear that materials provided parochial school students were loans and not grants. But as Congressman Goodell stated: "The record is clear that the Administration intended that it be a grant to the school or library."

Dr. Flemming also gave fuzzy answers on the question of taking public services to the child in the private school. After he and Congressman Goodell engaged in an exchange on the issue, the Congressman bluntly told Dr. Flemming: "You have kind of gone around the question, but your final statement seemed to me to say it makes no difference where they go as long as they are making public school services available to students regardless of whether private or public, and it is all right. Under that standard you set, I think they could probably go to the private school and teach English or history."

Dr. Flemming responded by saying that he really did not consider Mr. Goodell's question a constitutional one, but that if he were a superintendent of public schools, he would as a matter of policy have the private students go where the public school facilities were available "so as to keep this line clean-cut."

Dr. Flemming concluded his testimony by offering to send by mail any "further thoughts that do occur to me on any of the points we have discussed for the committee's consideration."

"We should be delighted to have that," Chairman Perkins accepted gratefully.

Goodell saw a chance to sink a political stinger into the fast-moving hearings. "The way the chairman is running," he remarked to Dr. Flemming, "I would advise you to call one of us. I don't know whether a letter will catch up with us."

A panel of religious lobbyists, church bureaucrats and clergymen followed Dr. Flemming to the witness table. Dean Kelley of the National Council of Churches, the panel chairman, gave this explanation to the subcommittee:

> The panel is mostly made up of constituents of the National Council of Churches. When your counsel asked me to convene this group to try to represent a broad spectrum of Protestant opinion. I did so within certain guidelines; namely that by and large we are all in favor of the bill with certain various minor modifications.

Second, we have reservations and opposition to direct aid to parochial schools, but by and large we are prepared to consider in a
broad sense various forms of aid to all children, including those
that attend nonpublic schools.

Kelley explained that the Baptist Joint Committee on Public
Affairs consisted of eight member conventions, some of whom
were in the Council, but the largest one, the Southern Baptist
Convention, was not in the NCC. Dr. C. Emanuel Carlson, as
executive director, would have to give voice to the ten million
Southern Baptists in his Joint Committee.

Dr. Philip Johnson, executive secretary of the Division of
Public Relations of the National Lutheran Council, also spoke
in part for a group that was not in the Council — the American
Lutheran Church, with 2.5 million members. The ALC, along
with the Lutheran Church in America with a membership of
3.2 million, make up the National Lutheran Council.

The other panel members were Dr. W. Astor Kirk, Director
of Public Affairs for the Board of Christian Social Concerns,
Methodist Church; the Rev. Richard V. Smith, representing the
Executive Council of the Episcopal Church, and H. B. Sissel,
Secretary for National Affairs of the United Presbyterian Church.

Dr. Carlson testified first. He warned the committee there
needed to be a distinction made "between the extension of services to the [private] schools . . . [and] the right of the pupil to
come into the public school to receive the services." The tone
of his testimony, however, indicated that he had no real quarrel
with the bill.

Dr. Johnson came down much harder on the same point:

This is a very dangerous thing to do with Dr. Flemming's interpretation, the interpretation on the transportation of public school
teachers to parochial schools, for example to offer regular courses.
I refer to possible infringement of proper church and state relationships. It would seem that this would obviously come under
the category of providing aid to the school rather than to the
pupil. . . .

Finally, I think it might be a service at this point simply to insert
the precautionary note that there may be a danger of rapid proliferation of what one of our reports called institutional creedal
rivalries if there is to be sufficient support for nonpublic education
at elementary and secondary levels, as to make establishment of
such schools economically feasible for many groups.

There are signs that the number of such schools already is growing
at an accelerated rate under the sponsorship of many religious

and other private groups. Obviously, such a development poses a serious threat to the quality of public education in a community where public schools would have many rivals.

"It would be ironic," he concluded, "if a laudable concern for improving the quality of education should, by stretching the pupil benefit theory to the limit, lead to the erosion of the public school system." The warning would seem even more timely in 1969 than it did in 1965 — with the NAACP charging that the program was not being properly administered. The organization asked that the government funds be used to support private schools in the ghettos.

Dr. W. Astor Kirk informed the committee that the Methodist Board of Christian Social Concerns "and, indeed, the general legislative body of the church, the general conference, have not had the opportunity to consider this specific piece of legislation." He said the general legislative body in May of 1964 had gone on record favoring increased opportunities for educating the economically and socially deprived. "Since this bill is geared to that need, or since it certainly emphasizes meeting that need, I would say that generally one would expect Methodists, or a good many Methodists, across the country, to support the objectives of this bill," Dr. Kirk said in one of the more ambiguously worded endorsements given the bill.

The Rev. Richard Smith stated that the Episcopal Church's presiding bishop had appointed a commission to make a study of church-state relations two years earlier. Mr. Smith said that the commission recommended including church-schools in certain governmental programs — pointing out that many church-related schools were already recipients of federal funds through the National Defense Education Act and the National Science Foundation Act.

"The primary effect of including church-related schools in such programs is not the advancement of religion through state action," Mr. Smith continued. "The inclusion of church-related schools in such programs is consistent with the American tradition of church-state separation and interaction."

Mr. Smith went further than had any of his colleagues on the Council of Churches panel by saying that the Episcopal Church's general convention the preceding fall had changed its former policy and had come out in favor of federal funds for textbooks and transportation for parochial children.

The Episcopal rector (associate at St. John's Church in Bethesda-Chevy Chase, Maryland), quoting his bishop, whose statement is a study in religious rationalization, read the following into the record:

> I should say that our schools have an obligation to cooperate in whatever national program is adopted and this would be a matter both of giving and receiving. If some of the national educational goals can best be reached by using existing church schools, then the schools should be used. I see no reason why Government funds should not be used. It is much more important to answer the needs than it is to quibble over who holds title to a building.
>
> I hope that something very much like the program proposed by the President will be adopted. I believe that the Episcopal Church and other churches will cooperate.

It was the kind of clerical backing that must have sounded like music in the ecumenical ears of President Johnson.

Congressman Hugh Carey of New York, reflecting the mood of the moment, commented: "On a personal note, I have met and heard most of this panel before at other times and, to me, this is really a day of 'aggiornamento' if I may be permitted to use that reference [made popular by Pope John XXIII].

"This is a very constructive panel," he continued. "The recommendations have been all very carefully weighed and they are in excellent style. I think a new day has come.

"At one of the last meetings we had under the general Subcommittee on Education, Dr. Sissel was with us. At that time he and I were expressing a belief, a common view, that we had hoped sometime during our lifetime we could see a general aid to education bill. We had misgivings about whether it would come to pass and I agree with him it is a wonderful day the drafters of this bill have brought to American education."

Congressman Goodell scolded Congressman Carey for his modesty. "It seemed to me the other day you said you were the drafter [of the bill]," he noted facetiously — while at the same time revealing that the parochial school position had been ably represented in the early stages of the bill.

"I do not think I could claim all of the credit," Mr. Carey replied in the same bantering tone. "It is not a total 'draft' but just a little 'breeze' in my case."

Congressman Goodell asked Presbyterian Sissel to elaborate his views on sending public school teachers into private schools, and Mr. Sissel said that under certain conditions — "provided it is temporary, rotating, mobile, provides a special service which is defined" — the public service could be given the private school.

Kelley, the panel chairman, hastened to interject that "if they [public school teachers] are going in and teach for the private school in any substantial way," it would not be permissible.

Mr. Sissel then underlined the bind in which all the church representatives were caught: "I do not think any of our communions represented here have faced squarely to this particular question," he confessed. "I know mine has not. We have to speak as individuals on this question."

Congressman Goodell's observation made it clear that he thought the church bureaucrats soon would have to deal with fact and not theory. "It is a point we are going to face after this legislation is passed," he said in his typical blunt fashion. "Probably you will have to deal with it ipso facto."

*　*　*　*　*

Unlike their "separated brethren," the Roman Catholic witnesses seemed much more certain what they wanted from the bill. Monsignor Frederick G. Hochwalt, director of the Department of Education of the National Catholic Welfare Conference (NCWC), a battle-scarred lobbyist, headed the panel of witnesses. He was accompanied by Msgr. William McManus, superintendent of the Catholic schools in Chicago, Msgr. John McDowell, superintendent of the Catholic schools of Pittsburgh, and Edward McArdle, a father of seven children, all of whom were attending parochial schools in Silver Spring, Maryland.

Chairman Perkins welcomed the panel, and to prove his fairness to all faiths noted, "Last year, if I recall correctly, we heard your group first and the Protestants in the afternoon. This time it is vice versa."

Msgr. Hochwalt made the formal presentation, outlining the Catholic position:

> Let me emphasize that the fundamental position of the NCWC department of education on federal aid to education is the same as expressed here in previous years. We reiterate that any federal aid to education program provided by the Federal government should include the children in private schools as a matter of justice.

Msgr. Hochwalt went on to embrace the bill — but at arm's length. "The formula for participation quite obviously is not based on equality of treatment nor does it pretend that it is," he told the committee. "The formula suggested is obviously an accommodation."

The Catholic spokesman insisted that private schools be consulted on the implementation of the bill on the local level. "There is one point, however, that should also be made," he said. "To carry out the intent of the legislation, there should be some kind of consultation with private school authorities on the types of programs offered.

"To move to Title II," he continued, "additional textbooks and instructional aids will enrich the education of both public and private school pupils. Trusting that the materials selected by state authorities will be satisfactory for all pupils, we endorse this title. We recommend, however, that there be consultation between public and private school educators or the efficient administration of this program.

"The door has been opened," Msgr. Hochwalt stated, "for full dress discussions of good school programs, aid to low-income areas, needs of libraries and textbook requirements and imaginative experimentation."

The subcommittee was then treated to a performance on the art of blowing one's own horn by the combustible Congressman from Harlem and chairman of the full Committee on Education and Labor, Representative Adam Clayton Powell, Jr. The minister of the Abyssinian Baptist Church, in a display of both ecumenism and the peculiar kind of modesty for which he is noted, beamed at the Catholic educators.

"Monsignor," he said, "I am very happy to have you and your associates here today. As you know, the concept of shared time on the federal level was originated by me, and you have participated in many of the conferences with Dr. Wolfe [the committee's education chief] and at subsequent hearings with Mrs. [Edith] Green."

Congressman Powell said he was just wondering how his little, old concept was working out in the field. After being reassured by Monsignor Hochwalt that in the State of Ohio where he went to school it had been working wonderfully since 1913 (considerably before Powell came to Congress), the Congressman continued.

"There has been some objection raised, as you know by now, by colleagues from the minority side that this would lead to federal control," the legislator said, in the sarcastic tone he reserves for white Republicans. "I think the greatest example of federal control was the Powell amendment in the Civil Rights Act which gives the Federal government the right to deny funds where there is discrimination.

"What do you think of the concept that I advanced the other day of operational centers which would also be on a shared basis, where a teacher could come and learn how to use these new media in visual and manipulative devices?" asked Congressman Powell — no slouch at operating "manipulative devices."

"That is an answer to the President and other educators who ask for an imaginative approach," Msgr. Hochwalt said, very much aware of whom he was addressing. "Surely that is imaginative and we would want to be a part of it."

Congressman Powell, now really warmed up to his subject, continued to interject irrelevant material into the hearing. "I believe that the preschool level should be lowered to, I hope, three years of age but at least four years of age rather than five," he told Msgr. Hochwalt, advancing another new educational "concept."

Congressman Powell was convinced he had found sympathetic ears for his new educational theory. "I believe your church has always recognized the importance of early training," he told the Catholic panelists. "Have you not said: 'Give me the child until he is seven'?"

Msgr. Hochwalt deflected the question by saying, "Our experience in teaching languages showed that the earlier you get them the easier it is to teach them."

Satisfied the committee had all the Powell theory of education it could assimilate in one day, the chairman of the full Committee on Education and Labor turned the proceedings back over to the chairman of the subcommittee.

Chairman Perkins asked the Catholic panelists the same question he had asked previous witnesses: "Do you see any language in this bill anywhere that would promote the teaching of religion?"

Msgr. McManus, superintendent of Catholic schools in Chicago, replied, "I certainly do not." He said his answer would apply to all the titles of the bill, "And I have read them very carefully."

Congressman Ford of Michigan complimented the Catholic panel, while basking in the warm sunshine of religious togetherness: "This has been a good day for us on the committee. I don't know whether you were present this morning, but we had the pleasure of hearing testimony which indicates to me that the effects of the ecumenical council and the new awakening of morality that the civil rights struggle has brought about are starting to be felt where they will do the most good. I see evidence of that again this afternoon from the testimony of you gentlemen."

Congressman Carey echoed the sentiment of his colleague from Michigan, adding that "I happen to belong to the same faith as the panel which is here today."

Msgr. McManus responded, noting this was the fifth time since 1946 that he had testified before the same committee. "I am thrilled beyond measure to be able to come in here today with a completely positive and constructive attitude and without fear and apprehension such as prevailed in 1946 that I might not make it out alive with the very suggestion that nonpublic schools participate," he commented, reflecting on the change in religious attitudes toward educational issues which impinge on the First Amendment.

The Catholic panelists, emphasizing that they recognized that the bill was designed to aid the educationally deprived child, explained how they thought the program should be carried out. "In theory we prefer to have the teachers come into our schools if that can be done, because it is done with less excitement — with less destroying of the order of the day," Msgr. Hochwalt told Congressman Carey. "You can follow your curriculum more closely without breaking the school day to travel some place else to get some good which might be offered to you.

"Where teachers can be brought in to do the job, we would like that surely," he added, conceding that this would apply only to remedial instruction.

Msgr. McManus, in trying to project how the bill could be worked out in an actual situation, explained: "My approach on that would be to take a census of the educationally deprived children who are in need of special services, like speech correction, to bring that information to the superintendent of the public schools, and say to him 'take your choice. Send a teacher to us and we will make the room available. Or, if you prefer, we will send the children over to the public school for the class. Whatever you do, please do it in accord with the strict interpretation of the law laid down by the attorney for your board, because we do not want to have children become, particularly the deprived children, victims of acrimonious legal controversy.' "

Msgr. McManus cited the experience of driver education in

Illinois, where the instructors were brought into the nonpublic schools to give the service required by law. "The authorities administering that program have found it much more efficient to do it that way, than to have the youngsters traipsing over to the nearby public schools for this instruction, so the efficiency of the operation has been the norm which has determined whether the children go to the public school or the teacher comes over," he stated, with an appeal to pragmatism.

Under further prodding by Congressman Goodell, the superintendent of Catholic schools in Chicago gave a succinct summary on the constitutionality of the practice: "I think that under the Constitution of the United States, it is legal for a public school teacher under public control and supervision to render a service within a privately owned structure."

Congressman Goodell pursued the constitutionality question further. "You limit that to the public school teacher constitutionally teaching geography, history, or English in private schools?" he asked.

"I think that would be possible, yes," Msgr. McManus replied. "I think that would be possible."

Conceding that they all were "exploring new territory," the New York Congressman continued his interrogation:

"What I am trying to do is to think ahead as to where the proper bounds are, assuming that this is within the proper bounds. How far do we go?

"We had a public school superintendent yesterday get himself sort of into a box where he appeared to draw the constitutional line between a remedial course and a nonremedial course. He said he thought it was all right for a public school teacher to go into a private school and teach a remedial course but a nonremedial course he was not all sure he thought was constitutional," said Congressman Goodell, who sort of got into a syntax box himself.

"You do not draw that kind of distinction?" he asked Msgr. McManus.

"No," the witness replied, "the legal principle here at stake is that the government may not do by indirection what is directly forbidden by law. . . . We are not making a plea — and I am sure I speak for my colleagues — we are not making a plea today for teachers to come into parochial schools."

At times during the legislative history of the bill, it became very confusing to determine the legal principles at stake. Msgr.

McManus stressed the need to find middle ground "on this vexing question of the relationship of the church-related school child to the Federal government. It is not an easy problem but we must, I think, move ahead on it. Otherwise, not only these children but the children in public schools are in danger of being deprived of urgently needed services because of our failure to strike a middle course on this important issue."

Representative Goodell steered around the possibilities of what would happen if the legislators failed to "strike a middle course" and asked Msgr. McManus: "Do you draw the line in the Constitution against grants to private schools to purchase textbooks approved by public school authorities? Do you say that would be unconstitutional to do it?"

"Let me see if I grasp your question correctly," Msgr. McManus replied. "Do I think it would be unconstitutional?"

"To have a direct grant to a private school," Goodell said.

"A direct grant to the private school?" repeated Msgr. McManus.

"To purchase textbooks, purchased by the school authority?" Goodell rephrased his question.

"I gather you mean then that a check would be sent to the nonpublic schools with which they could choose then to purchase books that have been authorized for the use of their pupils?" Msgr. McManus asked Congressman Goodell.

"That is right," the Congressman agreed, delighted the prelate was at last beginning to get the drift of his question.

"By state authorities?" Msgr. McManus asked, cautiously treading his way through a possible legally entangling thicket.

"That is one way it could be done; yes, sir," Goodell said.

"I really do not know which way should be chosen," Msgr. McManus explained. "I think this is a technical question, but that method could be utilized. . . . My only concern . . . is that the books are there for the children to use."

Congressman Goodell said that an Administration spokesman had testified that the grant could go to the school or to the library itself to pay for the books. "Then the question comes up," Goodell continued, "whether it is a critical point one way or the other; secondly, whether it makes any difference whether the check is sent directly to the school or the books are sent to the school in the value of the check, or, as was suggested this morning, that the critical point would be whether the ownership goes to the recipient."

"A detail," Msgr. McManus told the somewhat surprised Congressman. "As far as I see it, it is a detail. Our main concern is that the children read the books and the means by which they are bought, made available to these pupils, is an administrative detail.

"For example," he continued, "in the school system in which I administer, at the beginning of every school year a whole set of library books is deposited in the Catholic schools for the use of the pupils. Children regularly draw these books out. It is more efficient for the public library to put the books into the school and let the children have them than to have the public library overwhelmed by more children than they can accommodate after school hours, coming over to take out books."

Congressman Goodell obviously was not convinced.

"You call it a detail," he told the clergyman, "but there are those very sincere people who testified this morning who thought it was a very constitutionally significant detail."

The Republican committee member moved into another area involving the sensitive church-state issue. He explained that out of the mouths of Administration witnesses it had been established that thirty-two states have legal or constitutional bars against giving aid to private schools in one form or another. He said five public school superintendents from big cities testified that it would be unconstitutional to give aid to private schools.

"The question I raised is not the constitutional one but whether you are really going to get anything in these thirty-two states that is meaningful for your private schools," he said.

"I recall the testimony of Commissioner Keppel who said, 'If you have any trouble, come to see me,' " Msgr. Hochwalt answered.

"You mean you are going to go to Commissioner Keppel yourself, or us?" asked Goodell.

"Maybe both," Msgr. Hochwalt replied with a smile. "It might be a good idea."

Msgr. McManus fell back on an analogy which became the catch-all answer to every argument in the 1960's: "It strikes me as rather extraordinary that the Government of the United States that has conquered space and is preparing to go to the moon, has called upon the resources of the nation's best scientists for our leadership in this highly technical area of science, and then to judge it incapable of working out a satisfactory, and I might even say a pleasant, plan where little children in a metropolitan area who happen to go to two different types of schools would all get some books," the prelate said — in a meandering sentence that never really ended.

Later Congressman Brademas, a proponent of public aid for private schools, got down to the nub of the matter. "Do I take it from your testimony that the NCWC endorses this legislation?" he asked Msgr. Hochwalt.

"It is a strong word, but it comes close to it," replied the director of the NCWC Department of Education, with a sly smile. "We look with favor upon these kind of provisions and hope they can be worked out successfully. To say we endorse the whole thing line by line is a little too broad for us."

"Monsignor, you should be a candidate for public office," Congressman Brademas commented, recognizing a politically astute answer when he hears one. "I think that sounds encouraging enough for me."

Msgr. McManus expressed his qualified support. "With no little anguish on our part, we look upon this measure as a compromise; not fully satisfactory to Catholics by any means, but, yet, a measure that comes to grips with a problem that every American, regardless of his religious affiliation, has to face," he said.

He also pointed out the heavy burden a superintendent of Catholic schools must carry out — and why any kind of relief would be appreciated. "In Chicago I will have to raise another $90 million next year to keep the schools going even though the bill is on the books," he said. "And yet, we feel now, as we did at the time of the federal impact legislation, that we must go along, even though the benefit to us is extremely limited, in the interest of taking care of these desperately poor children in both metropolitan and rural areas."

Perhaps the Catholic attitude, as reflected in testimony before the subcommittee, was contained in a meaningful metaphor made by Congressman Carey during a friendly exchange with Msgr. McManus. Recognizing that the bill was not completely satisfactory to the administrators of money-starved parochial schools, Mr. Carey commented: "If I may suggest, the reference might well be made that Rome was not built in a day."

"I will take the allegory as you state it," Msgr. McManus concurred.

"We have put a couple of good building blocks in this bill," Congressman Carey said, implying he believed the opening wedge had been driven into the public treasury which would release a flow of funds to parochial schools. His figure of speech reflected things to come.

What Congressman Carey may have overlooked — although as an attorney it seems highly improbable — was that the blow that knocked the bung from the money cask would jar loose a string of court cases stretching across the length of the land. The constitutionality of some provisions of HR 2362 was still unresolved as late as the fall of 1969. The funds and materials made possible by the ESEA continue to flow, however, while the bulky machinery of the courts gear up to rule on the school cases appearing on their dockets with increasing regularity.

* * * * *

The Roman Catholic Church operates 90 percent of the private schools in the U. S. The most ardent advocates of HR 2362, however, were spokesmen for the Orthodox Jewish faith in the persons of Rabbi Morris Sherer, executive vice president of Agudath Israel of America, and Dr. William W. Brickman, educational consultant of the National Society for Hebrew Day Schools.

Rabbi Sherer rejoiced to see the day the Federal government would enact a bill which would "lift millions of poverty-stricken Americans out of their rut of despair." The only criticism he had was that the poverty-income factor of $2000 was too low — he thought it should be altered upward to "a realistic criterion which relates to the size of the family." As did his Catholic predecessors, he emphasized the need for the bill to contain language making it imperative that there be "consultation between the public and private school authorities concerning the practical arrangements of the various programs offered in this bill. We strongly urge its enactment," he concluded.

Dr. Brickman said the National Society for Hebrew Day Schools included 272 elementary and secondary schools in 95 cities in 27 states. He noted that more than 90 percent of all Hebrew day schools are conducted under Orthodox religious auspices. In reference to Title II, which makes instructional material available to all students, Dr. Brickman suggested that private school representatives join with public school authorities "in the specific selection of the textbooks and instructional materials available."

Rabbi Sherer, although he did not use the phrase, also predicted that HR 2362 could become an instrument of reconciliation. "In my opinion, Congressman," he told Mr. Carey, "the enactment of this bill, and its fair application in everyday life, would do away with many differences we have today between various faiths and religions."

Congressman Carey wanted to know if Dr. Brickman thought HR 2362 "would be in keeping with our historic concept of church and state?"

"As I was reading the bill, I had no feeling at all that it was in any way contradicting our historic principles," Dr. Brickman said. "As a matter of fact, I see the possibility of reinforcing that famous statement made in the Northwest Ordinance of 1787, and I quote, and I believe accurately, that 'religion, morality and knowledge being necessary to good government, and the happiness of mankind, schools and the means of education shall forever be encouraged.' "

Congressman Carey in his enthusiasm for HR 2362, and encouraged by the friendliness of the witnesses, thought he saw some kind of parallel between the Russian government, which makes it difficult for Soviet Jewry to maintain their institutions. and a Congress which would deny aid to parochial schools. "If we continue to pass legislation of this kind to assist only secular functions of public education without regard to giving any kind of treatment to your schools for the secular purpose of our educational system, would we be moving these schools in this country toward the same kind of an unwelcome situation as those in the Soviet Union?" he asked, freely using the forbidden word of "schools" while apparently forgetting the Administration's argument that HR 2362 would benefit pupils not schools.

"There is no question but the Jewish system in this country suffers in a very great degree from the inequitable treatment that it receives on the part of the Government as far as the secular programs are concerned, as far as the budgets are concerned," Rabbi Sherer agreed. "However," he continued, "I feel that since this particular bill does not relate to the school system, or to the very good schools, it is on an individual basis for the American child, we should try to leave this outside the overall realms of the problems of the school. Sometime when the committee will be taking up some overall direct aid for federal aid for education, we will perhaps talk to this particular area," he gently chided Congressman Carey for his far-fetched parallel."

Congressman Goodell also took issue with his colleague's analogy. "I must express a little concern over the context in which the Soviet treatment of religion was placed," he said. "I certainly do not think it is relevant at all to the discussion of the constitutional aspects of this particular legislation."

Dr. Brickman joined the fray, muddying the waters in the process: "May I comment, Mr. Congressman, about the reference to Soviet education. Perhaps the methodology differs, but the objective might be the same if the disadvantaged children and the disadvantaged schools continue in that status. There is a possibility," he warned, "there will be no children in the schools at all, and the religious private independent school which has existed in this country from its very founding in the seventeenth century will tend to disappear, and perhaps a kind of atheistic society might result, but I believe both the Congressman and I would oppose that. I think that was the inference of the question."

At this point, Congressman James H. Scheuer of New York, one of the quieter members of the majority, made an eloquent protest against the tenor of the hearing.

"I am somewhat disturbed with the state of the record at this point," he said. "We have not had a major federal aid to education bill in 150 years. I am in favor of this bill. It is an excellent bill meeting a desperate need. Yet, somehow or other we have managed over a century and a half to sustain a society where every religious group is flourishing, where young people in each of the great religious denominations learn the tenets of their faith without the slightest disapprobation on the part of our government or our society.

"I think from what I know of the situation in the Soviet Union, if the Jewish community there was to achieve the situation that we have now in the United States, they would consider it Nirvana. What they are looking for is not the assistance of their government, even in the education of the child, but indeed the very hands-off policy which our government has maintained under our Constitution since the Founding Fathers wrote that great document.

"I think it would be unfortunate if there were any implications that the absence of direct federal aid to children in nonprivate schools, and I repeat I favor such aid, were to be construed in any way as having encouraged, or led to the development of an atheistic society.

"The absence up until the present time of a direct federal aid program to children in parochial schools, which we all favor on basis of need, has in no way led to the development of a situation comparable to the condition of the tragic condition of the Jewish community in Soviet Russia.

"May I also add to your statement, Professor Brickman, that the great religious faiths have not objected to this bill. I think we can go even further than that. We have seen a heart-warming array of witnesses from the great major faiths in the last few days; we have heard magnificent statements from representatives of the Catholic educational hierarchy and from the National Council of Churches of Christ in America, in which they have endorsed, with only minor reservations, the towering moral purposes of this bill. As has been stated on previous days' testimony, there has been a soaring ecumenical spirit present in which the representatives of the great religious faiths have not only refrained from descending into the ancient quarrels, jealousies, and resentments of bygone years, but, on the contrary, have reaffirmed with spiritual fervor the moral imperative of educating every American child to the limit of his potential.

"There has been a spirit on the part of the great religious representatives whom we have heard, of tolerance, of some compromise in what each of them would consider the ideal, which all of us, I think without exception, have found deeply moving," Congressman Scheuer ended in a flourish of rhetoric.

CHAPTER IX

A Dubious Consensus

Rabbi Richard G. Hirsch, director of the Religious Action Center of the Union of American Hebrew Congregations (Reform), eased his small frame into the witness chair. Rabbi Hirsch usually finds himself in the forefront of fights for social justice but unlike many religious activists he keeps in view two basic points of reference — the Old Testament and the Constitution.

"It is a privilege to appear in support of the broad principles of federal aid to education and improvement of educational opportunities," he addressed the chair.

> We commend President Johnson for placing federal responsibility for improving education at the top of the nation's agenda. However, we are concerned that in our nation's desire to raise educational standards and ameliorate conditions of poverty, we may trample on precious principles and diminish cherished institutions.

> This legislation raises serious questions of public policy which deserve careful deliberation before precedents are established from which it may be impossible to withdraw. A great society must adhere to great principles.

> Our organizations are deeply committed to religious liberty and to the majestic concept of separation of church and state. We believe that this tradition of separation is the mandate of the Constitution, the lesson of history, and the absolute precondition to religious liberty and interfaith harmony.

The articulate rabbi then got down to cases — and ruffled the feelings of certain committee members.

> This bill includes precisely the kind of aid to religious institutions which President John F. Kennedy stoutly rejected as violative of our constitutional liberties. Why did the two education bills submitted by President Kennedy fail to pass Congress?

He ticked off the answers to his own question:

> There were undoubtedly many factors, but chief among them was the opposition of those who refused to support legislation unless aid was given to private as well as public schools. But as we have heard, last year's opponents of federal aid to education are among this year's supporters. We must ask why? Have they suddenly altered their position?
>
> Not from the statements made in public and before this committee, where they steadfastly continue to maintain that federal aid should go to nonpublic schools "as a matter of justice."
>
> Obviously, they must find in this bill a means of achieving their original objective — if not entirely, then in part; if not immediately, then eventually.
>
> Conversely, many of the groups which heretofore refused to support legislation if aid were given to private education, have now endorsed this bill. For them, this year's urgent public school needs have taken precedence over last year's reluctance — and they are now willing to yield in their opposition to federal support of private education.
>
> We deceive ourselves as a nation if we use semantics to conceal what has actually occurred. Both the language of the bill and the language of those who support it tend to create the illusion that it is the child, not the school, to which federal aid is to be given. However, in the guise of aiding the child, this bill does aid the school. Merely to insert language directing that tax moneys be "for the use of children and teachers" rather than for schools does not change the essential character of the recipient of the use to which the money is put.
>
> An end run around the principle can advance the ball of federal assistance just as far as a direct plunge through the middle of the line.

Rabbi Hirsch said that Jews in America out of a sense of religious responsibility created a vast network of private educational institutions for the perpetuation of Jewish religious values — all without the assistance of the Federal government.

"This network of schools is expanding and there is no reason why it should not continue to expand and flourish if people who have religious faith are sufficiently concerned about perpetuating their faith and give the money that it requires," he told the committee.

Rabbi Hirsch proved thoroughly ecumenical in his criticism. "The temptation to sup at the trough is not one to which most religious denominations have shown any exceptional resistance, and Jews are no different, as you have just heard," he said, using a figure of speech that caused some to wince.

Rabbi Hirsch argued that the use of tax money for private schools would dilute support of public schools. He also charged that many parents send their children to private schools to remove their children from public schools in neighborhoods where there are heavy concentrations of minority groups.

Chairman Perkins interrupted Rabbi Hirsch to announce that other witnesses would be heard later in the evening but that the testimony of the American Civil Liberties Union would be taken the next day.

Congressman Goodell, who had been chomping on his cigar, filed another political criticism of the hearings. "May I just once again express my concern and my protest over this procedure," he told Chairman Perkins. "The chairman has been very, very considerate in hearing every witness, but to hear them at 8 o'clock at night and make them sit here all day with eighteen witnesses scheduled is not proper."

Chairman Perkins replied he had been extremely flexible in permitting committee members unlimited time to interrogate witnesses.

"Mr. Chairman, you have been eminently fair within the limitations of one simple requirement, and that is, we conclude hearings February 1," Congressman Goodell said.

"We are not concluding hearings today [Feb. 1]," Chairman Perkins stated.

"We are going over until tomorrow now," Congressman Goodell admitted. "I think it is a matter of a day or two. I think it is unfortunate that we should gang up on eighteen witnesses in one day in order to hit an arbitrary deadline."

Rabbi Hirsch broke up the argument between the chair and the Congressman with a pun: "I know we all feel somewhat like Egyptian mummies pressed for time." He then became serious again to continue his criticism of the bill. He said he opposed the concept of public school administrators having to consult with private school officials in order to obtain funds and formulate a program. He said that Title II in the bill, dealing with library and instructional materials, did not make it clear who owns the books to be used in private schools or how they are to be distributed, and he charged that both Title II and Title III, dealing with supplementary educational centers, diminished public authority over the expenditure of public funds.

He also urged that a provision for a judicial review of constitutional questions be written into the legislation, in order to repair any constitutional damage the bill might produce. "The problem of education is urgent, but it is unwise to proceed before a genuine discussion and debate on the implications of this bill can take place," he told the committee.

"The overwhelming support for federal aid to education reflects a spirit of compromising and tolerance. But compromise is possible without compromising basic principles, and tolerance is more profound where expressed in respect for these basic principles. To paper over deep issues, in the name of a dubious consensus, is to do a grave disservice to future generations.

"A good bill with a major defect is about as serviceable as a majestic luxury liner with a hole at the waterline," he told the Congressmen who were attempting to get HR 2362 out of dry dock and into the water as quickly as possible. "The time to repair that defect is now."

It was the strongest criticism the committee had heard from any spokesman for the major faiths. Congressman Brademas attempted to recover from the onslaught by defending the testimony of previous church groups. (Congressman Brademas was by far the most ecumenical member of the entire committee. He made it a point to inform church witnesses early in the hearings that "I happen to be the Methodist son of a Greek Orthdox father and a Disciple of Christ mother and I taught at a Roman Catholic college before coming to Congress.")

"Would it be unfair of me to suggest that another interpretation of their [other church witnesses] position might be that they think this bill is not unconstitutional?" Congressman Brademas asked Rabbi Hirsch.

"I think there are many groups who have changed their position out of political expedience," Rabbi Hirsch insisted. "I think there are others who perhaps have had a different interpretation of the principle."

Congressman Goodell, complimenting Rabbi Hirsch for his "excellent testimony," said he touched on major issues the subcommittee members should consider. "One of the chief concerns we have is that it is not easy for the Supreme Court to get a case to pass upon in this particular issue," he explained. "Therefore, the primary obligation of interpreting the Constitution in these fields is upon Congress and upon committees such as this."

Rabbi Hirsch admitted that there was no clear line of demarcation on the church-state issue and that inconsistencies were inherent in any position one might take. "The lines between education and welfare are already blurred," he said. "One of the things I am concerned about is that this bill will blur them even further."

The outspoken rabbi agreed with previous witnesses that "there is a new spirit in the country. I think," he continued, "that we should be able to sit down and discuss our viewpoints but I do not think we can do it in two weeks or ten days of hearings. I do not think that such —"

That was a bit too much for Chairman Perkins. "Let me say to you, Rabbi Hirsch," the Kentuckian interjected, "have you attended any hearings in Congress that have been more comprehensive than these hearings . . . ? Are you insinuating that these hearings have not been comprehensive? Is that what you want to say?"

Rabbi Hirsch can be gracious as well as aggressive.

"Not at all, Mr. Chairman," he apologized. "If you get this connotation from my remarks, I withdraw them. I was not impugning your conduct of this hearing." But he adamantly refused to back away from his basic position. "I do feel, however," he said to the chair, "that we have not had sufficient time as a group to study all sections of this bill. We did not get the bill until the President sent it up, which I think was on the 12th, and today is only the first of February. We have standing committees which deal with these questions. We have not even had time to call a committee meeting." Rabbi Hirsch was voicing a complaint many of the church spokesmen must have felt when they were asked to testify on such short notice. Their general approval of the bill, however, overcame whatever reluctance they may have had on procedure.

Chairman Perkins, not one to hold a grudge, asked Rabbi Hirsch if he would agree with Dr. Flemming that HR 2362 could be an instrument of reconciliation?

"As far as I am concerned," Rabbi Hirsch said, "never before in history has there been such a fine relationship between the Protestant, Catholic, and Jewish communities. This relationship has been increasingly a cooperative one, and we have not had to pay the price of financing the sectarian schools in order to get this cooperation and this reconciliation.

"We can cooperate with the Catholics and the Protestants, as we have done on civil rights legislation," said the scrappy rabbi. "We have presented joint testimony with them. But we can come before this committee and say we disagree wholeheartedly and adamantly with their position on this particular legislation."

Chairman Perkins extended a verbal olive branch to Rabbi Hirsch with a diplomatic dismissal: "I can appreciate your views and you have been very helpful to this committee." There was almost a note of relief in the chairman's voice.

*   *   *   *   *

Howard M. Squadron, chairman of the National Commission on Law and Social Action of the American Jewish Congress, represented that organization's view before the subcommittee. As with most witnesses, Squadron favored federal assistance to public schools but opposed the shared-time requirement, grants to sectarian schools, and the establishment of consortiums to provide supplementary educational services and grants without proper safeguards.

In elaborating his three major points, Squadron said that he believed shared-time creates the danger of dividing the public school community into two parts, based upon religion — the general student body and the parochial school group. He said experience proves that the parochial school students enter the public school as separate groups. Squadron said the AJC saw no difference "between the grant of federal funds to sectarian schools to purchase instructional material and library materials and equipment [under Title II] and the grants of such materials themselves."

Warning that this kind of grant could disenfranchise the public schools, he gave the following example:

> Consider what happened in the Netherlands. Before tax-raised funds were made available to confessional schools, only one out of five Dutch children attended such schools, and the other four attended public schools. When, after almost a century of pressure, the Dutch constitution was changed to provide for government financing of confessional schools, the ratio was almost reversed. Today, about three out of four children in Holland attend confessional schools. . . .

Squadron even went so far as to predict that religious groups would develop bitter rivalries "in seeking a 'fair share' of the pie. One can expect high-priced lobbyists to represent various private school systems," he said, "and perhaps even the formation of religious political parties to push for government funds."

In reference to supplementary educational centers, Squadron stated that they should include no religious symbols and that no teacher should wear a religious garb or identify with a religious group. He said that the consortium concept, which would include representatives from private schools and community educational and cultural institutions, should be rejected. "The idea of a partnership between church and state in education is not only unprecedented in American history since the establishment of the public school system but is directly contrary to the entire philosophy of the First Amendment," he insisted.

He also inserted in the record a letter, dated January 20, 1965, to Rep. Adam Clayton Powell, Jr., chairman of the House Committee on Education and Labor, from Dr. Joachim Prinz, president of the American Jewish Congress.

The letter included strong objections to the rush treatment accorded witnesses. Wrote Dr. Prinz:

> I wish to state, most emphatically, that the proposed schedule of hearings is manifestly inappropriate for these bills. The President's proposals have presented to the American people a totally new plan for dealing with a pressing national issue, a plan that raises serious questions under the constitutional requirements of separation of church and state. The specific terms of the bill have been available only in the last few days. In short, the American people have had no opportunity even to begin to give this matter the attention it requires.

Alas, Dr. Prinz's plea would suffer the same fate as those entered previously — filed in the record but unheeded. The deadline set by the White House would be met — even if it meant hearing eighteen witnesses in one day and continuing the hearings late into the night.

Perhaps the most significant and effective testimony was given by Dr. Leo Pfeffer, who though legal counsel for the American Jewish Congress, testified as an individual. Dr. Pfeffer, chairman of the Department of Political Science at Long Island University and at the time of the hearings visiting professor at the Law School of Rutgers University, is a constitutional lawyer of great distinction. The respect he rates was attested to by the fact that his testimony was the only one that all members of the subcommittee attended. Dr. Pfeffer did not lobby the committee in behalf of a religious group, but it would be a grave omission in a section devoted to church-state relations to omit his scholarly and lucid testimony. Dr. Pfeffer appeared before the committee on February 2 — the last day of the hearings. But because his testimony has close affinity with the testimony given earlier by representatives of Jewish organizations, it is included at this point.

Conceding that the "purposes of this measure are noble" and that he had long strongly advocated public aid to education, Dr. Pfeffer said that nevertheless as a lawyer he felt there was "an obligation on the part of this committee to examine and to consider constitutional questions which arise in any legislation. The duty of acting within the limitations of the Constitution, of the Bill of Rights, is not," he emphasized, "limited to any agency of government; it binds the legislature as much as it binds the executive and the courts.

"So what I propose to do," he explained, "is to make some comments as to what appear to me to be serious constitutional questions with respect to this measure."

Dr. Pfeffer said if Title I could be separated from the remainder of the bill and passed independently, he would be much more at ease. He did, however, question the shared-time aspect of Title I. If that program "were effectuated and practiced as it is set forth in theory," he said, "it would pass the constitutional test." But too often the program in actual practice varied radically from what was set forth in theory.

Dr. Pfeffer's primary criticism centered on the other titles of the bill.

Title II, he said, dealing with library resources and instructional materials, rated special attention. Referring to the "euphemism of private nonprofit schools and nonprofit agencies," Dr. Pfeffer warned that the innocuous description could give Congress cause for embarrassment:

> Theoretically a court could, in applying this act, interpret private nonprofit elementary and secondary schools as meaning nonreligious elementary and secondary schools. Such interpretation would undoubtedly avoid constitutional questions. We would have to close our eyes to the fact that is not what this legislation intends. The legislative history of this testimony given here by the remarks of the members of the committee, leaves no doubt what the bill intends is primarily religious schools and not secular public and nonprivate elementary schools. But the very use of that terminology may, in another way, cast some question regarding this title, specifically.

(The Senate committee report on the bill, quoting a letter from the Department of Health, Education, and Welfare, stated:

> As originally introduced, Title II of HR 2362 authorized the making of grants for the acquisition of books and instructional materials for the use of children and teachers in "public and nonprofit private elementary and secondary schools." The House deleted

the word "nonprofit," thereby extending the benefits of Title II to all children in private schools. The purpose of this amendment was to assure that under Title II, which is designed to benefit all children and not schools, certain children would not be discriminated against merely because they attend a private vocational, trade, or other school which meets state standards but is operated for profit.

The nonprofit limitations were not removed from Title III, however, apparently through an administrative oversight according to Dean Kelley of the National Council of Churches.)

Dr. Pfeffer gave the subcommittee an abbreviated lecture on U.S. Supreme Court decisions applying to the church-state question:

> This title [Title II] is apparently based on the position of the Supreme Court in 1930, in the case of Cochran against Louisiana in which the Court upheld a state statute providing secular textbooks for children in secular schools. The decision was handed down in, I believe, 1930, before the Court had held that the restrictions of the First Amendment with respect to religion were applicable to the states under the Fourteenth Amendment; therefore, no party raised, nor did the Court consider, the question of whether the statute violated the no-establishment clause of the First Amendment.

> The Court did give full consideration to the meaning of the no-establishment clause in the Everson Bus case in 1947. It did not rely on, or follow the Cochran case, but explored a different approach of constitutional reasoning and so, while often the approach of the Cochran case is used, the fact that it is attributable indirectly to the child-benefit theory, this is utilized to justify a measure such as this. It is probably an inaccurate use or an inaccurate interpretation, I think, of what the courts thought in 1947.

> The distinction of the Everson case, as I read that, is not indirect benefits but the nature of the service which the Government is providing. The Everson case was upheld by the majority not because the benefits were indirect — rather they were direct — but it was upheld because the benefits were welfare benefits. The justification of the rationale of the decision was that the purpose of the New Jersey law was to provide safety to insure the safety of children crossing the streets, and there is obviously no constitutional question as to the power of the state to appropriate money for that purpose.

> The four judges who dissented . . . agreed that a statute whose purpose is to protect the safety of children does not fall within

the provision of any constitutional provision. Their interpretation was based on the interpretation of what the purpose of the statute was. They thought the purpose of a statute was to help the school in meeting its budgetary problems, its financial problems. This, both the majority and the minority agreed, the state could do.

It was the opinion of the majority that the application of that principle to the fact before the Court was permissible, so I think it is fair to say that under constitutional law today, the question is whether the use of state funds in respect to church schools depends on whether those funds are used for *an educational purpose or for a welfare purpose* [italics mine].

Moreover this title [Title II] goes considerably further than the Cochran case. It refers not merely to books, but to instructional material. The testimony of the Commissioner of Education indicates they interpreted that to include not only printed material, but photographs and magnetic tape materials also. That realistically can't be considered to be of benefit to the child, except as all education is of benefit to the child. It makes no difference whether you give money to buy a laboratory, a classroom, a microscope, or a magnetic tape recorder. They are all of benefit or none of benefit.

I think the indications are that realistically this title does not — its purpose is not the child, except insofar as all education is for the benefit of a child.

Perhaps we made a mistake in 1791. Perhaps we should today change the Constitution to provide that government funds be used to finance parochial school education. But if it should be done, I think it should be done the way Congressman Becker sought to do with respect to the *Prayer* decision, which was a constitutional amendment. . . . This places a high responsibility on this committee and on the Congress to avoid violating the Constitution.

Dr. Pfeffer, making a title-by-title criticism of the bill, charged that Title III "permits in various ways the actual channeling both of money and equipment to parochial schools." He raised questions about the so-called consortium, which he described as a partnership between representatives of the two types of educational systems — private and public. "This creates a partnership which I think is forbidden by the Constitution," he said bluntly. He also said he had grave doubts about the constitutionality of Title IV with respect to direct aid to nonprofit institutions, universities, and colleges. But he acknowledged that the approval of the titles "may be the price we have to pay to get approval of Title I. We all know the realities of life," he concluded, "yet we have to consider whether we cannot get what is so sorely needed without compromising a constitutional privilege which has stood as well for 175 years."

In an exchange with Congressman Goodell, Dr. Pfeffer said he "would be inclined to doubt" that it would be constitutionally permissible for public school teachers to go and teach in private schools—whether the subject being taught was remedial or non-remedial.

Dr. Pfeffer also suggested that the bill include a judicial review provision permitting the school board to go to court to get a judicial determination on the constitutionality of the bill. "The only power of judicial review here is the state agency and that is very limited," Dr. Pfeffer stated. "Of course it is also unlikely to be effective."

The committee members spent so much time picking Dr. Pfeffer's fertile brain that the questions and answers consume twenty-eight pages in the subcommittee hearings record.

The subcommittee got hit with the second round of a double-barrel assault on the bill in the form of a thirty-one-page critique submitted by the American Civil Liberties Union. Lawrence Speiser, director of the Washington office, and George R. LaNoue, the consultant to the Commission of Religious Liberty of the National Council of Churches and a member of the ACLU'S Committee on Church and State, testified for the ACLU.

At this stage of the bill's history, the cumulative impact of testimony—primarily of the Jewish agencies—had caused the committee to decide informally that the materials allocated by Title II should be owned by public authorities. As Mr. LaNoue told the committee: "Having had the education of almost two previous days of testimony I have gathered that there is now a growing consensus on the committee that it should be clear that title [to materials] should remain in public hands." Mr. LaNoue explained, however, that the question of who holds title to the instructional materials is not the real issue. "As was mentioned yesterday, we can have the fiction of the 99-year lease," he said. "At some point the issue is not really title but whether the books are made on valid loan concept."

Mr. LaNoue also came down hard on the suggestion by Commissioner Keppel that community "centers will be administered by a partnership including the local educational agency."

"When I am speaking of partnership," said Mr. LaNoue, "the kind of partnership that I see embodied in this bill is the concept of partnership which includes joint authority and responsibility for the distribution of public funds. Unless changes incorporating the protections we have made or some similar changes are made," he admonished the Congressmen, "and here I am speaking for the Civil Liberties Union as a whole, we believe Titles II and III to be flatly unconstitutional as within. And we feel obliged to oppose the bill."

Congressman Carey, upset by the bluntness of the testimony, took the witness to task. "That is a rather strong ultimatum to the committee," he said, "that unless we adopt your language, at least your principles as you see them, and you spoke as an individual as well as a member of ACLU, that you will be forced to oppose the bill."

"The purpose of congressional committee hearings is so that individuals can express themselves," replied Mr. Speiser. "I think that candor requires us to tell you that this is our position. I trust that a citizen or a group of citizens in presenting its view and taking a position on legislation can do that without being accused of delivering ultimatums to Congress," he added.

Congressman Carey let the witnesses know that after listening to ten days of testimony he was convinced the consensus made it plain that the bill was acceptable to most segments of society. "I hope you would not think this committee to be delinquent in its obligations if we choose the first consensus even at the cost of losing the support of the second [ACLU]," he said, with pointed sarcasm.

Chairman Perkins tried to place the ACLU witnesses on the defensive by stating they disagreed with the former Secretary of Health, Education, and Welfare, Dr. Flemming, in connection with Title I.

"In what way, sir?" asked Mr. LaNoue.

"As spokesman for the National Council of Churches," replied Chairman Perkins, evading the alleged point of disgreement.

"In what way did I disagree?" Mr. Speiser interjected.

"As I understand your testimony," Chairman Perkins said, softening somewhat, "you are dissatisfied with the present language in Title I insofar as dual enrollment is concerned."

But Mr. LaNoue would not be caught off-base by the chairman. "If I may say," sir, the educator explained, "having some familiarity with the National Council's system of testimony, the Secretary was speaking as an official spokesman of the Council, and the Council does not have policy on every single aspect of the bill. Therefore, he [Dr. Flemming] confined himself to areas where the Council did have policy. On questions like whether a public school teacher could teach in a parochial school, he said the Council did not have policy and that although he personally thought it was not a good idea, he thought it would be constitutionally all right.

"I do disagree with him on that, yes, sir," the Assistant Professor of Government and Education at Columbia University informed the committee.

The ACLU testimony received much more sympathetic attention from the next witness than it did from Congressman Carey. The hour was growing late and it was the last day of the hearing, but at the insistence of Congressman Goodell, the U.S. Commissioner of Education, Dr. Francis Keppel, was recalled to the hearing room. Mr. Goodell was outside the room when Dr. Keppel arrived and Chairman Perkins had the New York Congressman paged. In the meantime, Mr. Perkins apologized to Dr. Keppel. "I regretted to call you back," he told Dr. Keppel. "I know you have been most helpful, that you will be most helpful to us again. Your testimony was so enlightening and was so detailed it could not be misunderstood when you were here before."

Other committee members interrogated Dr. Keppel while waiting for Mr. Goodell. The colloquy with the education commissioner illustrates the fluid state of the bill at the time, and the impact the ACLU testimony made on certain Congressmen.

Congressman Brademas said he was especially concerned about the misapprehension of the ACLU witnesses on the constitutionality of Title III and with respect to the governing board policy of the supplementary educational centers called for in Title III.

Dr. Keppel admitted that the problem "is to get a [governing] body which represents the educational resources that are not usually called school and bring them to bear on the improvement of the quality of the school system." He noted there had been a remarkable growth across the nation in the number of museums, symphony orchestras, and theatrical groups. He said all those kinds of educational resources should be used to enrich education at the secondary and elementary level.

"I have been looking very hastily at the language which the Civil Liberties Union has suggested and I hope that the chair-

man will permit us to comment on this at a later time," Dr.
Keppel said. "I have a high regard for the Civil Liberties Union
as a guardian of our freedom."

"We will permit you to do that in executive session," the chairman agreed.

Dr. Keppel reiterated that the purpose of Title III was not to
set up a parallel federal school system alongside the public school
system. He said that while both the private schools and public
schools would be represented on the consortium, "it certainly was
not the intent to put private schools in charge of this group or
consortium. But it seemed appropriate to us," he continued, "that
they bring strength to this enterprise."

A question by Congressman Carey illustrates how laws are
shaped by discussion with witnesses who have strong convictions
on a subject. During the discussion with Mr. LaNoue, he said,
"we reached an understanding that was acceptable at least to the
members here that they could see no difficulty with the loan of
a book for the duration of a semester. As an educator, now, would
that be a workmanlike arrangement?"

"I do think it would be a workable yardstick, sir," agreed Dr.
Keppel.

Later during the exchange, Dr. Keppel explained the mechanics
of how the federal money would flow down to the local school
district to aid the deprived student by repeating testimony he had
given earlier. "Funds will be transmitted to each state educational agency," he stated. "The state agency will in turn transmit
authorized amounts to each local educational agency operating
a state-approved program. The state will make the necessary
suballocations where there is more than one school district in a
county—and when census data are not available to help the Office of Education in HEW publish an allocation for school districts
within a county."

Congressman Ford of Michigan sought a clarification. "Isn't it
correct then that when the State of California...through its state
agencies has determined how much each of the districts within
the county of Los Angeles is to get, that ultimately the money gets
down to the county as a lump sum?"

"That is right," Dr. Keppel confirmed.

"And it is the local school district within Los Angeles county,
local board rather, that would determine which of the schools
within that school district they would spend the money in, is
it not?

"That is correct," Dr. Keppel again replied, "but the school district would present a plan to the state."

Although the Congressmen had had a long day — or perhaps because of it—they still found time for humor in the hearings. Congressman Carey unintentionally led the committee into a word game with a serious plea for summer enrichment programs in New York City under the provisions of the proposed legislation.

"Would there be some hope that an ongoing program of great cultural attraction in my own city, which has had great difficulty in getting off the ground, would be assisted, possibly, as one of the cultural contributions in this title?" he asked. "I am referring to Shakespeare in the Park."

"You touch me on a sensitive nerve," Dr. Keppel admitted. "I hope so, Mr. Carey."

"And all children could participate because it would be held out in the music grove or on the stage, wherever it is decided to be placed," Congressman Carey continued.

"Think how much better that is than to have somebody solemnly read Shakespearean plays that I suffered through when I was in school," Dr. Keppel stated, shuddering at his unhappy childhood experience with the English bard.

"If this bill will help to get Shakespeare off the ground—"

Congressman Carey was interrupted by Rep. Scheuer.

"I think what my colleague from New York wants is Shakespeare ON the ground, right in the middle of Central Park."

"It is, I take, 'As We Like It,'" Dr. Keppel responded, indicating that his solemn readings of Shakespeare were not a complete literary loss.

"In some cases, I might say there has been 'Much Ado About Nothing,'" Congressman Carey added to the list of Shakespearean titles.

"I shouldn't have started this, Mr. Chairman," Dr. Keppel apologized for the literary lapse. "I am sorry."

Chairman Perkins had his mind on more mundane matters— such as getting Congressman Goodell into the hearing room. The Congressman arrived a few moments later, and Chairman Perkins greeted him with a needling welcome on his tardiness: "Let me say that about an hour and a quarter ago I called the witness and I stated that he was recalled at the special request of our good friend from New York, Mr. Goodell."

"Thank you," the unruffled Mr. Goodell responded, as if he

had just been given the red-carpet treatment. "There have been just too many balls in the air this afternoon."

Congressman Goodell sparred briefly with Dr. Keppel before getting to the real reason why the education commissioner had been recalled—to discuss the so-called slip of tongue by Dr. Cohen when he said that schools rather than individuals would get text-books.

"Let me ask you with reference to Title II generally, and I understand you have covered this," Mr. Goodell began. "As you are aware, I am sure, I have quoted back to the testimony of you and Mr. Celebrezze and Mr. Cohen a number of times, on how you intend to administer Title II, particularly in those states where they feel there is a constitutional or other legal bar to their handling funds, giving books to the private schools.

"We have revolved around this question almost continuously in these hearings. Is it your view that a direct grant to a private school or to a school library is constitutional for the purchase of books approved by the public schools?" he asked, looking directly at Dr. Keppel.

"I think it might be worth trying, sir, to get the record straight as we understand it," Dr. Keppel said. "This issue, if I remember, came up, as I think you said, on the first day of the testimony. At that time, Mr. Celebrezze, Mr. Cohen, and I were responding."

What followed is almost unbelievable. For the entire nine days following the "slip-of-tongue" incident, Congressman Goodell had used Dr. Cohen's explanation to make political hay and em-barrass the Administration forces. One would have thought that when a second chance was afforded to rectify the error, Dr. Keppel would have gladly embraced and expertly exploited the oppor-tunity. Instead he only compounded the error.

"I remember when I first went to work as a dean, my chief, Mr. Conant, said that a wise administrator wore a worried frown on his assistant's face," Dr. Keppel said. "I wonder if I could extend Mr. Conant's remarks to Mr. Cohen and ask Mr. Des-Marais, who is Mr. Cohen's assistant, to deal with the record on this." (Why Dr. Cohen was not called to interpret his own state-ment is a mystery the record makes no pretense at solving.)

"We don't have the exact transcript here," Mr. DesMarais be-gan, fumbling the ball at the outset, "but I took a look at it in the clerk's office, and I believe the question was, 'The Commis-sioner would make the grant directly to the private schools for textbooks. Is that a correct statement of what would happen?'

"Mr. Cohen responded, and this is the way *it now reads in the record being printed for this committee:*

> That is correct; this is one possibility. Under Title II, students in nonpublic schools would be eligible to receive the books used in the public schools of their state. Our present thought is that these books would be made available by the publishers with payment to them coming from the Commissioner of Education.

"If you look at the language on page 23, line 17, in the bill on this matter, it says:

> The Commissioner shall arrange for the provision on an equitable basis of such resources as materials, or both, if necessary, for such use, and shall pay the cost thereof for any fiscal year ending prior to July 1, 1970, out of that state's allotment. The library resources in printed and published instructional materials made available pursuant to this subsection shall be limited to those which have been approved by an appropriate state or local educational authority for use, or are used in public elementary or secondary schools of the state.

"It is on the basis of that language that Mr. Cohen responded as to how he thought the Commissioner might handle this," Mr. DesMarais said, with the air of a man who believes his repair job is better than the original work.

Congressman Goodell exploded. "Are you saying the record has been corrected since he spoke, that it now stands this way, or is that your understanding of what he said?"

"That is our understanding of what Mr. Cohen was *trying* to say," Dr. Keppel said.

"Was TRYING to say?" Congressman Goodell shot back.

"Said," Dr. Keppel retorted.

Congressman Goodell seemed temporarily thrown off by the inadequacy of the explanation.

"I don't want to get into a fine discussion on this, but I have the record in front of me, and I think—well, are you contending he did not say there would be a different payment to private schools for books in those states where the state—"

Dr. Keppel interrupted. "I was present, Mr. Goodell. I realize the difficulty of recording these things, but I think Mr. Cohen was attempting to point out that, beginning on page 23, where the Commissioner is authorized to make these grants, arrange for or provide for, Mr. Cohen was attempting to point to the way in which it was done.

"I cannot myself recall the precise language," Dr. Keppel said, as if there were no record available.

"I take it Mr. Cohen is correcting the record as he *intended* to say it."

"I will just read for the record what he said, and we can pass to something else," said a flabbergasted Mr. Goodell. "It is not necessarily a matter of how you think it should be done."

He then read back the record which included the question by Mr. Perkins, "Isn't it true that the aid goes to the pupil and not to the school?"

> Mr. Cohen: We have to be sure we are talking about the correct title, Title I. When we talk about Title I we are talking about federal funds to go to public educational institutions. That is a federal financial payment to a local school district, and the point we were discussing with Mr. Goodell only had to do with how that public educational body used its public funds. That is a separate question. The other question Mr. Goodell developed had to do with Title II, the library resources, in which there is a somewhat separate situation, in which the state law, the Constitution, the law and the practice and the policy prohibit the use of federal funds to the state for this particular purpose or purposes. Then the Commissioner can make a grant directly for them.
> Mr. Goodell: To the school or to the library?
> Mr. Cohen: To the school or to the library; yes, sir.

"I think the record is pretty clear that at least as set up here, his [Cohen's] concept of it was that there would be a direct payment to the school or to the library, either in books or in cash, but in any event to the school or to the library," said Mr. Goodell in the tone of a lawyer who knows when he has the facts on his side.

"If he has revised his remarks or that is not the way you want to interpret it, that is fine," Congressman Goodell conceded. "I don't want to make a point of that. I am concerned as to how it is going to be done and whether we can work this so that the private school students can constitutionally share equally in this."

Dr. Keppel, apparently unaware of his chance to correct or at least put a more acceptable construction on Dr. Cohen's statements, simply moved to another point. The record remained muddled—for reasons known only to Secretary Celebrezze, Dr. Keppel and Dr. Cohen.

*   *   *   *   *

The evangelical or conservative Protestant viewpoint at the

hearing was presented by Dr. Arthur M. Climenhaga, executive director of the National Association of Evangelicals (NAE). Dr. Climenhaga had one advantage over his liberal colleagues in that the NAE executive committee had met January 25 to consider the President's education proposals and to stake out a position.

Commending the committee for providing educational assistance to poverty-impacted areas, Dr. Climenhaga followed with NAE's reservations:

> It is inherently wrong and therefore improper for the Government to take tax money from a Roman Catholic and use it to support a Baptist school, or vice versa. The Supreme Court has said repeatedly it is unconstitutional and, therefore, illegal.

> We, therefore, recommend that you and your colleagues insist on the elimination of every provision from HR 2362 that provides aid in any amount, directly or indirectly, to nonpublic schools.

> We deeply regret that the desirable aspects of this bill are being used as cover for all of these highly questionable features.

> Why not separate the latter from the bill in order that they may stand or fall on their own merit? In any case, as a further safeguard, we request that a provision be included in the bill for a judicial review that will permit its constitutionality to be tested in the courts.

Dr. Climenhaga was dismissed without so much as a question except to be asked by Congressman Carey how many denominations there were in NAE. Dr. Climenhaga replied that NAE represented 2.5 million people in forty-one denominations.

*   *   *   *   *

The next witness looked even more dour than usual. C. Stanley Lowell, associate director of Protestants and Other Americans United for Separation of State and Church (POAU) was no new face to many of the educational subcommittee members. The blunt-spoken POAU official, more concerned with possible constitutional infringements than sharpening HR 2362 as an instrument of reconciliation, enjoys verbal combat.

Submitting a rather brief written statement in behalf of POAU, Lowell launched into a criticism of the bill.

"I think there is real danger in this bill," he told the committee. "There are provisions that where the state law will not permit the school board to carry out the practices suggested in the legislation that the federal agencies should do this, anyway, and deduct so much from the allocation of the state.

"I wonder whether this is wise procedure in federal legislation, whether it does not trespass upon local control of education, upon the functions of the local school boards.

"Of course, we have most serious reservations in regard to Title III, which seems to provide—and there has been a lot of testimony about this—for a sort of hybrid school agency. This is something new, a private school agency supported by federal funds," he added, sarcastically.

Lowell then referred to statements prepared by attorneys from the Justice Department and HEW under President Kennedy when he started to formulate his program of aid to education—which did not include assistance to private schools.

"I have heard this memorandum alluded to three or four times in these hearings," Lowell said pointedly. "I have yet to hear it quoted. I think that it should be quoted. I think we should remember that President Kennedy's church-state policy in aid to education legislation was predicated and formulated on the basis of this legal memorandum.

"I think that this memorandum very plainly would bar as unconstitutional certain forms of aid to parochial schools that are provided in this legislation," he continued. "I think particularly Title II, with its provisions for the building up of libraries and the providing of educational materials for church schools would come under this ban."

Congressman Carey, whose dislike for Lowell's position was obvious, tried sandbagging the POAU associate director by engaging in an irrelevant discussion on POAU's mailing privileges.

"I have read a good deal of material sent out, and unless I am very much mistaken, you qualify for second- or third-class mailing privilege as an organization," Congressman Carey began, boring in. "It happens I believe that you also indicated in response to a question by my colleague, Mr. Hawkins, back in 1962 that you do enjoy tax-exempt status as an organization," he said, displaying an amazing memory of facts that indicated the Congressman was well prepared to grill the imperturbable Mr. Lowell. (Congressman Carey hit closer home than he realized. The tax-exempt status of POAU would be discontinued in 1969.)

Lowell replied that while POAU pays taxes on its property, it did have a nonprofit tax-exempt standing with the Internal Revenue Service.

Congressman Carey then embarked on a long dissertation on the research he had done to determine the amount of postal subsidies for religious organizations.

"Can you distinguish for me the benefits accruing to a religious organization that accrue from a postal subsidy and the child who goes to school with a standard textbook?" the Congressman asked.

"It seems to me you confuse two things," Lowell responded. "You are dealing with postal rates, where they have first-, second-, third-, and fourth-class rates, and then you are dealing with the issue of aid to the teachings of religion as such."

Congressman Carey said the intent of Congress through postal subsidies was to assist in education by making available the printed page to all segments of the population. He said it seemed to get down to whose ox was getting gored whether a subsidy was constitutional.

"We are dealing with channeling funds into parochial schools on the basis that we want to help poor children in the schools," Lowell contended, getting back to the purpose of the hearing. "I am saying there are better ways of helping poor children than channeling the funds through the churches. You can assist them in other contexts. This is a question in itself. I do not think it is involved with postal rates, which would be a different issue."

Congressman Carey said he planned to do nothing about the benefits the POAU received from the post office but requested Lowell to share with the committee any method of helping disadvantaged children his wisdom and understanding of the Constitution could come up with.

"I would be happy to do it, and in my statement I have done so," Lowell said without hesitation. "I have made specific recommendations which I hope will be helpful to the committee."

"No further question," said Congressman Carey, recognizing a worthwhile adversary in the POAU associate director.

The last witness to appear before the weary subcommittee— around 8:30 p.m. on February 2—was Dale L. Button, chairman of the church-state committee of the Laymen's League, Unitarian Universalist Association, representing both the League and the Association. As Button told the committee, it was a Massachusetts Unitarian, Horace Mann, who championed the public schools as religiously neutral and free to children of all faiths and classes. Standing in that tradition, Button asked the committee if encouraging shared-time experiments by the Federal government could not be "stimulating proliferation of church schools to the eventual detriment of the public schools."

He also urged the legislators to write into the bill a provision which would give a citizen "standing" in court so an individual could institute a suit to test the constitutionality of aspects of the bill.

"We would counsel caution to the writers of this legislation, lest, in their determination to solve the problems of cultural and educational deprivation and of poverty, they contribute unwittingly to the erosion of the constitutional safeguard which has made it possible for the poor in America to receive free elementary and secondary education—not as a privilege, but as a right," Button concluded.

It had been a long eleven-hour day. The hearing room was nearly empty and the clock was pointing at 8:40 p.m. Chairman Perkins gratefully dismissed Button and then asked unanimous consent that the record remain open for ten days so that any statement any member of Congress, or any individual, would wish to make could be inserted in the record.

"I know these hearings are about to come to a conclusion," the subcommittee chairman said, "and I do want to state that in my judgment the subcommittee has endeavored to make these hearings as comprehensive and as thorough as this complex subject requires. Perhaps these hearings have been more comprehensive than any we have held in the past."

The chairman then reminded the committee of the next order of business—"marking up" the bill. He said the subcommittee would meet in executive session at 10 a.m. the next day to "write a bill for the benefit of the school children of America."

Congressman Carey proved he is never at a loss of words—even at the eleventh hour. "From the great cities, from the major states, from the rural areas, from all walks of life," he told Mr. Perkins, "men of good counsel, and men of authority have come before the committee and unhesitatingly and without any equivocation have endorsed the spirit and the terms and the operation of this legislation."

He said he agreed with Chairman Perkins that the hearings had been comprehensive and they had "not been in a sense of haste," Republican Goodell to the contrary. "As a member of the subcommittee, Mr. Chairman," he added, "I wish to express to you my sincere appreciation for your fairness and for your courtesy and your devotion to the rules of the committee and in the conduct of these hearings."

More grateful that Congressman Carey had stopped talking than impressed by the content of his complimentary remarks, Chairman Perkins adjourned the committee. Stuffing his papers inside his briefcase, he must have felt that he had kept the faith, for he had come within one day of meeting the Administration's deadline of February 1—even though the committee had heard more than 2000 pages of testimony, which when compiled by the U.S. Government Printing Office would weigh more than four pounds.

* * * * *

Chairman Perkins' job, however, was not finished, since he had to keep prodding the subcommittee to "mark up" the bill as hurriedly as possible. Dean Kelley and Professor LaNoue in their analysis of the subcommittee's action in "The Church-State Settlement" observe that the cumulative impact of witnesses caused the subcommittee to make several changes having church-state implications:

(1) New language was included in Title I making it clear that the ownership of property and the administration of projects would be in public hands.

(2) A new section was drawn up for Title II stating that library resources and instructional materials obtained under the title would be limited to those approved by the state or the local educational agency (the local school board). Ownership would be vested in the public agency. The same concept was reflected in Title III in a clause governing ownership of any supplementary educational facilities constructed with federal funds.

(3) The "marked-up" bill also elaborated on the benefits available to children. In Title I, the word "equipment" was added, providing that children attending private schools could share in Title I benefits "such as dual enrollment, educational radio and television, and mobile educational services and equipment."

(4) The subcommittee expanded Title II so that instructional materials bought with public funds would include "textbooks" in addition to "library resources and printed and published instructional materials" already in the title.

(5) Sensitive to the strong protest lodged against the consortium concept during the hearings, the subcommittee gave public school boards sole administrative responsibility for Title III grants for supplementary educational services. "Community participants would propose but the school board would dispose," Kelley and LaNoue point out.

(6) The committee report, which explains the intent of the

bill (legislation is seldom noted for its lucidity), further clarified
the child-benefit concept:

> The bill does not authorize funds for the payment of private school
> teachers. Nor does it authorize the purchase of material or equip-
> ment or the construction of facilities for private schools. . . . The
> bill does not anticipate broadened instructional offerings under
> publicly sponsored auspices which will be available to elementary
> and secondary school students who are not enrolled in public
> schools.

(7) The report also emphasized that "library resources, textbooks, and other instructional materials" are to be made available to children and teachers and not to institutions. And the
materials would be made on a loan basis only.

The Republicans boycotted the subcommittee meeting at which
the bill was approved on a 6-0 vote. Rep. Goodell explained that
the Republicans stayed away to protest the "hasty and superficial
consideration given the bill" by the subcommittee. It was a valiant
but vain attempt by an ineffective minority to register its opposition.

The full committee marked up HR 2362 in executive session
between February 25 and March 2. The committee made one
major change by counting families on welfare receiving $2000, or
less, in determining the Title I federal contribution to counties or
school districts. The committee ordered the bill, with amendments, reported on a 23-8 vote. The question now before the
House was: Could the Administration forces keep the church-state
compromise from becoming unglued in the heat of a possible
floor hassle?

Early in March, Dean Kelley got an unexpected but urgent
telephone call from one of the most influential members on the
Committee on Education and Labor—U.S. Rep. Edith Green,
Democrat of Oregon. Mrs. Green, a school teacher for eleven years
in Oregon before going to Washington and a former public relations director for the Oregon Education Association, is a strong
advocate of local school control.

"Are you aware of the church-state implications of that bill
(HR 2362) as reported out by the subcommittee?" she asked
Kelley. Without waiting for an answer, she continued: "I think
you ought to know about this. I want to point out where your
concerns are affected."

Kelley was aware that many members on Capitol Hill believed
Mrs. Green was jealous of Congressman Perkins and critical of his

subcommittee. Others felt she was determined to leave her own peculiar stamp on all major educational legislation. Although a liberal, Mrs. Green is a strong states' righter as far as schools are concerned. She favors aid to education without strings attached. Honest convictions, however, as well as personal ambition, may have motivated her to call Kelley.

Kelley arranged for a meeting the next day at the NCC Washington office. He contacted members of his church-state consortium, including Dr. Carlson of the Baptist Joint Committee on Public Affairs and Rabbi Hirsch of the Reform Jews Religious Action Center. Mrs. Green was accompanied by a contingent of Congressmen including Republican Albert H. Quie of Minnesota.

"She passed out a committee print of the bill—a rare thing to do," recalls Kelley. "A print is a marked-up bill as re-written by the subcommittee before it has been adopted by the full committee. It is supposed to stay in the committee."

Kelley had learned from H. D. (Jack) Reed, Jr., counsel for the subcommittee, that Mrs. Green wanted the committee to assure her that public school teachers would not be sent into private schools. Kelley also had a quick conference with Msgr. Francis J. Hurley, associate director of the Catholic Office of Education, before meeting with Mrs. Green's group. "The Catholics were not entirely satisfied with the bill — and neither was the National Committee of Churches," Kelley said.

"As Mrs. Green talked," Kelley continued, "it was obvious that she was trying to drive us apart and break up the shaky religious coalition. During the conversation, Dr. Carlson, with his benign smile, said, 'You know, Mrs. Green, this bill gives me much less trouble on that subject [church-state] than does your Higher Education bill.' She spluttered and said the two were in no way similar," Kelley said. The coalition continued to hold.

The Education Subcommittee, headed by Senator Wayne Morse of Oregon, began hearings on the Administration bill (labeled S 370 in the Senate) January 26. The Senate subcommittee was determined not to disturb the church-state settlement.

Both Kelley and Dr. Flemming of the NCC had expected a full-blown interrogation on church-state questions similar to the House subcommittee hearing. "We expected Dr. Flemming to be raked over the coals in the Senate," Kelley admitted. "But he was only asked two questions on the church-state issue." The two questions were: Had he seen the revised House bill? (he wasn't called before the Senate subcommittee until February 11) and

Was he satisfied with the revisions? He replied in the affirmative on both questions, and the subcommittee members then turned to educational rather than constitutional issues.

The Senate subcommittee heard so many of the same witnesses who had testified before the House subcommittee that at times the hearing sounded like a rerun. HEW Secretary Celebrezze explained the purpose and operation of the bill to the Senators as he had to the Representatives. Msgr. Hochwalt showed up to say, "we indicate our willingness to cooperate with this legislation proposal because of the assurance that all children in need will benefit from the program."

Harrison J. Goldin, representing the American Jewish Congress, said AJC supported federal aid to education "but opposed the measure in its present form." Rabbi Morris Sherer of Agudath Israel of America countered by saying his organization endorsed the act as "a major step forward in meeting the educational needs of the school children of the nation."

Sargent Shriver, as director of the Office of Economic Opportunity, testified that the big guns in the War on Poverty were educational programs, such as Headstart, tutoring, remedial education, and summer programs. He said that if the educational bill would perform these services, then OEO funds could be put to other uses.

The Rev. C. Stanley Lowell of POAU took another whack at the proposed legislation warning that portions of the bill providing assistance to students in private schools would "deteriorate our country's constitutional tradition of church-state separation." The Senators were no more impressed than had been the Democratic majority on the House subcommittee.

In the meantime the church lobbyists' "acknowledged church-state expert," Dr. C. Emanuel Carlson of the Baptist Joint Committee, was sending back a glowing report on HR 2362 to his constituents. "Few education bills have been given a larger measure of goodwill," he wrote in an article entitled "Revised Bill Seeks to Relieve Church-State Tensions" in the March, 1965, issue of *Report from the Capital* — "so much so that even the subcommittee members from the opposition party did not vote in opposition to the measure." (His facts were correct, but the reason hardly coincided with that given by Congressman Goodell that minority members abstained from voting as a form of protest against the "hasty and superficial consideration given the bill.")

"The responsible representatives of the major Protestant churches and their organizations are satisfied that this bill will aid the educational opportunities of the next generation," Dr. Carlson continued. "Their concerns for full public responsibility and public control have been heard and incorporated into the bill."

Dr. Carlson dismissed three opponents of the bill — ACLU, POAU and the Anti-Defamation League of B'nai B'rith — in a rather offhanded manner. "There is a prevalent view that these question marks [from the opposing organizations] arise from a misunderstanding of the operation of the proposals," he stated.

Dr. Carlson seemed to lean toward Dr. Flemming's point of view that HR 2362 was an instrument of reconciliation forged in the warm sunshine of ecumenical understanding. "In the matter of interfaith controversy regarding education, this bill may contribute more toward the solution of the problem than it does to the opportunities of the professional advocate or the exhilarating experience of tension," he told his constituents. "The bill does seem to be an honest effort to meet the needs of our day."

*   *   *   *   *

The Democratic party leadership apparently was not as convinced as Dr. Carlson that the bill would be hailed from both sides of the aisle as a "measure of goodwill." The House Democratic whips of state delegations, keenly aware of the federal aid failures of the past and the efficacy of power politics, called a strategy meeting. They were determined that all amendments to the bill on the House floor would be opposed. The Democrats outnumbered the Republicans 295 to 140. The leadership, however, wanted to make sure the shaky coalition did not break up on the jagged points of church-state issues and the Title I allotment formula.

Congresswoman Edith Green, who also was chairman of the House Special Education Subcommittee, strongly opposed the Administration formula which stipulated that a state would receive funds equal to half its average expenditure per school child multiplied by the number of pupils from low-income families. Opponents argued that the formula discriminated against the poorer states. Mrs. Green offered an amendment calling for a straight $200 grant for each child from a low-income family. She was encouraged in her attempts to effect changes in the bill by Republican Congressmen Goodell and Albert H. Quie.

When Mrs. Green's amendment was defeated on a 136-202 teller vote, Congressman Goodell stoked the fires with a recommittal motion. The Democrats held the line by defeating the motion 149-267 on a roll-call vote.

Congressman Quie took his turn next, offering a substitute for Title I which provided $300 million a year in federal funds for the establishment of pre-school and special educational centers for impoverished three-to-seven-year-old children. The Quie formula allocation to the states was based on the number of impoverished children from families with annual incomes below $3,000. His motion was shouted down by Democrats in a voice vote.

In a persistent attempt to penetrate the united front on her own side of the aisle, Mrs. Green compiled figures showing that under the Administration formula Mississippi would get only $120 per child compared with $283 per child for New Jersey.

An articulate woman who doesn't hesitate to scold members of her own party, Mrs. Green lashed out at the stubborn stance taken by the Administration supporters:

> I really am serious in saying to my liberal colleagues, those of you who honestly and sincerely have been terribly concerned about the events in Mississippi during the last two or three years. Are you really shedding crocodile tears? Are we making pious statements about how awful things are and how we really want to do something about it, and then, when we have a bill that is before the House, we do the least for those states of any single state in the nation?

The Administration supporters, comfortable in the security of their numbers, informed the lady from Oregon that it costs more to educate a child in the North than in the South and therefore the formula really was not inequitable. They also countered her argument by proving that the percentage of increase in school budgets caused by the influx of Title I assistance would be considerably higher in the South than in the North.

Having lost that battle, Mrs. Green turned to another controversial aspect of HR 2362 — the limited provision for judicial review to test the constitutionality of the act.*

---

* In 1922, the U.S. Supreme Court ruled in the case of Frothingham vs. Mellon that taxpayers do not have sufficient standing to challenge the constitutionality of a federal appropriation. The Supreme Court's position was that a single taxpayer's stake was too small to support a suit contending that a federal expenditure exceeded Congress' general powers. The ruling blocked

On February 26, the National Council of Churches, while approving the child-benefit theory, called for an adequate judicial review provision. Dean Kelley said the NCC legal counsel advised that there were ways of getting into court even under the limited provisions of the Education Act. (The act permits a state to go to court if dissatisfied with the action of the U. S. Commissioner on the state's application.)

"Mrs. Green and company wanted to use the proposed judicial review amendment as a divisive tactic," Kelley said.

While the bill was being debated on the House floor, Kelley got a call from Dr. A. Dale Fiers, influential member in the "inner council" of the NCC and executive secretary of the Christian Church (Disciples of Christ) — of which Mrs. Green just happens to be a member. Dr. Fiers informed Kelley he was not satisfied with the limited judicial review provisions. "Dr. Fiers said he was going to send wires to all the Congressmen quoting NCC to the effect that the bill should include an adequate judicial provision," Kelley said.

Kelley's Irish temper flared, and he called Dr. R. H. Edwin Espy, the National Council's general secretary, to ask, "Since when does a head of a member denomination determine NCC policy?"

Dr. Espy called Dr. Fiers and warned him that he could not "unilaterally set policy." The NCC officials, however, could not prevent Mrs. Green from exploiting Dr. Fiers' statement by reading it into the record.

"We felt she was dragging NCC in by the tail," Kelley said. "The statement seemed to give the impression NCC was pressing for the amendment."**

In a desperate attempt to offset Mrs. Green, Kelley dictated a hurried letter from the NCC Washington office to his secretary in New York stating that while the NCC did in fact favor a judicial

---

the path for challenging the growing number of federal programs involving church-state issues.

A breakthrough in the "standing" test was scored in June of 1968 by Mrs. Florence Flast, New York City housewife, and six other taxpayers who argued that tax money used to pay for tutoring in parochial schools was a violation of the First Amendment prohibition against "an establishment of religion." The case was originally dismissed by the federal court in New York for lack of "standing." The Supreme Court, by an 8-1 vote, held the New Yorkers were entitled to their day in court to try to show that Congress really had violated the First Amendment.

** In Cincinnati, in October of 1969, Dr. Fiers told this writer that Kelley later conceded that his (Fiers) position was correct. At the request of Dr. Fiers, Ian McCrae of the denomination's Department of Church in Society wrote the author a letter, dated October 15, 1969, which states, in part:

review provision, the Council was convinced the bill made allowance for limited review. Kelley did suggest the bill's review provision "might include local boards, so as to give them standing for filing suits." His secretary typed the letter, had 435 copies made (for each member of Congress), stuffed them, and then brought the whole batch by plane to Washington.

"Before distributing the letters, I called Douglas Cater [White House legislative assistant] and told him about it," Kelley said.

Cater wasn't too happy. "That sounds like grudging approval to me," he told Kelley. "Can't you do something better?"

"That IS our policy," Kelley replied.

Kelley later contacted a member of the House committee staff for his reaction. "I would think you wanted the bill amended," the staff member said after reading the letter.

"I went back to the office and threw all the letters in the wastebasket," Kelley said. Then he got Cater on the telephone again.

"We will forget about the letter," he told Cater, "if you can give us some assurance you will get something in the record showing Congress rejected a judicial review provision, not because they were against it, but because they didn't think it was necessary."

Cater promised Kelley he would contact the Justice Department immediately to see "if they could tool something up." This they did overnight, and Rep. Emanuel Celler, chairman of the House Judiciary Committee, agreed to give the speech, saying that a judicial review provision was unnecessary.

Cater asked Kelley if the NCC would take some kind of action indicating that the bill was acceptable on that basis.

Kelley, who still chuckles over his part in the behind-the-scenes church-state intrigue, arranged to get the NCC office to send a wire to Majority Leader Carl Albert (D., Okla.) approving the bill based on Congressman Celler's speech. "We will send the

---

Our original reaction to the bill was to support it provided that a judicial review section was added. It was our conviction that the bill moved us into a significantly new era in church-state relations and we felt that it was important to clarify the matter in the courts before practices were well established.

While I would have to say that we have not been able ourselves to follow the application of the bill in detail, it is our conviction that our original position was correct. We are convinced that a number of the grants which have been made under the bill are of highly questionable constitutional validity.

It is our understanding that a number of persons who supported the bill without the judicial review section in it now agree that a review process would have been very helpful in clarifying where we are going to go in church-state relations.

wire to the Majority Leader, in care of me," Kelley told Cater, "and I will sit in the front row of the members gallery with the telegram in my pocket." Kelley agreed to release the telegram as soon as Celler gave his speech — but not a minute before.

On March 26, 418 of the 435 members of the House of Representatives met for final action on HR 2362.

Congressman Celler got up and made a short statement, but Kelley didn't hear it. He turned to Cater, sitting next to him, and asked, "Is that his speech?" Cater didn't know, either. He called Celler from the floor, who explained that he had just gotten permission to extend his remarks "so I can put the speech in the record in case I don't get to give it."

Cater looked hopefully at Kelley: "Now that it is guaranteed to be in the record, can we have the telegram?"

"No," Kelley stubbornly held out. "The telegram refers to Celler's speech and he hasn't given it yet."

Kelley had thrown 435 letters into a wastebasket, but he was not going to release a telegram until the Administration lived up to its part of the agreement.

As the evening wore on, however, he relinquished and gave the telegram to Jack Reed, counsel for the Subcommittee on Education. Reed was sitting next to Perkins, the floor manager of the bill.

"It was Friday," Kelley said, "and the Tuesday-to-Thursday Club was getting impatient. Both sides were trying to wear down the other side — waiting for the others to go away. About 9:30 p.m. Judge Smith [Rep. Howard W. Smith of Virginia] got up and offered a judicial review amendment. Then Congressman Celler got up, pulled out his speech and read it word for word to a hushed House."

Congressman Celler spoke as if he were reacting to Rep. Smith's amendment — even though Celler's statement had been carefully prepared hours before. The gray-haired New York Congressman told the House that judicial review was unnecessary because "there is no aspect of this bill which raises issues of any significance in the field of church and state that will not be subject to judicial review. . . . State and federal law already make available judicial remedies against executive action in practically every situation where a remedy could, as a constitutional matter, be provided. . . .

"Unless there is a 'case or controversy,' that is, unless the suit is justifiable," Celler continued, "the Constitution forbids the federal court from considering the matter. If the case is justifiable and a constitutional question is involved, like church and state, whether we accept or reject the amendment providing for review, the case will be adjudicated. . . ."

Kelley had to suppress a loud laugh when Rep. Smith, looking at Rep. Celler with absolute amazement, asked: "I just now wrote this amendment out on the back of an envelope. How did you have such a response ready so quickly?"

"As an attorney of long standing," the venerable New York Congressman replied, "I believe in being prepared."

Majority Leader Carl Albert, who finally had been handed the NCC telegram of endorsement, got up to read it.

"Then Adam Clayton Powell pops up and asks for a vote," Kelley recalled with disgust. "Albert never got to read the telegram. So the bill passed without all our valiant effort."

Kelley did give copies of the telegram, however, to Congressmen Goodell, Quie, and Mrs. Green. He thought it better to give them away than to toss them into the wastebasket — although the results were the same.

*   *   *   *   *

The House passed HR 2362 by a 263-153 roll-call vote, and the Senate passed it April 9 by a 73-18 roll-call vote, clearing it for President Johnson's signature two days later.

When LBJ tied a political knot, he made it tight. The Senate subcommittee Democrats voted down twenty amendments to the bill offered by the five Republican members. The minority charged that "by decree of the President of the United States . . . this important and complex piece of legislation . . . is to pass this body without a dot or comma changed; this by fiat from the Chief Executive."

By passing HR 2362 in the exact form it had been approved by the House, a House-Senate conference to resolve differences was avoided. Senator Wayne Morse of Oregon, the bill's manager, said President Johnson agreed with the majority that the bill should be passed without any amendments to avoid "possible risks that are always involved in connection with an education bill in conference sessions."

President Johnson's signature made HR 2362 the law of the land — in theory. In fact, the U. S. Office of Education administers the Elementary and Secondary Education Act and in so doing writes its own regulations as to how the bill should be implemented. "Imagine the surprise of the church-state specialists, then," exclaim Dean Kelley and Professor LaNoue in their article, "when they obtained copies of the first draft of the administrative regulations late in the summer and discovered that many of the central terms of the church-state settlement were completely missing from the draft regulations."

Men familiar with the working of the intricate machinery of national government should not be surprised. Often what is written as law on the Hill is ignored by the professionals who execute the bill — and who may have helped draft it in the first place. Bureaucrats are not inclined to let Congress rewrite or tamper with their regulations. And local school administrators would have to live with the Office of Education regulations rather than the actual act itself.

A strong protest was made to Commissioner Keppel, by members of Congress and lobbyists. John Gardner, the new Secretary of Health, Education, and Welfare, made the decision that the language of the Senate committee report would be the basis of the regulations of the sections involving the so-called church-state settlements. The regulations were revised — but many church lobbyists who had supported the bill still were apprehensive.

CHAPTER X

A Second Look at the Church-State Settlement

Dean Kelley of the National Council of Churches was furious. He felt the church lobbyists had been double-crossed by the Administration and he had prepared an angry article for *Christian Century* magazine to blast the U. S. Office of Education for its watering down the church-state settlement.

Other lobbyists were saying the same things in more gentle terms. In January of 1966, Dr. C. Emanuel Carlson of the Baptist Joint Committee on Public Affairs, wrote in *Report From the Capital* that the focus of the educational act had shifted from Washington to the local school board. An editor's note explained that "Dr. Carlson's study reveals that 'regulations' and 'guidelines' from a church-state standpoint, seem not to be as precise as the legislation enacted by Congress and signed by the President."

In January of 1966, HEW Secretary Gardner named Yale-educated Harold Howe II the U. S. Commissioner of Education. Kelley met with Howe shortly after he was sworn in to impress on him the need for the Office of Education to carry out the precise intent of the church-state settlement in HR 2362.

In the meantime, Kelley had sent a copy of his magazine article to Douglas Cater, White House assistant, to get his reaction. "Cater saw Jim Hamilton and me in the White House," Kelley said. "Cater came over to us and told me, 'That article hit me like a ton of bricks.' He then sent us over to talk to one of the under secretaries of education." Kelley also called several Congressmen — including Representatives Brademas of Indiana and Thompson of New Jersey — to protest the casualness of the Office of Education toward the church-state settlement. Kelley's lobbying of Congressmen and Administration officials did result in a tightening up of regulations — enough to make him rewrite his article but not enough to take the sting out of it.

Kelley explained that church-state safeguards had been written into the act and into the Senate and House committee reports enabling

> defenders of the act to reassure many who feared lest it have the effect of contributing to the "establishment" of religious institutions through tax aid. The National Council of Churches, the Baptist Joint Committee on Public Affairs and many of the Protestant communions were able to support the Elementary and Secondary Education Act on the basis of the child-benefit concept as formulated by Congress under the leadership of the Johnson administration.

> How is the act working out in practice? . . . From the federal and state regulations and the state plans approved by the Office of Education it is possible now to ask whether the child-benefit concept is eroding into a school-benefit result, contrary to the assurances given by the administration to those who wanted to support the act.

Trying to change legislation after it has been passed and signed into law is a frustrating, fruitless experience, the church lobbyists found. Government bureaucrats are a separate breed of men who often are impervious to the pressures and cajolings of lobbyists — even those motivated by the highest ideals.

By the spring of 1967 there was widespread dissatisfaction among the church lobbyists over the way the U. S. Office of Education was executing the ESEA. "In looking back with 20-20 hindsight, I think there are a number of things about which we now might have a little different attitude," Hamilton of the NCC Washington office told me. Robert Jones, the affable executive secretary of the Washington office of the Department of Social Responsibility for the Unitarian Universalist Association, called ESEA "a real behind-the-scenes deal. It made a lot of us pretty mad," he said. "It was a slap in the face of American Protestantism."

He conceded, however, that there was not much he could do. "There has been a real change lately in the feeling of our people," he said. "They used to get real excited about church-state principles. Now it's just a big boring subject. Civil rights and the ecumenical movement may have drained it of its importance."

* * * * *

Dr. Carlson of the Baptist Joint Committee was still concerned in March of 1967 about Title II of the bill, which provides library resources and instructional materials. "Here we wanted public administration, which was provided, but we questioned how it could be implemented," he said. "Will they put the materials in public libraries for all children and teachers or try to build up private school libraries? I don't think they are out of the woods on this one yet. Suppose you buy encyclopedias and put them in the private school library. Is this an aid to the student or to the institution? I think the courts will be working some time on this," he predicted.

Rabbi Hirsch wasn't being smug, but he couldn't completely hide his "I-told-them-so" attitude. "The Protestants made a mistake — they were well motivated but they didn't use their intelligence," he said, pointing to his head. "If they would have put up a bigger yell they would have gotten more emphasis on what are our basic concerns. But once the Administration comes out with a bill, they have everything pretty much going their way and all the pressure groups caved in along the way. The President didn't have to make the church-state compromise he did in order to get the bill passed. It was an Administration Congress — the votes were there anyway. I think the record shows now that our position was justified," he affirmed with conviction.

The Rev. C. Stanley Lowell of Protestants and Other Americans United for Separation of Church and State, explained how he viewed the ESEA of 1965 two years later. "If you put administrative discretion in the saddle, you can count on getting a wrong result," he noted with finality. "I think the National Council of Churches just couldn't envisage a permanent conflict with the Catholic Church in an ecumenical age and they [NCC] were willing to make concessions."

In April of 1967, Congressman Goodell's office reflected little of the liberal image he attained so rapidly in 1969. His picture-lined office wall included conspicuous portraits of President Eisenhower, Senator Kenneth Keating of New York and Senator Barry Goldwater of Arizona. Lighting his cigar and propping his feet on his desk, the Congressman forcefully expressed his views on ESEA in a late afternoon interview.

"We elected the most pro-federal aid to education Congress in 1964 that we ever had," he said in his typical blunt manner. "Otherwise, things might have been a little different.

"It is generally accepted that before the Administration makes any proposals on education it gets representatives from the National Catholic Welfare Conference to work it out.

"The National Council of Churches tends to divide [weakening its bargaining position].

"The bill was an interesting cover up," he said. "The Administration didn't want to delineate too carefully what the bill would do. Public school advocates might get concerned about teachers going into private schools to teach. The private school people were sold, believing it would do more than it really would do."

He stopped to collect his thoughts before revealing why he opposed ESEA.

"My primary objection to ESEA was the overcentralization in Washington and then the categorical grants. I'm very sympathetic to more aid to private schools," he quickly added. "And for poor kids — hell, who wants to be against poor children during this poverty fever? Most of the money is in Title I and will go to some of the richest school districts in the country — many of whom don't need it. The distribution formula is questionable."

Representative Goodell conceded that Congress gave wide latitude to the Office of Education in implementing the act. "I don't think Congress was very clear on its intent," he continued. "The scope that was left open to the Commissioner [of Education] permits him to go in a variety of directions. But the White House took the view that this piece of legislation had to go through as written. The Senate passed it without changing a word, comma or period [a slight overstatement]. This has never happened before during my career here," he said flatly.

Sam Halpern, deputy assistant secretary for legislation in the U. S. Office of Education, gave the Administration point of view on ESEA. "President Johnson says this is where he gets his greatest kicks," Halpern explained. "He has tripled government investment in health and education. ESEA was cleverly contrived," he continued with a satisfied smile, "to break through a series of roadblocks—Catholics versus Protestants, rural versus city, general versus categorical aid. Each part was tailored to win support of certain segments. We never thought Catholics would be able to support the bill the way they did. They helped pass it.

"We consulted with all kinds of pressure groups. We always asked the question 'How far can you guys go without being clobbered by your own people?'

"I feel very strongly the Catholics did not get what they wanted," Halpern said. "They wanted parity with the public schools. But they did get a federal principle established that all kids should get aid."

Halpern agreed with Congressman Goodell that Congress worded HR 2362 so loosely that it gave the Office of Education considerable flexibility in writing up the regulations. "Congress never really said what it meant about the church-state issue," Halpern said. "But an all-time record was set in getting the bill passed in three months. Everybody worked around the clock and everybody worried that if it didn't pass, we would have a new holy war on our hands," he added, indicating the depth of concern felt by the Administration.

The "holy war" almost erupted again in 1967 despite President Johnson's cautioning his opponents not to disturb the precarious church-state settlement contained in ESEA of 1965.

In the spring of 1967, Albert H. Quie, the lanky Congressman from Minnesota, was ready to take a stand and slug it out with the Administration forces on federal aid to education by attempting to make changes in the bill passed two years earlier. His proposed amendments to the ESEA of 1965 drew withering fire from President Johnson, Democratic Congressmen, and newspaper pundits.

"The Quie bill would bring down in a crash the structure of the 1965 settlement of the church and state school issue," solemnly warned Walter Lippmann in his "Today and Tomorrow" column. President Johnson, speaking at the dedication of the Crossland High School in Camp Springs, Maryland, appealed for support to oppose what he called a "reckless" Republican move to amend ESEA. Lumping both Democratic and Republican opposition into the same bag, he admonished: "They are raising the same roadblocks which halted federal aid to education for twenty long years. I hope Congress will stop, look, and listen before they march down this blind alley." He said his opponents were trying to revive bitterness between church and public school leaders, and between poor and wealthy states.

Congressman Quie, who left his 240-acre dairy farm in 1958 to take his seat in Congress, had grown accustomed to political infighting, but the partisan position of the church lobbyists both baffled and dismayed him. "The more the church is included in all phases of our society, the more it has the responsibility to lobby," Quie, a Lutheran, explained to me in his office in April of 1967. "But I think the churches should limit their lobbying to the way issues affect them and not take a particular partisan position — but they do."

He described the ESEA of 1965 as a "house of cards."

. Explaining why he voted against HR 2362, Quie stated: "Title I gives more to the rich than to the poor. On a per-poor-child basis, Mississippi would get $129 while New York would get $364.

"There is not sufficient state participation," he continued. "Only the states are sensitive enough to know where the real need is. We want to provide for more state direction and let them zero in on the greatest need.

"The language is the same in my bill as in the present act, so there would be no church-state issue."

In another interview, he said: "Johnson has got the big city superintendents thinking they'll get less money under my plan and the rural school people thinking they'll get cheated. He's got the private and parochial school people afraid they'll lose out, the civil rights backers afraid of less action against segregation and the segregationists afraid my plan will cause more rigid enforcement."

Even the astute Walter Lippmann tended to see the political school battle as between Catholics and anti-Catholics. "There is under serious attack the measure which may well come to be thought of as the greatest single peacetime achievement of the Kennedy-Johnson Administration," Lippmann wrote. "This is the Education Act which was passed in 1965. This act opened the way through the conflict between the Catholics and anti-Catholics, the conflict which has been so stubborn and perplexing an irritant in the life of the American people."

(To describe the political and philosophical differences on federal aid to education — and especially aid to students in private schools — as a conflict between "Catholics and anti-Catholics" misses the real issue. Would the columnist argue that the American Jewish Congress, the American Civil Liberties Union and even Dr. Leo Pfeffer, the constitutional lawyer who opposes the bill as an individual, were acting out of anti-Catholic bias? Mr. Lippmann knows better.)

"Since 1965 the old controversy has subsided," Mr. Lippmann continued. "The anti-Catholics [he insists on using the term] have accepted the Act, which provides Catholic children with educational advantages. [Also Lutheran, Episcopalian and Jewish children, Mr. Lippmann.] The Catholic hierarchy and the Catholic community have been satisfied, although the parochial schools receive no direct aid.

"Mr. Quie proposes to unsettle all this," the columnist asserted. "Not that he wishes to spend less money. He is asking for a total authorization of three billion dollars while Rep. Brademas' bill, which is the Administration bill, would come to about $3.3 billion. Mr. Quie has fixed his attention upon the control of the funds to be allocated for aid to education. As against the principle of the Act of 1965, the Quie bill is based on the plausible slogan that the states should themselves distribute education funds.

"But the constitutions of some 20 states bar the use of state funds for parochial schools," he warned, as if he had never heard of the "bypass clause" contained in both the Administration and Quie bills. "If the funds presently administered by HEW were to be given over to the states, the whole church-state question would be reopened."

President Johnson's unrelenting counter-attack on the Quie bill was not without good and sound reasons. The President knew a Republican victory on education had broad implications for all of his Great Society programs.

Congressman Quie admitted as much in his interview with me. "If we're successful here, then we'll have a greater opportunity for our Opportunity Crusade which Goodell and I worked out," he said in his open, honest manner.

Earlier, Congressmen Quie and Goodell had announced that their proposed Opportunity Crusade "would completely dismantle the Office of Economic Opportunity under Sargent Shriver, eliminating or redirecting existing programs." (Republicans would have to wait for President Nixon to get elected before their aims would be achieved by executive order.)

"The Opportunity Crusade builds upon the solid foundation of a free enterprise economy," the two Congressmen had stated. They proposed cutting federal allocations $300 million below President Johnson's budget and replacing them "by involving private industry and states." Thus the conflict between federal government and private enterprise served as a backdrop for the fight on how federal funds could best be channeled into the local school districts. And because of Congressman Quie's basic, although enlightened, conservatism, liberal church lobbyists found themselves coming down on the side of the Democrats — as they did on most issues during the 1960's.

Rabbi Hirsch of the Reform Jewish Action Center, not one to lock step on a cause merely because it's backed by liberals, brought the issue into focus:

"It's pretty clear to me that Congressman Quie is no great lover of federal aid to education. (Quie admitted this. But once the aperture was opened for federal funds, he went on record as saying that the Federal government should guarantee the states $5 billion a year.) "There is a very serious civil rights implication in the Quie bill," Rabbi Hirsch continued. "His bill would weaken the control of the federal establishment [Office of Education] over which the civil rights groups [including church lobbyists] do have some influence.

"I attended a civil rights conference this morning and the gist of it was how are we going to block the Quie Amendment.

"You just can't talk about principles outside of the context in which they operate," the rabbi concluded. "You have to make up your mind on which specific bill you believe will do the job."

(Congressman Quie believed that "the churches would rather deal with one national commissioner of education than fifty separate state commissioners.")

It should be pointed out, in order to place the Quie bill in proper perspective, that the Republican minority in 1967 was not trying to abolish federal aid to education. By 1967, the first federal aid to education bill had been in operation for one full year, during which time more than 22,000 projects were conceived and carried out and more than 500,000 parochial and private students benefited under Title I of the act. Republicans recognized that federal aid in some form was here to stay. Representative Quie's bill reflected the view of the "school lobby," which preferred a system with greater state responsibility. The education organizations also preferred block grants rather than the submission of tens of thousands of separate projects to the Office of Education in Washington. Both the National Education Association and the Council of Chief State School Officers favored increasing the state's role in handling public funds.

The Quie amendments, often referred to as just the Quie Amendment, admittedly would have weakened federal control of education in Title III, with state plans replacing the federal selection and approval of local projects and supplementary centers. The states, under ESEA of 1965, lacked legal authority to coordinate the number, location, and functions of federal Title III supplementary centers with their own state-wide systems of similar units.

Professional educators feared that the U. S. Office of Education, by an expansion of its personnel in federal, regional, and subregional offices, would reach down into the local and state levels

with its money-tinted tentacles and usurp the authority of local
officials.

Msgr. James C. Donohue, the chief education spokesman for
the U. S. Catholic bishops, charged the Quie bill proposing
block grants be turned over to the states would kill the aid program for parochial schools. "If it is passed, we believe that private
school participation in the federal school aid program would
become all but non-existent," he said.

The Republican leadership in the House called a conference
of Catholics and private school representatives on April 25, 1967,
to convince them that the Quie bill contained iron-clad provisions guaranteeing that funds to students in private schools would
not be reduced.

The conference produced a short-lived but sharp division
between the aggressive Citizens for Educational Freedom (CEF),
the Catholic-dominated private school lobby, and Monsignor
James C. Donohue, the national spokesman for Catholic education. (It also resulted in red faces for certain CEF staff members.)
Before the CEF leaders could be whipped back into line, however,
telegrams had been sent out to CEF state presidents urging them
to mount a campaign in behalf of the Quie Amendment. It
looked as if the Republicans had gained the backing of the CEF
and stolen some of the educational thunder from the Johnson
Administration.

*   *   *   *   *

Stuart Hubbel, CEF vice president, emerged from a meeting
with the Republican leadership — including Rep. Gerald R.
Ford of Michigan, House Minority Leader; Rep. Melvin R.
Laird of Wisconsin, Minority Whip; and Congressman Quie — to
announce that CEF was not only dropping its opposition to the
Quie bill but might even back the GOP measure over the Administration's proposed extension of the 1965 ESEA.

The abrupt reversal of field by CEF appeared to be a political
miracle wrought by the persuasive powers of the Republicans.
CEF had spearheaded strong opposition to the Quie bill, especially in the midwest. Congressman Quie, who had attended
church in his home town the previous Sunday, had been deluged
with protests at church from fellow Lutherans who operate a
number of private schools. They clearly had gotten the CEF
message.

The experience may have had some impact on Congressman

Quie. He seemed to go to extra lengths in meeting with the private school lobbyists to meet their objections. The smiling Minnesotan seemed so eager to please that some church school educators suspected a doublecross. The affable Congressman reminded the doubters that he had cast the deciding votes for church-school participation in other federal programs under discussion in the House Education and Labor Committee. The private school lobbyists seemed satisfied.

Rep. Quie's original amendment would have wiped out the categorical aid — grants made for specific programs — and substituted block grants. Block grants gave state school superintendents nearly complete control over the funds. The private school administrators, aware of the constitutional bars against church-school participation then existing in thirty-three states and mindful of the state superintendents' long-standing tight-fistedness in sharing with private schools, demanded changes permitting funds to be given to private schools.

Congressman Goodell, in reconstructing the event in his office a month later, stated: "They [church-school educators] raised their objections to mixing federal funds with state monies. Al [Quie] agreed to change. CEF then said it would not only withdraw its criticism but would come out for the Quie bill. Stu Hubbel said he wanted a letter from Jerry Ford that the changes were supported by the Republican leadership — and he got it."

It looked as if the Republican gamble was going to pay off. Congressman Quie made far-reaching compromises — changing his amendment so much that it was only a pale facsimile of his original.

In place of block grants, Quie agreed to substitute specific goals. Quie's amended amendment, prohibiting the mixing of state and federal funds, bypassed those state constitutions which barred public aid to private schools. U. S. Commissioner Howe not only was given power to bypass state departments of education but he also could dock their federal allotments if they did not include private school students in their programs.

Hubbel, won over by Congressman Quie's generous concessions, sent telegrams to CEF state presidents urging them to pull out all stops in support of the Quie Amendment. The telegrams were sent out over the signatures of CEF president Paul Mecklenborg of Cincinnati and CEF executive secretary Jeremiah Buckley. Hubbel did not get Mecklenborg's consent until AFTER the telegrams had been dispatched. The telegrams stated:

Our negotiations with Congressman Quie on his amendment of ESEA here resulted in major success thanks to your efforts. Stop all opposition to Quie Amendment. Quie proposal, with our additions, now so favorable must begin major effort to obtain support of Quie proposal. Important you commence immediate telegrams and calls to Democratic Congressmen in support of this proposal. Congratulations on magnificent job. Details follow.

Hubbel, a veteran officer of CEF in charge of legislative matters, had unwittingly set the scene for a dramatic power struggle among CEF staff, officers, and board members. Religious lobbyists can play as rough as their secular counterparts if necessary.

Msgr. Donohue met with the Republican leadership the same day. Publicly, he failed to follow Hubbel's lead. But Congressman Goodell claims that the Catholic educator had his mind changed at the White House, after conferring with the Republicans. "We called in some people from the U. S. Catholic Conference and except for Bud Consedine [legal counsel], we had them convinced," the New York Congressman said. "Msgr. Donohue said he would issue a statement saying the Quie Amendment provides for private school kids.

"Then he went down to the White House and came out against the Quie Amendment."

Msgr. Donohue left the Republican leadership session to attend a Democratic strategy meeting in the White House. Following that meeting, he said he would continue to oppose the Quie bill. "I'm willing to admit they have made an effort to include us, and that they have good will, but I still feel that their bill is not a good bill," he stated. "We still have two basic objections." He outlined his objections:

(1) "Determination of the use of funds is still in the hands of chief state public school officers. For the past fifteen or twenty years, their association has passed resolutions opposing any kind of participation by private schools. Only last week the New York superintendent repeated this stand.

(2) "One of the geniuses of the present act is that it allowed for a new spirit of cooperation and understanding at the local level. This local cooperation is now gone."

Msgr. Donohue had other complaints. "This is now the third version written in less than a week," he said. "You don't write good legislation that way. We have been unable to study it thoroughly, to confer with our colleagues, or to testify."

The Administration was shaken by the inroads made by the

Republican leadership. And the Democrats began stalling for time, in order to shore up their position. The Republican advance was quickly repulsed. The telegrams sent out by the CEF staff and officers infuriated the CEF board members — one of whom was Congressman Hugh L. Carey, who had so ably represented the private schools in the hearings in 1965. Carey and other board members — including Jewish rabbis — insisted that the telegrams be retracted and that CEF continue its opposition to the Quie Amendment.

Two days later, a properly chastised Stuart Hubbel smartly executed another about-face. "There remain certain fundamental difficulties with the Quie Amendment which remain unsolved, despite his suggested improvements," he said. "Unless they are met we will be unable to withdraw our objections to his general proposals."

Hubbel demanded that Congressman Quie stipulate that public funds be divided between public and private schools according to the proportion of public and private school students in a state. It was a far-reaching concession, which even the Administration bill did not include.

"That's going too far," Rep. Quie objected. "That's not even in the present act."

Hubbel made his face-saving demand the same day he was to confer with the CEF directors — April 28. At least he didn't have to face the angry board members empty handed.

Two years later — November, 1969 — Mecklenborg, no longer CEF president, gave this behind-the-scenes account of what took place in 1967.

"We had really started to get serious with the Republican contingency in the House," Mecklenborg says. "We got to know Congressman Quie pretty well, along with Laird and Ford, and Goodell to a lesser extent.

"From our particular standpoint — a political standpoint — we started to see what we could get out of the Republicans. Whereas the Catholic group [meaning Msgr. Donohue] had been so tied down with the Democratic Party that they — and I very frankly think this is a big mistake on their part — kept working with the Democrats [Mecklenborg is a Catholic].

"We were able to get enough concessions on the wording of the Quie Amendment that we thought this was good enough to start backing it to get the Democrats out of the woodwork in order to get more out of them," Mecklenborg explained.

"When we started to publicize our support for the Quie Amendment, all hell broke loose on the thing," he continued, chuckling at the incident.

Mecklenborg says Hubbel sent the telegram "because at the time he thought we were at the point where something had to be done and done quickly.

"Buckley and I then got together over the telephone — after the telegrams had been sent out. After he explained what had happened, I remember at the time I did agree with it [sending out the telegrams] based on the information I was given."

Why did CEF later reverse its field and oppose the Quie bill?

"There was some real struggling going on there," Mecklenborg recalled. "There is a Catholic majority of members in CEF but the board is set up where the Jewish and Protestant element have proportionately more control than their numbers warrant — and still do. And it's really the board membership — and primarily the executive committee — [who make the decisions] in this kind of thing.

"And then Congressman Carey on the board. This was the way they got to some of us, very frankly, through Carey. And then the Orthodox Jewish element got involved and basically the Jewish element in CEF is Democratic.

"So we really got into a partisan interplay there in our own group," the ex-president stated.

"It's just a shame that the Catholic group has not learned to play the game across the board with both parties, because they've got leverage — more leverage than we will ever have in CEF," he said of the U. S. Catholic Department of Education.

On the same date that CEF's Hubbel met with his directors and agreed to "go and sin no more," Msgr. Donohue wrote letters to all parochial school superintendents stating why the Quie bill was inimical to the best interests of Catholic educators.

In an attempt to neutralize Msgr. Donohue's unfavorable interpretation of the bill, two Catholic Congressmen were called on by the Republican leadership to write to the school superintendents — and to editors of newspapers — stating why they endorsed the Quie Amendment. The two Congressmen from rock-ribbed Republican districts — John N. Erlenborn of DuPage County, Illinois, and William J. Scherle of Iowa — mailed their letters May 2 and 3. The letter to the parochial school superintendents, on Congress of the United States stationery, stated:

Dear Monsignor:

Monsignor James C. Donohue has been so courteous as to provide us with your address and a copy of his letter to you, dated April 28. We seek to lay directly before you, for your earnest consideration, a detailed account of the Quie Amendment of the Elementary and Secondary Education Act.

Let us say, first of all, that we are Roman Catholics, and that we are both products of parochial schools. Let us say further that all of us who foster this amendment are convinced that it is in the best interest of education, both public and private.

We also say to you, in all candor, what has been said to Monsignor Donohue and his associates: That we regard their interpretation of the Quie Amendment as inconsistent with the facts. We say this with utmost respect for Monsignor Donohue.

The Quie Amendment was drafted with an intent to exclude any doubt about the participation of parochial schools in the benefits of Federal programs in education. It is supported by the leadership and most of the Republicans in the House of Representatives, including Roman Catholic members.

It incorporates many specific suggestions of officials of the Citizens for Educational Freedom. It extends the formula for benefits to parochial school children while, at the same time, freeing State and local education from burdensome, unnecessary and often self-defeating Federal restraints.

Representative Quie has suggested a precise and carefully conceived amendment to accomplish these purposes. We ask that you read the enclosed analysis, bringing to the effort your understanding, your attention to the full provisions of the amendments and your best judgment.

The analysis, a page and a half, made three major points: (1) "The proposal works to the advantage of parochial school children"; (2) "the 'general tenor' of the amendment is not a 'public school' bill — but a flexible bill that guarantees private school participation"; and (3) "the amendment is in the best interests of all education."

The letter and analysis illustrated two political realities: that the backing of church lobbyists — all church lobbyists — is earnestly coveted by the legislators on Capitol Hill and that two years after the 1965 ESEA had been enacted, the fine constitutional distinctions between federal aid to "private students" vis-à-vis "private schools" no longer seemed so important.

The Scherle-Erlenborn analysis included open references to private schools, such as the following: "The amendment expands the coverage of the Title II programs to include '*laboratory and other instructional equipment'* — which should be an enormous added benefit to your schools." Also, "The 'general tenor' of the amendment is not a 'public school bill' — but a flexible bill that guarantees *private* school participation" (italics mine).

Perhaps the lesson is that constitutional principles having been once violated, even for the highest of motives and in the best of disguises, never again seem quite as important as when the violation first took place.

Congressman Erlenborn, a personal friend of this reporter since the middle 1950's when that gentleman was then State Rep. John Erlenborn, told me: "I've got lots of mail from churchmen on the Quie Amendment. Msgr. Donohue and Consedine seem to think the 1965 ESEA is their baby.

"I don't think my letter changed many minds," he admitted. "But I told Msgr. Donohue if he would stay out of politics, I wouldn't insist that priests remain celibates."

Rep. Erlenborn made the point that while churchmen have the right to speak out on issues — such as the principle of federal aid to education — they should avoid partisan positions.

A Republican colleague, Representative Robert Taft, Jr., revealed that he had felt church pressure on the Quie Amendment. "I got a direct call from the Cincinnati Archdiocesan office asking me to categorically vote against it," he said. "Actually, Ohio would get $60,000 more under the amendment than under the present act."

Private school administrators obviously were more concerned about how the public funds would be dispensed than the amounts. They had their feet in the vault door, and they would not remove them on the basis of political promises — even from members of Congress of their own faith.

Because the Republicans failed to win Catholic support for the Quie Amendment, it looked in late May of 1967 as if a Republican-Democrat donnybrook was shaping up in the House. Braced for a frontal assault by the Republicans, the Democratic leadership suddenly found itself outmaneuvered in a flanking movement by one of its own members — none other than the redoubtable Rep. Edith Green of Oregon.

It happened so fast that it caught both the Democrats and Republicans by surprise — although the GOP members quickly gained their balance to begin cheering their new-found ally. Mrs. Green stood up in the well of the House to offer a series of amendments. While the Democrats listened in stunned silence, the

Republicans gaped in amazement. When Mrs. Green ran out of time, gallant Republicans jumped to their feet to offer her their time. The mild-mannered Chairman Carl Perkins was caught off balance, and Mrs. Green continued in her best classroom fashion to proffer her amendments.

The Quie Amendment guaranteed that private school students would participate in publicly financed programs. Mrs. Green's amendments offered no such safeguards. Administration forces, upset by the position taken by the maverick school teacher from Oregon, found themselves in a box. They could attack the Quie Amendment with partisan fury. But they were not so eager to tangle with Mrs. Green.

As the House neared the showdown during a two-day debate on May 23 and 24, the Administration forces were lined up to extend the ESEA to 1969 to the tune of $3.4 billion. Most of the Republicans were behind the Quie Amendment. Despite a series of caucuses, the Southern Democrats were undecided which way to go.

All this placed Mrs. Green in a strategic position. Some of her amendments appealed to the Republicans — the strengthening of state departments of education — and some to the Southerners. She asked for "the opportunity for a hearing" for local school districts before depriving them of funds under Title VI of the Civil Rights Act. Her suggestion to bypass U. S. Commissioner Harold Howe II as the arbiter of state plans for "supplementary education" under Title III, warmed the hearts of the Dixie Congressmen. Commissioner Howe had become the symbol of the forced integration of Southern schools, and Southerners held him in the same regard most Georgians do General Sherman.

If the Democratic leadership was caught unprepared by Mrs. Green's flanking action, the same could not be said of Msgr. James C. Donohue, director of the U. S. Catholic Department of Education. In a letter dated May 22 and addressed to Representative John Brademas of Indiana, influential spokesman for the private schools, Msgr. Donohue wrote:

> Dear Congressman Brademas:
>
> We understand that during the House of Representatives debate on HR 7819, the Elementary and Secondary Education Act Amendments of 1967, an effort will be made by Mrs. Green to change Title III (Supplementary Educational Centers and Services) into a totally State-operated educational program without the quality control features now inherent in the program. We are

totally and profoundly opposed to such an amendment and urge you to reject it.

The emerging operation of Title III programs across the country has been encouraging. For the first time, in community after community, public and private school educators are sitting down together to work out supplementary programs for children, regardless of the school they attend. We believe that the cooperation now engendered by Title III into a totally State-run operation inevitably would diminish this cooperation and result, in many States, in minimal services to children in private schools.

A State-plan operation would ultimately result in greater State interference in the entire workings of the Title III program. It would raise new and serious questions as to the equitable participation of children in private schools in more than thirty states with strict limitations on state assistance to nonpublic schools. Furthermore, such a fundamental change in the program would undoubtedly result in administrative changes which would operate to inhibit today's encouraging cooperation between public and private school educators. The vast majority of local school district administrators favor the present arrangements, fearful of negative forms of interference by state agencies.

Mrs. Green started the proceedings May 23, 1967, by explaining the intent of her amendments, namely, that the Office of Education when issuing guidelines would cite the statute on which the guidelines were based, and secondly, that the guidelines or regulations be administered uniformly in all fifty states.

Surprisingly, Representative Perkins did not oppose the Green amendment. Strong supporters of private schools openly expressed their dismay and puzzlement at the threat to the 1965 Act. "Mr. Chairman," said Congressman James G. O'Hara of Michigan, a member of the full Committee on Education and Labor, "I think I ought to begin by admitting that I am not sure I know what the amendment offered by the Gentlewoman from Oregon does. But it is my suspicion that the amendment is either meaningless or mischievous." Congressman Brademas quickly seconded the speech of Congressman O'Hara: "I, too, share the puzzlement of my friend from Michigan, who is a first-class lawyer."

And Congressman Thompson of New York took the floor to express the same sentiments: "Mr. Chairman, I join the gentleman from Michigan and the gentleman from Indiana in expressing reservation, and indeed a complete lack, really of knowledge, specifically and categorically of what the gentlewoman's amendment would do."

Mrs. Green in her firm, icy manner explained again to her

baffled colleagues that all "I am simply trying to say is that if we have discrimination in a city that is not in one of the seventeen Southern states, and if that discrimination does indeed exist and if we are going to promulgate guidelines, rules, and regulations, that they apply in every one of the fifty states, and that is what my understanding is of equity and fairness under the law."

Republicans and Southerners eagerly joined with Mrs. Green, the Republicans seeing an opportunity to get half a loaf if they couldn't get the whole Quie Amendment. Congressman Quie himself said, "After listening to the debate, I very strongly support the amendment."

Congress continued its deliberations until 7:30 p.m., May 23, but "came to no resolution thereon" as the *Congressional Record* phrases it. Consideration of both the Green and Quie amendments were held over until noon the next day.

The Democrats the next day decided to dispose of the Quie Amendment before turning their attention to the more knotty Green amendments. Once again the church-state issue permeated much of the deliberations.

Congressman Erlenborn of Illinois, speaking in behalf of the Quie Amendment, revealed the intensity of the lobbying then going on by church educators.

"The church-state issue gives us an interesting study in contrasts," the Catholic Congressman stated.

"I see in my mail, letters from Catholic schools saying, 'We are advised that if the Quie Amendment is adopted all aid to parochial schools will be shut off.' One of the nuns of my district sent letters to all of the parents of the students in her school saying, 'If the vicious Quie Amendment is adopted, our school will no longer get any federal aid.' And then she pointed out that they had received $750 for one program and $2000 some odd for another program.

"This is the sort of information they have been receiving, that they will be shut off from all aid," the Illinois Republican stated.

"On the other hand, I received a letter from a Baptist Joint Committee, and they fear the Quie Amendment because they understand it is going to expand the aid which is going to parochial schools, and they are fearful of the church-state issue.

"It is not possible to have it both ways on the church-state issue," he concluded.

The church-state issue, injected back onto the floor, produced flowery oratory from two veteran antagonists, Congressmen Goodell and Carey.

"I must express my admiration, regretfully, sadly, but my admiration for those who have raised this issue," Congressman Goodell, in top form, began. "They certainly have created a fantasma with reference to church-state issue. It is not there. I marvel particularly at the metaphors — the mixed metaphors if you will of my colleague, the gentleman from New York, [Carey] who speaks on this subject.

"He says if we inject this vandalism [referring to Quie Amendment] into our politics, we will set this war afire. And that it would be a Trojan horse, a pig in the poke, a bonanza and a hot nugget when it gets down to the school districts," Congressman Goodell said.

When Congressman Carey reminded Goodell that he was the one who used the term "holy war" in 1965, Goodell retorted: "I do not know whether the gentleman from New York gets his inspiration from Calliope, the mythical muse of eloquence and epic poetry, or from Terpsichore, the muse of dancing." He sounded as if he had been researching Greek mythology just for Congressman Carey's benefit.

Congressman Brademas said if there were no church-state issue involved in the Quie Amendment why had the National Council of Churches, the Synagogue Council of America, and the U. S. Catholic Conference expressed strong opposition to it? He put in the record the full copy of Msgr. Donohue's letter opposing the amendment. The Catholic educator said that "the latest version does not eliminate the dangers to the interests of the children enrolled in private schools which I have earlier expressed more extensively in other communications."

Time had run out on the Republicans. The ill-fated Quie Amendment was rejected 197-168.

The weary Congressmen earned their salaries on May 24. The often acrimonious debate continued to 1:49 a.m. the next day, before the members voted to adjourn.

Although the Quie Amendment was defeated, Mrs. Green had managed to win amendments strengthening state departments of education and providing uniform guidelines on desegregation for all fifty states and the opportunity for hearings for local school districts before they would be deprived of funds under the Civil Rights Act. With these amendments, the House passed

HR 7819, the Elementary and Secondary Education Amendments of 1967.

Despite his personal defeat, Congressman Quie interpreted the Green amendments as a Republican victory. In the May 29 Republican Congressional Committee *Newsletter,* he was quoted as saying: "Much of what we set out to do now has been accomplished in that only one title of the Administration bill will now be directly controlled by the Office of Education."

The same newsletter acknowledged the political clout of the religious lobbyists:

> Quie charged that its defeat [the defeat of his amendment] was chiefly due to misinformation spread among church groups by the Administration that private and parochial schools would receive less money under his plan. Actually, they would have received somewhat more.

Such are the vagaries of politics that even in the ashes of defeat one can often construct a Phoenix-like victory. Mrs. Green succeeded in amending the 1965 ESEA where Mr. Quie had failed — effecting many of the same things the Minnesota Congressman was attempting. She returned funds to the state departments of education which had been bypassed under Title III for supplementary education centers. She noted that the U. S. Department of Education, which had only 555 employees in 1955, had over 3,198 in 1967 to administer 77 different programs costing $3.3 billion. She said she thought at least one of the programs could be taken away without doing violence to the U.S. Office of Education. (The purpose of Title III funds was to encourage local school districts to make use of new methods and techniques in teaching.)

Congressman Carey made an impassioned plea — including an implied political threat — to those voting for the Green amendment: "In doing what we have done tonight, I hope we will go on record and vote in a separate vote on this Green amendment. I warn my colleagues if you do this, keep in mind you may be taking a step backward, regardless of what has been said about the church-state relationship not being involved.

"Keep in mind," he warned even more ominously, "that those who are responsible for children in the nonpublic schools have spoken with one voice that this amendment as presented by the gentlewoman from Oregon has put them at a disadvantage, and they have opposed this amendment. Are we about to destroy in a separate vote the carefully constructed accommodation and arrangement that it took twenty years to put together?"

But Carey's warnings went unheeded and the Green amendments were adopted.

* * * * *

What has been the impact of the Elementary and Secondary Education Act on church-state relations?

Has the act in fact served as an "instrument of reconciliation" in our polarized society? Or has it invited sectarian conflict at the expense of our public school system?

Has the legislation eliminated or even loosened "the tap root of ignorance" among the nation's poor?

Are tax funds being used to support private schools in a fashion that threatens to undermine the First Amendment?

Are the church-school lobbyists satisfied with the way the act has been implemented by public school administrators?

Did the Protestant church lobbyists compromise on important constitutional principles in the name of ecumenical expediency?

Even four years later, December, 1969, there are no clear-cut answers to all these questions. There are some troubling signs on the horizons, however, which may presage far-reaching implications for the public school system.

A national survey made by the American Jewish Congress, released in August of 1969, shows that forty-one cases involving church-state issues — a record high — await decisions in federal and state courts. The survey states furthermore that the largest number (fourteen) of pending federal and state cases involves the question of public aid to sectarian schools. Of these, six are federal cases arising under the 1965 ESEA.

Dr. George R. LaNoue of Columbia University, who testified in behalf of the American Civil Liberties Union on the bill in 1965, studied sixty cities two years later to see how the act was working. His conclusions, as reported in the *New York Times*, August 21, 1967, were the following:

(1) The location of the program determined whether reasonable aid was provided to individual children from all schools or degenerated into direct aid to parochial schools. One recurrent problem was that parochial schools, because the federal programs cost money to implement, demanded and often got salaries for coordinators and secretaries who were recruited and hired by the parochial school authorities.

(2) The publicly purchased equipment "loaned" to the church

school often became a de facto grant because the equipment was loaned indefinitely. Some private school administrators even ordered the equipment directly from the supplier.

(3) ESEA programs in parochial buildings failed to promote racial, religious, and class integration as the law requires.

Dr. Virgil M. Rogers, former president of the American Association of School Administrators and a special project director of the National Education Association, told strongly biased church-state separatists in Cincinnati in February of 1968:

> Legislation has been stimulated in many states, partly due to the influence of the ESEA, to expand the child-benefit theory; therefore, it is safe to assume that a long period of struggle is inevitable before the courts provide more clear-cut guidelines on this issue.

> At the very time in American educational history when the parochial school concept is coming under increasing scrutiny by its patrons and leaders, when the one significant group of church-controlled schools — the Roman Catholic — has ceased to grow and in many places is on the decline in enrollment, when many parochial educators are speaking and writing in a manner to indicate that they have growing misgivings as to the value to the church of the dual system, a carelessly managed federal support program could prop up for generations what may have become an anachronistic institution in an ecumenical one-world society.

In an interview in *Look* magazine in October of 1969, Monsignor Donohue seemed to be having some second thoughts on federal aid while recalling some of the things alluded to by Dr. Rogers in his speech. Concurring that Catholic schools were losing both students and teachers, Msgr. Donohue said: "Unless we change, we'll wither away, we'll die. We might as well experiment."

Msgr. Donohue, who pumped vigorously for federal aid in 1967, told the magazine that money was not the answer to his Church's school problems. "We have to determine what the teaching mission of the Church is for the decades ahead," he said. He said Catholic schools should offer an alternative to the public school. "Instead, they have become a carbon copy." He also stated he would reject federal aid if it prevented experimentation. "What price the federal buck," he asked, "if in accepting federal aid we have to dilute our concept of what a religious-oriented school is? If we do, then I say we ought to get out of the business."

Looking ahead ten years, he foresaw a much smaller Catholic

school system, "that is hopefully the leading edge in experimentation and quality, and that offers a real alternative to public education." He added, "If we lose just numbers, I don't think we have lost too much."

*   *   *   *   *

Paul Mecklenborg disagrees with Msgr. Donohue's priorities in Catholic education, believing that ESEA helped start a trend on the state level — using tax funds for private schools — that will ease the burden of the Catholic parent.

Catholic schools, he pointed out, have not shared in Title I funds the way they should have. For example, the Catholic schools in Cincinnati, one of the largest Catholic school systems in the nation, did not get any Title I funds. "There was a real disappointment in that, but our attempts to get across those points to the people at HEW didn't get too much sympathy," Mecklenborg stated.

The CEF lobbyist now believes, however, that Ohio has become a leader in the amount of tax funds it appropriates for private schools. And he predicts that even bigger and better things are in the offing in that state, crediting ESEA with helping to widen the public funds aperture for private schools.

The emphasis on public aid to private schools caused the *New York Times* to editorialize in the summer of 1969 on "Holding Church-State Line":

> New formulas, based on Supreme Court-approved theory of aid to children rather than institutions, have been devised in recent years to relieve the financial plight of non-public institutions, without violating the constitutional prohibition on public subsidies for religion. The Elementary and Secondary Education Act of 1965 combines support of disadvantaged children regardless of the church schools' budgetary plight.
>
> But the very fact that such constitutional means have been found for aiding children in religious schools has encouraged deliberate efforts to gain subsidies of a kind that would erode the essential principle of church-state separation. Renewed pressure for direct state and Federal financing underscores the growing threat to a philosophy of government basic to the protection of both public education and of religious liberty. The parents' right to favor religious schools for their children is an essential freedom but the costs of operating such schools cannot be underwritten by government without making religion itself an establishment of the state and subject to its power.

Perhaps one of the most foreboding developments growing out of the passage of the ESEA of 1965 has to do with the possibility of using Title I funds to found private schools.

In November of 1969 the NAACP Legal Defense Fund and a Washington, D. C., research project published jointly a 137-page "Title I" report. The report concentrates on the "injustices and inequities" of the title. This study, noting that $4.3 billion had been spent on Title I in the past four years supposedly for disadvantaged children, charges that the money was "wasted, diverted, or otherwise misused by state and local school authorities."

The report includes the following recommendation: "Alternative vehicles for operation of Title I programs should be provided where state and local officials are unable or unwilling to operate effective Title I programs." What the report suggests is that if public schools can't do the job of educating the poor, then private schools or private industry should be paid to take over.

Several witnesses who appeared before the Perkins subcommittee warned that federal funds could be used to perpetuate segregated schools under ESEA. At the time, they had Southern-style segregation in mind. But the NAACP report raises the possibility that ghettos would take over their own schools, removing them from the public school system. If the predominantly black ghettos are permitted to use federal funds in this manner, what would prevent white supremacists from doing the same thing?

In an article published in November of 1969, William Steif, a Scripps-Howard staff writer, reported:

> House members such as Reps. John Brademas (D., Ind.) and Ogden R. Reid (R., N. Y.) are readying legislation to permit private companies to take on responsibilities of ghetto public schools which aren't doing a job. In places where high school youngsters can barely read or write, schooling would be thrown open to competitive bidding, and the contract would demand attainment by testing.
>
> An extension of this idea is a bill which nearly passed the California legislature this year and is a cinch to pass in 1970, according to Willie Brown, a black assemblyman from San Francisco.
>
> State-school funds would follow the child "so that parents in Watts, for example, could start their own school," Brown says.

Rep. Brown explained the program this way:

> Parents would be given a voucher, and federal Title I money to

help the child from a poor family would be included. It would be good for the public schools to have competition, and at the end of the school year the children would have to pass basic achievement tests.

"It is no accident," writes Steif, "that Lewis Butler, assistant secretary for planning at the Health, Education and Welfare Department, is intensely interested in these experimental ideas. He is a former law partner of Rep. Paul N. McCloskey, Jr. (R., Cal.) and now is trying to pry funds out of Congress to rev up competition to the public schools."

Dean M. Kelley of the National Council of Churches and Dr. George R. LaNoue may have been far more accurate than they realized when they predicted in 1965:

> The Elementary and Secondary Education Act of 1965 is the beginning of a stream of legislative enactments that will have more impact on the future of education than any previous legislation in the history of the country.

There are signs that the prophecy already is beginning to be fulfilled. Whether the public school system will be strengthened or weakened by private competitive schools is an open question at this point. Most Americans undoubtedly feel that our public schools, with all their flaws, have stood the test of time and afford the best system for educating our children. This is not to say the system cannot be improved. That should be a continual process. The question church lobbyists now must ponder is: Have they helped sow the seeds of destruction of the public schools by endorsing the legislative mechanism through which tax funds can be channeled into private schools, secular and religious?

The U. S. Constitution is silent on education. And obviously the First Amendment is subject to varying opinions — even from Supreme Court justices. But it seems safe to say there was some "game playing" with the Constitution in the enactment of the 1965 ESEA. Assistance to private schools, under any other name, is still assistance.

Both the constitutional purists and the aggressive private school lobbyists may be doing a disservice to the nation. Neither group is facing the problem of federal aid realistically. The facts are that private schools do educate about one in seven of all American school children. It seems evident that church schools are going to be around for a long time. And they do save the taxpayers millions of dollars annually. It appears logical then that some fair plan should be worked out, in the public forum, to openly assist private schools rather than continually looking for cracks in the church-state wall of separation through which tax funds can be leaked.

It is stretching a point to argue that private schools have a legal right to public funds because parents of parochial school children pay taxes. The answer to that is simply that their children have the right to go to public schools the same as anyone else. But that does not mean private schools should be denied tax funds. They provide a service and Americans are accustomed to paying for services rendered.

Whether church schools should receive federal aid is a moot question. They already do under a dozen different guises. Why not stop the sham and openly give the funds for the proper reasons — for the services they provide rather than for some fictitious legal right? The greatest rends in our national garment are caused when we say we are doing one thing (assisting poor students) when in fact we are doing another (assisting parochial schools). Hypocrisy, under any other name, smells the same. And no one should know this better than religious lobbyists.

CHAPTER XI

Priority for Peace

President John F. Kennedy relayed through his press secretary Pierre Salinger early Monday, October 22, 1962, that he would appear on television at 6 p.m. to speak on a matter of "highest national urgency." The announcement followed a weekend of mounting tension. The President met around the clock with the National Security Council and Democratic and Republican Congressional leaders. Hard-nosed newsmen covering the Capital tried without success to learn what national issue President Kennedy had in mind. In a city noted for its news leaks, frustrated reporters could not produce even enough facts to write an authoritative story attributed to the traditional "usually reliable sources."

President Kennedy was unusually somber as he walked in front of the battery of television cameras to reveal to millions of nervous Americans the indisputable proof he had that Soviet Russia was at that moment shipping long-range ballistic missiles for emplacement in Communist Cuba. Such weaponry, he said, brought the entire North and South American continents under the reach of Russian missiles. The young President then outlined the steps he was taking to intercept the missile-carrying ships to make sure the deadly rockets never reached their destination ninety miles off the coast of Florida.

President Kennedy hardly had finished speaking when "Students for Peace" appeared on the darkened side of Pennsylvania Avenue in front of the White House. Equipped with signs and placards, they objected to President Kennedy's tactics for meeting the Russian threat and urged that he instead initiate diplomatic relations with Premier Castro of Cuba. The Soviet Union accused the U.S. of taking steps which could lead to thermonuclear war and called on the UN to intervene. Warsaw Pact countries were placed on a war footing. As the Soviet ships plowed through the Atlantic toward Cuba, concerned Americans wondered if the two most powerful nations in the world were headed inexorably toward a collision of such force that the entire planet might be blown up. One noted commentator ended a special newscast on the tense international situation with the pessimistic promise he would return tomorrow "if there is a tomorrow."

As an entire nation held its breath, fearing the worst but hoping for the best, and as President Kennedy met in secret sessions with the National Security Council, a deeply troubled church secretary in the Methodist Building across from the Capitol Building called an emergency session of his own.

Herman Will, Jr., is a veteran attorney who carries the laborious title of associate general secretary in charge of the Division of Peace and World Order of the United Methodist Church — a heavy responsibility indeed in October of 1962. "The people down here were really shaking in their boots, and we knew we had to do something," Will recalled as he talked with me in his third-floor office overlooking the U. S. Supreme Court and the Capitol. "When you have a responsibility you just can't sit on your hands. You have to do something constructive."

There may be those who feel church bureaucrats really are not qualified to advise the President in a national emergency. Will was not beset with such misgivings. "We didn't have time to go into the field and get a reaction that would mean anything because the situation changed so quickly," he conceded. "But here in Washington we tried to interject some constructive ideas into the discussions of the government leaders."

Will, a pacifist, though not in an absolute sense, is a former member of the peace-plugging Fellowship of Reconciliation. "Although I'm a pacifist, I know most of the country is not, and you have to suggest something in line with national policy," he said realistically. The church secretary plotted his strategy for peace at the same time President Kennedy and his advisors prepared for the possibility of war. Will consulted with members of his own staff and colleagues on the General Board of Christian Social Concerns housed in the Methodist Building.

The Peace Division staff was convinced that if the U.S.-U.S.S.R. confrontation continued, the United States would attempt to destroy the missile sites in Cuba. The church bureaucrats reasoned that a first strike at the sites would inevitably result in some Russians being killed. This would create a situation which would demand a response on the part of the Soviets — and the church staff predicted that the response would be in nuclear terms. (Needless to say, other persons felt the same way in those dark days in October.) The staff concluded that restraint on the part of the U. S. was more in order than rocket rattling.

The Methodist secretary went beyond the circle of his church colleagues in seeking information and advice on a sensitive subject of international import. He conferred with professors of international relations in the Methodist-affiliated American University located only four blocks from the White House. He also met with Dr. John C. Bennett of Union Seminary and with Dr. Benjamin Spock, both of whom later would lead the list of the most outspoken critics of the U. S. involvement in Vietnam.

Will's peace team went into action. After hours of agonizing appraisals and brainstorming, the group came up with a plan. The churchmen decided to urge President Kennedy to propose a ten-day cooling-off period during which time UN General Secretary U Thant could act as mediator between the two superpowers. The proposal was put into writing.

Then came a question almost as difficult as the first: How to get the peace plan into the hands of the President, who was holding around-the-clock conferences?

It may be an office joke, but "where there's Will, there's a way." Every lobbyist, whether he represents the church or the oil industry, must have contacts on the Hill to operate effectively. Will had his. He called a friendly administrative assistant of Senator Hubert H. Humphrey, Democratic Majority Leader, who was sitting in on President Kennedy's war councils. The assistant promised to pass the proposal along as quickly as he could.

Will wanted to make doubly sure the President would have the benefit of the church group's advice. And he reasoned that the plan would have a better chance of penetrating the security curtain surrounding the President if the proposal were sent through bipartisan channels. He then devised an ingenious, albeit circuitous, method of contacting Senator Leverett Saltonstall, influential Republican from President Kennedy's own state of Massachusetts.

The Methodist church secretary called the Rev. James K. Mathews, Methodist bishop of Boston and president of the Massachusetts Council of Churches. Will explained the peace plan and what he was attempting to do. The Bishop agreed to use any influence he had to relay the plan — after he had given it careful consideration — on to its final destination. Bishop

Mathews discussed the plan with Dr. Harold Case of Boston University and with several members of the University's political science faculty. 'They thought the idea a good one," Will said, with a certain amount of understandable satisfaction.

Bishop Mathews was in a pivotal position to assist Will, for he was a friend of Senator Saltonstall's son, who promised to give the plan to his father and ask him to present it to the President and his advisors.

"We assumed it got to the individuals we intended to reach, but we don't know whether our plan ever was discussed by the President and his advisors," Will admitted. "But it was an attempt at being relevant during a national crisis," he said, and "being relevant" ranks as the highest of holy callings among most church lobbyists.

(Former Vice President Hubert H. Humphrey, in answer to a letter by the author, revealed that Will's message had indeed gotten through. "I did receive the suggestion," Mr. Humphrey wrote me Dec. 30, 1969, "but I was convinced that President Kennedy was following a proper course of action — a judgment vindicated by subsequent events.")

Attempts at being relevant by church lobbyists are seldom staged under such dramatic conditions as those existing in October of 1962. Newspapers pay more attention to mass marches than they do to the less spectacular day-to-day lobbying for peace carried on by numerous church organizations. Among the numerous issues to which church lobbyists have addressed themselves, none has rated higher priority during the last half of the sixties than has peace. It also has been the area where churches have been least effective. One reason of course is that the American public holds a wide variety of views on the subject. The church also has failed to be effective in the pursuit of peace because church lobbyists confuse "prophetic ministry" with attempts to give advice in military and international matters in which they have no unusual expertise.

Dr. Peter L. Berger, who teaches sociology in the Graduate Faculty of the New School for Social Research, stated it this way in an article in the March 6, 1967, issue of *Christianity and Crisis:*

> Then, a word to the churches: in making political assessments the churches are essentially in the same position as everyone else. They can appoint study committees, make carefully balanced public statements, lobby in Washington, etc. . . . Whatever may be

the merits of this sort of activity (and I am willing to concede all kinds of merits) let us not confuse it with what is, often so lightly, called the "prophetic ministry" of the Church. "Prophecy" is not the result of expert consultation or of committee work. It appears only where there is the conviction of apodictic moral authority — in other words, where somebody finds the courage to say "in the Name of God—No!" I am suggesting that, if there is such a thing as prophetic ministry in our churches, Vietnam is an appropriate occasion for its exercise.

Failure to achieve the elusive goal of peace caused the Washington-based church lobbyists to focus even more sharply on policy decisions rather than on moral principles. At a symposium in Washington, the Rev. Richard John Neuhaus, a leader of the National Emergency Committee of Clergy and Laymen Concerned About Vietnam, was quoted in the *New York Times* (Dec. 3, 1967) as stating that for churchmen to espouse specific policy changes was self-defeating. He said the Administration merely replied to the specific recommendations and "neglected the main points, which were moral."

At the two-day symposium on "Who Speaks for the Church?" Msgr. George G. Higgins, director of social action work for the U. S. Catholic Conference, read a paper stating that he "seriously" doubted that the overall U. S. policy in Vietnam was "so absolutely clear-cut from the moral point of view that the Christian response to it is immediately self-evident." The Catholic prelate also criticized the "Selma syndrome," which he defined as the "almost irresistible compulsion to stage clerical rallies and demonstrations at the drop of a hat just to prove that the church is relevant."

Dr. Paul Ramsey, author of "Who Speaks for the Church?" criticized the World Council of Churches and other religious organizations for being too quick off the drawing boards with statements on social issues in which the church lacks special competence. He went even further to declare that church endorsement of specific policies was wrong, not only strategically, but also in principle. "We must make a distinction between what the Christian says as Christian and what the same person would say as a citizen in a democratic society," he said. "Even if the churches had a solution for the current Middle East crisis, that's not their business. We should not baptize a 'citizen' view of things."

Dr. Carl F. H. Henry, founding editor of the conservative Protestant journal *Christianity Today,* told the group that churchmen "should either say the war is just or it's unjust and then leave the rest to military experts."

But the bureaucrats manning the peace stations in Washington appear congenitally unable to react in the manner recommended at the symposium. They seem compelled to stage seminars, issue statements, approve resolutions, wage write-in campaigns, testify before Congressional committees or get influential clergymen to personally contact legislators so that they might by all means persuade some Congressmen.

One of the most active mainline Protestant denominations in the path of peace is the now 11-million-member United Methodist Church. Although not a "peace church" in the historic tradition of the Quakers — who incidentally are often the behind-the-scenes prodders of the larger denominations — the Methodists do have a pacifist "strain," and Herman Will, Jr., is the primary carrier — a description which that dedicated churchman surely would consider complimentary.

In the fall of 1961 in Salt Lake City, the Methodists entered the "Race for Peace." The campaign started in Salt Lake City in a true enough church setting — the program was bathed in prayer. In November at Omaha, the Methodist Peace Division issued the call to action in these rallying words: "As children of God we are under compulsion to be consumed in the tasks of peace lest man be consumed in the fires of war." (Sloganeering is just as essential for peace as it is for war.) Hundreds of "Prayer Vigils for Peace" would be held across the nation for the next two years.

Methodists are as irresistibly drawn to organization as a moth is to a flame — and sometimes the results can be strikingly similar. The Rev. J. Elliott Corbett, director of the Washington Study Programs in the Peace Division, wrote the following in a paper in which he alluded to the Race for Peace:

> It would seem that another essential ingredient for a church peace emphasis would be an organizational structure that could be used to quickly mobilize the church for action. In this instance, the Methodist Church with its Boards of Social Concerns in Annual Conferences, district directors and local church Commissions on Christian Social Concerns prove to be a most useful instrument.

Mr. Corbett, as a staff man, modestly conceded that an aggressive staff also is essential:

> Secondly, for effective peace action a church needs an aggressive, well-educated and dedicated staff. In the Methodist Race for Peace

such a staff proved a most useful instrument for implementing a tremendously demanding program. Staff needs to be sufficiently realistic so as not to waste its time in windmill charging, yet idealistic enough to be adventurously imaginative. A wise staff will know how to live under its mandate, when to go through appropriate channels, and the right time for exercising independent judgement.

"Such personnel should be sufficiently well trained that they may take their place among secular counterparts and not be discounted," Mr. Corbett continued, reflecting the philosophy of the professional church lobbyist. Most church bureaucrats certainly do not lack in training or political sophistication. But are those the proper tools of the church, or do they merely place the churchman on the same level as his secular counterpart — thereby diminishing his prophetic voice based on moral authority?

In 1961, the Methodist Church had 104 Annual Conferences in the United States, and each Conference had a Peace Division Chairman. The original design was to have leadership-training conferences at scattered sites throughout the United States on the disarmament pacts as related to the United Nations and economic aid. The leaders attending the training conferences were to return home and teach small groups in their own churches.

The small group was to serve as yeast for peace in the community by taking the message to (1) members of important opinion-forming community secular groups; (2) editors of newspapers; and (3) members of Congress.

The Rev. Rodney Shaw, director of disarmament education for the Methodist Board of Social Concerns, told how the program worked at a Conference on Disarmament and World Peace held in Washington, February 4 and 5, 1965. (The conference was sponsored by the Union of American Hebrew Congregations and included, along with top-ranking clergymen, such well-known government officials as Secretary of State Dean Rusk, Ambassador Averell Harriman, and Senators George McGovern of North Dakota and Jacob K. Javits of New York. Church bureaucrats move in influential circles.)

"This [Race for Peace] sounded tremendous," Mr. Shaw said. "I spent thirty consecutive days in the Western states meeting every day with several groups in leadership-training, and I came back feeling that the Western delegation in Congress was taken care of.

"Then a year passed and I got no correspondence from the

West giving me tales of victory and paeans of joy about the editors, the veterans, leaders, and Congressmen with whom they had met.

"So I took another ten days following that February of training and made a spin around the same states. I soon discovered the reason why there were no letters and no results. Our church people had the habit of sitting down and studying within their own church framework. We were asking them to go outside the normal church framework and contact people whom they were not in the habit of contacting.

"We were asking them to do this in a highly controversial area, about which they were terribly uncertain," the church official explained. "As one very capable minister, who had just been through one of the most extensive training seminars told me: 'I just haven't the nerve to sit down with a veteran or a Congressman or an editor and talk to them about this — they've got forty problems for every one answer that I have.' "

Mr. Shaw elaborated on what has been adopted as the primary operating principle of the majority of church lobbyists who are not required to answer to the people they purport to represent. "So we have discarded the idea that we have to involve massive numbers of people in order to do this task," he stated. "We have begun to accept the principle Dr. Arnold Toynbee points out in his study of history — that the move from plateau to plateau of civilization has not come because the masses of people were informed, committed, and organized but because a small portion of the people were informed and committed to an idea for which the time was ripe.

"We are now doing things differently," Mr. Shaw emphasized, giving examples to illustrate how differently.

"In West Virginia, for example, instead of mounting a big education program through all the churches there, we have found ten ministers and as many laymen, who are interested, capable, and able to articulate, who will sit down at least once every six months with their Congressmen and Senators.

"I am convinced that if this is done, they will have substantial impact upon the thinking of those men," he asserted.

"We have discarded the idea that we can get this job done with letters, with speeches, with meetings," he continued. "Meetings such as this one are important, but only if you go home and decide that you will relate yourself to the *centers of power* (italics mine) where the decisions are being made in our society."

Mr. Shaw then let his listeners in on the nitty-gritty of the church lobbying operation:

"Last November [1964], we learned on a Friday that there would be a Congressional Conference Committee to work out a compromise between the money voted by the Senate for the Disarmament Agency budget and the money approved by the House.

"Twelve men, seven from the Senate and five from the House, were to make this decision on the following Tuesday. Normally, a conference would end up in a compromise. The only problem was that on this conference committee were three men who were opposed to the Disarmament Agency altogether and who had voted against its existence. Furthermore, there was not one person on the committee who had ever given any evidence of concern for the agency's continuation! The situation looked desperate. There was not time for a massive letter appeal."

Mr. Shaw then listed another basic principle of effective church lobbying: Make your effort ecumenical. "We spent a day-and-a-half calling men in key positions first, like Rabbi Richard Hirsch and men in the other church offices. We asked them — 'Do you have somebody in your state whom you can get to telephone his Congressman or Senator who may be on the Conference Committee?'

"They went to work. The Committee met. Before any public announcement was issued of the results, I received a long-distance call from a minister who came from the district of one of the three Congressmen who had spoken against and voted against the continuation of the agency.

"The minister had said to the Congressman: 'I simply wanted you to know that the seventy Methodist churches in this district are part of a denomination which has been committed to the principle of disarmament since 1940. We are concerned that this agency grow — not that it decline.'

"This minister had just received a call from the Congressman in question saying, 'You will be very happy to know that the committee voted the entire permissible amount!' Other calls had been made, including five from the West Coast. I am sure that not more than six phone contacts were made to each one of these twelve men.

"This proved," Mr. Shaw concluded, "that a wheelbarrow of letters is not as important as a direct contact with the *centers of power.*

Mr. Shaw failed to mention that while the Methodist bureaucracy may have been committed to disarmament since 1940, it is extremely doubtful if the members of the seventy churches referred to had a similar commitment. It was a bit awkward in World War II to convince either government or the man in the pew that the United States should disarm. And it was even more difficult to convince Hitler he should go and do likewise.

The Methodist Church adopted its first major official statement on Vietnam in February of 1964. In November of the same year, the Peace Division sent urgent memos to the various church judicatories expressing concern at the course of events in Vietnam and urging action to halt the war.

In 1965, the Methodists escalated their campaign against the U. S. position in Vietnam. In contrast to the single statement and the sending of memos in 1964, the church in 1965 took separate actions. On February 8, 1965, a telegram, signed by the officers of the General Board of Christian Social Concerns, was sent to President Johnson requesting the President to resort to the United Nations in preference to unilateral actions.

Nine representatives of the Interreligious Committee on Vietnam — including three Methodists, Bishop Charles F. Golden, Dr. A. Dudley Ward, and Herman Will, Jr. — had a conference with Secretary of Defense Robert McNamara on May 12. The Methodists spared no effort in an attempt to convey their view on what the United States should do about Vietnam.

The Methodists cooperated with eleven other denominations, the Central Conference of American Rabbis, and the National Council of Churches, in arranging a Washington visit by religious leaders concerned about Vietnam. Once again this ecumenical committee was heavily fortified with Methodists — twenty of the sixty persons. The church leaders spent the most of three days conferring with Vice President Hubert H. Humphrey, White House and State Department staff, and key members of Congress.

More than seventeen similar types of action were taken by the Methodists in 1966. This included sending out literature, supporting peace candidates, and active cooperation with the interfaith "Wednesdays in Washington" program. The program was designed to encourage churchmen to come to Washington and attend a briefing session, participate in a morning worship period, and then go calling on Congressmen to try to convince them of the folly of the U. S. involvement in Vietnam.

Although the Methodist Church was not officially connected with the Clergymen and Laymen Concerned About Vietnam, that group did use an empty office in the Methodist Building during some of its demonstrations in Washington. "Lots of our people were involved in the demonstrations," Will said. "We gave assistance but we didn't take responsibility."

Will said his Division does not make a "Methodist pitch" to the Congressmen. "We don't try to work Methodist-to-Methodist," he explained. "We are here to represent all the people.

"We do have a fall-out effect from our Washington seminars," he added. "Persons attending them often go over and talk to their Congressmen." It's only a short walk across the Capitol Grounds from the strategically located Methodist Building.

The Methodists continually pressure, criticize, and suggest solutions to the knotty problem of achieving peace in Vietnam. On February 10, 1967, Secretary of State Dean Rusk was called to task in a telegram signed by Bishop Charles F. Golden of Nashville, Tennessee, and the indefatigable Herman Will, Jr.

While others may question the expertise of a bishop and a bureaucrat in the art of international diplomacy, Bishop Golden and Will obviously experienced no such qualms. The telegram is worth quoting in full to illustrate how churchmen not only criticize stances taken by governmental officials but also offer specific policy suggestions in an area where the church officials' qualifications may be suspect. The telegram stated:

Dear Mr. Secretary:

We are deeply troubled by your statement on Viet Nam in the February 9 press conference. It would seem you are actually asking North Viet Nam to stop sending men and supplies into South Viet Nam in exchange for no more than a halt of the U.S. bombing of the North.

How can Hanoi be expected to leave its forces and others associated with them in South Viet Nam without support unless the U.S. is willing to take similar action by halting the sending of its own men and supplies into South Viet Nam? We earnestly hope you will clarify this question.

If our understanding of your statement is correct, we believe you have hardened the U. S. position and made the securing of negotiations more difficult at precisely the moment the other side appears to be showing increased readiness for the conference table.

Added to a sequence of past events in which U. S. military escalation has seemed to coincide with and to help frustrate opportunities for negotiation, this hardening of position can only con-

vince Hanoi and the world that the U. S. is interested far more in
military victory than in peace through negotiations.

We hope further action by the Administration, such as an indefinite extension of the truce and of the cessation of bombing in the
North will remove the serious doubts about U. S. intentions in
Viet Nam and will show that the U. S. is ready to take the risks
for peace that the world would properly expect.

The telegram reflects what some might call arrogance — or at
least presumption — on the part of the two churchmen. Did they
have classified intelligence denied to Secretary Rusk? If not, how
could they so readily read Hanoi's mind to the extent they could
write, "... we believe you have hardened the U. S. position and
made the securing of negotiations more difficult at *precisely the
moment* the other side appears to be showing increased readiness
for the conference table." Subsequent events proved it took a long
time to bring Hanoi to the conference table and up to December
of 1969 the only thing that had been decided was the shape of
the table.

The tone of the telegram, had it been sent by a a professor of
international studies or a seasoned diplomat, might have carried
weight. It would seem more proper for churchmen, however, to
deal with the morality — or gross immorality — of the war rather
than scold Secretary Rusk for his inability to detect the "increased readiness" of the enemy to head for the conference table.
Do bishops and bureaucrats possess some kind of ESP denied ordinary government leaders involved in the day-to-day intricacies of
international diplomacy?

In April of 1967 at a meeting in Portland, Oregon, the entire
Methodist Board of Christian Social Concerns adopted a strong
resolution urging withdrawal of all U. S. forces in Vietnam.
The resolution, submitted by a board member, Dr. Robert W.
Moon of Sacramento, California, had been prepared by the staff
of the Division of Peace and World Order back in Washington.
This is a common tactic of church bureaucrats. What often
appears as a resolution or statement threshed out by delegates
in a heated floor debate really is a paper prepared by the staff
of a church bureaucracy seeking official approval for what it
planned to do anyway.

In the publicity release containing the Methodist Board of
Christian Social Concerns statements on "Vietnam and other
military matters," it was pointed out the "board speaks only for
itself and not The Methodist Church as a denomination." But

even such sophisticated agencies as the Religious News Service failed to mention that disclaimer in its report on the meeting. And in most of the secular press, the resolutions came across as the official position of all Methodists. The fact is, disclaimers to the contrary, the only reason the Christian Social Concerns board would rate any coverage at all is because it is an appendage of a large denomination. The bureaucrats are aware of their privileged position and exploit the situation to their fullest advantage.

The preamble to the Vietnam statement spoke the language one would expect to hear from a church group:

> The situation in Vietnam has reached the point where most of our people are almost frantically seeking an early end to the involvement. Proposals for negotiations with varying conditions and assumptions, many from recognized leaders in the world community, have proved fruitless. Meanwhile, the killing and maiming and the wanton destruction of property continue at an increasing pace until the world is aghast.

> The Board of Christian Social Concerns of The Methodist Church is convinced that this carnage cannot be the will of God and that we must, with all our energy, demand that it cease.

Couched in that kind of moral language, the statement is difficult to fault. While the observation that most of the people were "frantically seeking" an early end to the war could be classified as an overstatement — unfortunately, from the author's view, not enough people have sought an early end to the war — the preamble pointed up those issues over which most believe the churches should be concerned.

But, alas, the statement didn't stop there. It went on to suggest three possible solutions — to dispose summarily of one and then elaborate extensively on the other two, which merged into the solution approved by the board.

The three possible solutions in Vietnam, as seen by the members of the Board of Christian Social Concerns (read the staff of the Division of Peace and World Order) were the following:

(1) The total obliteration of all those who oppose U. S. forces.

(2) The total removal of all U. S. military forces from Vietnam with the greatest speed consistent with their safety.

(3) A vigorous program of peaceful initiatives to bring about negotiations.

The board rightly labeled the first alternative as unthinkable. It stated that "unilateral withdrawal would be preferable to a policy of total obliteration" and also would be preferred to continuing the war for five or ten more years.

"We believe that neither withdrawal nor negotiations can be considered apart from each other," the resolution continued and then went on to outline specifically the board's plan:

> Any policy regarding withdrawal would require negotiations concerning the military forces of the National Liberation Front and the Saigon government, the timetable for withdrawal, amnesty for prisoners and guarantees against reprisal.
>
> We urge the U. S. government immediately to initiate necessary steps leading to the withdrawal of all its forces from Vietnam in a manner to be determined by negotiation.
>
> These steps should include an acceptance of the U. N. Secretary General U Thant's proposals. Specifically, this means:
>
> (a) An announcement by the United States and South Vietnam governments of a unilateral cease-fire and stand-fast upon a specific date.
>
> (b) An announcement that the United States and South Vietnam are ready to negotiate with all interested parties including the National Liberation Front.

Never let it be said that the Board of Christian Social Concerns left the U. S. military and diplomatic leaders operating in a vacuum, without detailed advice on how to accomplish their goals. The board's detailed resolution declared that negotiations should seek agreement on the following matters:

(1) The demilitarization and neutralization of Vietnam.

(2) The establishment of a government that represents all the people of South Vietnam, either through a coalition arrangement, or a free and possibly internationally supervised election.

(3) An amnesty for all political and military prisoners.

(4) A guarantee of no reprisals against participants in the current hostilities.

(5) A commitment by the U. S. to provide assistance through international channels for the reconstruction of both North and South Vietnam.

Even a superficial reading of these five points clearly shows that they are much easier to put on paper than to put into action. But that is the advantage of being a church bureaucrat. One doesn't have to follow through on one's proposals, and even more important, one doesn't have to suffer the consequences if the recommendations were erroneously conceived or are misdirected. That awesome responsibility rests squarely on the shoulders of those in government who are not permitted the luxury of re-solving complicated world problems in three-day conferences.

The Methodists rounded out their peace activities for 1967 in November at a four-day conference of the Council of Bishops of the Methodist Church and the Board of Bishops of the Evangelical United Brethren Church in Miami Beach. (The two Protestant denominations later would merge, becoming the United Methodist Church.) The bishops of both communions called on the United States to "implement verbal offers of negotiation" in the Vietnam war "with concrete action."

In their statement, the bishops first commended President Johnson for continuing to call for negotiation in the Vietnam war and for his repeatedly expressed offers to go anywhere, anytime, to make such talks possible.

The bishops then proposed that the United States and the South Vietnamese governments declare that on a specific date they would:

1. Initiate a cease fire, with the maintenance of positions for the safeguarding of life and order, and

2. Send to a neutral place a top-level team of negotiators to meet, under the auspices of the United Nations or the Geneva Conference, with all parties to the dispute, including the National Liberation Front. We believe that the United States, at the same time, should affirm its belief that

(a) the purpose of negotiation should be to establish the right of self-determination for the people of South Vietnam, and

(b) that the negotiations should consider the phased withdrawal of all foreign troops and bases with arrangements for asylum for those who may require it.

Apparently the resolution of the tragic conflict in Vietnam appeared much more simple to churchmen in the warm climate of Miami Beach than it did to the President of the United States in the frigid climate of Washington, D.C.

The Rev. J. Elliott Corbett, director of the Washington Study Programs, argues that church bureaucrats, like their governmental counterparts, do have to consider the likely consequences of their acts. He quotes Dr. Ernest W. Lefever, who stresses "calculation of the probable consequences of competing policies." In Dr. Lefever's view, "No statesman can make policy from principles alone. He must relate goals and ideals to the political facts of life. This means calculation. And calculation is the foundation of strategy and tactics — policy." Mr. Corbett says the Methodist peace staff "accepted his premise of the importance of such an assessment."

He also quotes from diplomat George F. Kennan's book *Foreign Policy and Christian Conscience* on the matter of consequences:

> I can testify from personal experience that not only can one never know, when one takes a far-reaching decision in foreign policy, precisely what the consequences are going to be, but almost never do these consequences fully coincide with what one intended or expected . . . [the statesman] is best off when he is guided by firm and sound principles instead of depending exclusively on his own farsightedness and powers of calculation.

Church lobbyists often act as if their resolutions and statements actually are going to influence foreign policy. There is little evidence, however, of church bureaucrats having made any impact on either the conduct or the shortening of the Vietnam war.

Herman Will's hard-working Division of Peace and World Order continued to plot for peace even as the military men in the Pentagon plotted their strategy for war.

The division's 1967-68 Action Project "Toward Security and Disarmament" makes an interesting study in the art of lobbying for these twin goals — some would argue that in our ideologically polarized world the two terms are mutually exclusive.

The format of the project was contained on a three-page memorandum. "It must be understood," the memorandum began, "that no significant progress is likely on either of the following two issues until the Vietnam war is ended. Thus the settlement of the Vietnam conflict will remain of paramount importance until it is achieved.

"These emphases in the action project will be set in a framework of encouraging alternatives to the unilateral national and military action in dealing with threats to peace or with revolutionary situations."

The paper set out a two-point emphasis:

> (1) Strengthening of international institutions for the achievements of peaceful change, peaceful settlement of disputes, and peacekeeping, including such steps as universal membership in the U. N. (especially the People's Republic of China) and increased authority, budget and staff for U. N. Operations.

> (2) Further steps toward world disarmament, such as inclusion of the People's Republic of China in conferences, agreements for

nonproliferation of nuclear weapons, denuclearization of specific regions, reductions in stockpiling and production of weapons, and a ban on underground nuclear testing.

Resource material for those involved in the action project would include information leaflets, discussion packets on China, disarmament, and the strengthening of the United Nations, guides for organizing a local World Understanding Institute, or a community survey on arms and the economy, and last but not least, a visit with a member of Congress.

The project would be worked out on four different levels, thereby adhering to Will's favorite dictum, "Peace comes in pieces." On the national level, the Washington peace staff planned a UN/Washington conference, Nov. 13-17, 1967, during the UN General Assembly disarmament debate. Those who attended the conference would be invited on a selective basis — Methodists from states having members on the Senate Foreign Relations, Armed Services, and Appropriations committees. The conferees presumably would use whatever influence they had to get their Senators on the three key committees to vote in a manner pleasing to the Methodist-sponsored conference.

On the local church level, the project called for a fellowship of churchmen "deeply concerned for peace education and action." The project included World Order Sunday observances to include "dialogue sermons between the minister and carefully selected and competent lay persons on some aspect of the action project."

The district judicatory leaders were instructed to conduct a district legislative seminar and to "make a special effort to involve the Congressman of that district, as one of the U. S. Senators of that state, as well as other key persons in that area." Representatives from local peace discussion groups also were to meet with the Congressman from that district. "Have the district chairman of that Congressman's party present," the memorandum advised, "as well as the mayor of any large city in the district." The conference leaders of the project — most Methodist conferences cover a state — were to set up meetings with the state's two Senators and the Governors, "in most cases meeting with each of the three separately." Furthermore, the memorandum continues, "in a meeting with a Senator, seek to have the state chairman of that Senator's party present. In states with more than one annual conference, it would be desirable to coordinate efforts in planning such meetings."

Members of the Division of Peace and World Order argue that in the strictest sense of the word their role in relation to peace issues is not lobbying. They point to the Bible of Methodist lobbyists — the political action pamphlet called *Register Christian Opinion*, which states:

> The activity described above [communication with legislators] is not lobbying in the sense of applying political and economic pressure. It is simply exercising responsible Christian citizenship. To do more than this might involve pressure tactics, but to do less would be to ignore our mandate — to subject all things to the judgment and redemption of God.

The key, according to the Division, is whether the activity involves self-interest. Because the church bureaucrat is not attempting to win economic concessions, he maintains that he is not lobbying. But under the generally accepted definition that a lobbyist is anyone who carries on activities to influence the decisions of Congress or government administrative agencies — or the President — then even members of the peace staff would have to be placed in that category.

No one could fairly accuse the Methodist Board of Christian Social Concerns with failure to keep contact with government agencies which implement U.S. foreign policy. The State Department Office of Public Affairs says the Methodist board arranges for more briefings for visiting Methodist groups than any other nongovernmental group.

By the late 1960's, even the most sensitive bureaucrat would not flinch at the word "lobbyist." Others were openly pumping for more vigorous attempts to influence the decision-making bodies and policy-implementing agencies of the U. S. government.

An article in *The Washington Post* in December of 1968 revealed how far the Methodist staff members had advanced in the art of lobbying. The Rev. Rodney Shaw, coordinator of the Methodists' "Vietnam Education Project," was quoted as saying the United Methodist Church spent $100,000 on the program. He called it a "new form of evangelism." Admitting that "we are not strictly objective," he said two project members worked to force the United States to recognize the National Liberation Front and to get out of Vietnam because "we have been defeated."

"I believe this is the first time a church has sought to directly influence foreign policy," Mr. Shaw was frank to admit.

Seeking to influence foreign policy may represent a questionable activity of the church and promoting the recognition of the National Liberation Front can hardly be classified as an evangelistic effort. Apparently Mr. Shaw is content to ignore the "thou shalt not employ pressure tactics" admonition found in *Register Christian Opinion.*

* * * * *

E. Raymond Wilson, executive secretary emeritus of the Friends Committee on National Legislation (FCNL), is a soft-spoken man with strong convictions.

"Lobbying is as American as celebrating the Fourth of July or eating hot dogs," says the dean of religious lobbyists in Washington. (The FCNL was the only religious organization in Washington in 1967 whose staff members registered as lobbyists with Congress.) "The churches exert about 10 per cent of the influence which they could or should be exerting in the fields of peace and social justice," he laments.

The FCNL operates out of austere, second-floor offices in the three-story building owned by the Committee at 2nd and C streets, N. E., in the Capitol Hill section. In 1967, the other occupants of the building included the secular SANE organization (National Committee on a Sane Nuclear Policy) and the pacifist-oriented Unitarian Universalist Association Department of Social Responsibility.

Mr. Wilson was one of the founders of the FCNL in 1943. The Friends then had a Quakerly "concern" about protecting the interest of conscientious objectors in the draft and were the first major denomination to support a full-time legislative staff for the specific task of lobbying. (Surprisingly, in World War II only about 25 per cent of Quaker young men of military age took the position of conscientious objectors. The other three-fourths accepted full military service — including Quaker Richard M. Nixon.)

The FCNL bears the indelible imprint of Mr. Wilson. An editorial in the November 1, 1963, "Friends Journal" referred to the FCNL "as the lengthened shadow of Raymond Wilson. It is his gift to the Religious Society of Friends, which they have now formally accepted with appreciation and gratitude."

The FCNL "Statement of Legislative Policy" declares:

> Our Committee does not, nor can any organization or individual, speak for all Friends. We endeavor to make this clear whenever witnesses testify before Congressional Committees. We recognize

that strong differences of opinion may exist on specific questions among sincere and thoughtful Friends notwithstanding their common religious heritage.

Mr. Wilson, as one would expect, has heard all the arguments against church lobbyists — "Lobbying is something nice people don't do," or "The church shouldn't get into politics," or "The issues are too complex for the individual to fathom."

"In answer," he replies, "one can say that at least the church can act on questions on which there is considerable consensus. And what better subjects for religious education could be found than those issues on which there is difference of opinions?" he asks, with a sly grin.

Mr. Wilson believes the man in the pew may not have his priorities properly arranged. "This is not to assume that church bodies can speak with the undiluted wisdom of God," he admits, "or that the church should impose its will on government. But it does mean that members of Congress and officials in other branches of government need the warmth of religious fellowship in discussing and arriving at the political decisions they are called on to make."

The Friends have a variety of ways to express this "religious warmth" — some politicians call it "heat." The FCNL hammers out a sixteen-page statement on legislative policy at the beginning of each new Congressional session to serve as a guide to the FCNL staff as the session progresses.

In the FCNL executive secretary's office, a huge chart, covering nearly one entire wall, contains the scoreboard on "Congressional Interviews for the Year." The names of legislators, when they were contacted for some Quaker-style "religious fellowship," and by whom — all this is recorded. The FCNL also periodically mails an analysis of Senate and House attitudes on Vietnam in which the Congressmen who have taken some action against the war are divided into three groups:

I — Those who voted against the Vietnam appropriations.

II — Those who have been consistent critics of Vietnam policy and/or have signed most of the critical Vietnam statements circulated by members of Congress.

III — Those who have signed one or more statements critical of U. S. Vietnam policy or have otherwise indicated their unhappiness.

FCNL staff also testify at Congressional committee hearings, sponsor seminars for visiting Friends, contact Congressmen in person and by mail, and spark interfaith peace projects. The Quakers exert influence greatly out of proportion to their number because of their dedication and skill in penetrating other groups to promote peace. Mr. Wilson serves on four levels of the National Council of Churches. He is a member of the Government Relations Committee, the Department of International Affairs, and the Program Board of Christian Life and Mission Division, and he represents the Philadelphia Yearly Meeting on the general board of the NCC.

Edward Snyder succeeded Mr. Wilson as the FCNL executive secretary in 1955 after having practiced law in Connecticut. He is a graduate of the University of Maine and the Yale Law School.

Sitting in his Washington office, Mr. Snyder explained that the "Friends' peace testimony is nothing less than the total elimination of war and the full lifelong dedication to that effort individually and collectively, with zeal, intelligence and persistence.

"Many non-Friends are subscribers and supporters of our committee," Snyder explained. "Two-thirds of the approximately 200 members of the committee are officially appointed by twenty of the twenty-six Yearly Meetings of Friends (the closest thing to a state-wide judicatory the autonomous Quaker meetings have), by one regional association of Friends and by nine Friends' organizations or committees. The Quakers are at ease with members of any denomination — or a humanist for that matter — as long as they are marching for peace."

The Quakers are sophisticated enough in the workings of the national legislature to know where to apply the political leverage. "We've come to the conclusion that the best way a Congressman can express his opinion on war is to vote against funds to finance it," Snyder said, pulling a thick twenty-two-page brief from his desk. "The brief will be circulated on the Hill to all those we think would give it some serious consideration."

Entitled "Brief in Opposition to the $12,300,000,000 Supplemental Appropriation to Carry on and Escalate the Vietnam War," it contained these two opening paragraphs:

> Congress now [February, 1967] has before it the President's request for the $12,300,000,000 Vietnam supplemental appropriation for fiscal year 1967. These funds will add to the billions already appropriated by Congress last summer for the 1967 fiscal year. They will be used to carry on and escalate the Vietnam war.
>
> This brief argues that the cause of mankind and United States

national interest call for a vote against further funds for this tragic war. Members of Congress are given special responsibilities under our Constitution to exercise their own best judgment on these questions on behalf of the nation and their constituency. They are answerable to their own consciences and to the bar of history as well as to the White House for their votes.

A synopsis and index appeared on the first two pages with such subheadings as "Failure of Our Vietnam Policy," "Public Opposition Grows," "Missed Negotiating Opportunities," and "Congressional Responsibility."

(It was a detailed argument logically developed, appealing to the conscience of the reader, but its impact was minimal. The appropriation passed.)*

Each year the Quaker-supported organization distributed the voting records of Congressmen and how they related to the Friends' position on peace, the draft, civil liberties and civil rights, disarmament, the distribution of food, and any other "concern" that might have a top priority during the legislative session.

In 1967, the Friends joined in a tandem effort with the Clergymen and Laymen Concerned About Vietnam. "The Clergymen and Laymen committee wanted to have a one-shot visible effort from January 31 to February 1, which would overlap our first 'Wednesday in Washington' project," Snyder explained. "So we had many people come in for both programs. We urged all who came to Washington to be actively involved in influencing legislation for peace." This meant lobbying to get the appropriations for Vietnam reduced.

Snyder briefed the clergymen and laymen who flocked to the Capital from all over the country. He also directed the committee preparing appointment lists by states for those planning to visit their Congressmen. "Some Congressmen had so many visitors they had to meet in Committee rooms because their offices were too small," he recalled.

To spur the activists and to smite the consciences of the American public on Vietnam, Snyder prepared a grim brochure that would find its way into the offices and meeting halls of the major denominations. Called "Vietnam: Challenge to the Conscience of America," the brochure's impact was heightened by a pencil

---

* It is interesting that three years later — May, 1970 — Senators opposed to the U. S. involvement in Cambodia adopted the same tactic Snyder proposed in 1967.

drawing of a weeping mother clutching her wounded, or dead, baby as a soldier walks by, his weapon on his shoulder. A second pencil drawing depicted a child with bandaged forearm and hand, hobbling along using a stick for a crutch. The brochure informed the reader that the war in Vietnam cost $24 billion a year — all of which had to be appropriated by Congress. That was the legislative Achilles heel at which the Quakers aimed to stop the military. "Your Senators and Congressmen must vote on these bills (appropriations) and on limiting amendments," the brochure stated. "You have a citizen's right to ask them to consider your views as they prepare to vote."

In typical Quaker fashion, the brochure contained an outline for three possible plans of action. First, readers were urged to visit their Senators and Representatives at home before they returned to Congress.

The second step of action encouraged attending a Wednesday in Washington program. The one-day schedule called for the following:

7:30 — 9 a.m. — Breakfast and briefing on Congressional visits.

9:00 — 4 p.m. — Congressional visits. (Write in advance from home requesting appointments.)

4:00 — 5:30 p.m. — Workshop on community action.

The third alternative urged joining with others at home to set up educational programs to build a climate of public opinion enabling members of Congress to express frankly their own views about the war. Two "outstanding opportunities" for community action consisted of "organizing broadly based delegations to visit members of Congress during the Easter recess" and "sending representatives to Washington in late April and May when the regular Vietnam war appropriations bill is expected to be actively under consideration."

Once again there was no evidence that the Quaker effort produced results. Congress continued to pass Vietnam appropriations.

Snyder said he first wrote "Vietnam: Challenge to the Conscience" in memo form to get the reaction of other social action people "whom we know on a first name basis. I discussed it a great deal with Herman Will of the Methodists."

The brochure was described on the back as the "cooperative effort" of twelve religious organizations and was "commended"

by the Commission on Social Action of Reform Judaism and the
International Affairs Commission of the National Council of
Churches.

The project is illustrative of the cooperative efforts of church
lobbyists who seek the broadest base possible for a particular
project and who usually consult with their peer group before
embarking on a campaign. Help is not hard to find. Is there a
church lobbyist who doesn't want to get "involved" — indeed who
does not feel compelled to do so?

"Our appeal is not based on numbers," Snyder insists, "but
on the rightness of ideas. We try to bring experts with first-hand
experience before Congressional committees. Our goals are far-
reaching and progress seems very small and modest. We don't
try to claim anything in terms of success. It's too difficult to
measure. I'm skeptical of the claim that the churches are responsible for anything. There are so many people involved and it is
usually a coalition of people working together that results in
success."

The Committee staff — usually augmented by volunteers —
leaves little to chance. Records are kept of visitors and of staff
members who conduct interviews with Congressmen. After an
interview is finished, the person who conducted it is asked to
return to the FCNL headquarters and write "the essence of the
interview." Snyder explained the purpose of putting one's im-
pressions on paper. "When the next man comes he can see the
file, find out how the Congressman feels on the topic, avoid the
pitfalls listed, and make a stronger case."

Quaker-style interviews total more than 600 in a year — which
means that every Congressman feels the fellowship of Friends at
least once annually and some more often.

Snyder produced the records of two interviews of March 3,
1967. A Winnetka, Illinois, man met with the then U. S. Rep.
Donald Rumsfeld, who eventually became director of the Office
of Economic Opportunity. The other interview was conducted
by a constituent of Rep. Ray A. Taylor of North Carolina.

The report on the Rumsfeld interview reveals the persistence
of a Friend with a "concern":

"Rep. Rumsfeld was up against a meeting of the Space Committee, and so had little time," the report began. "He also mentioned seeing several other people from the AFSC and FCNL; to
the extent that I simply had to sit down without invitation."
Undaunted by the cool reception, the Quaker continued:

> In the course of my presentation of the case against the appropria-
> tion, he interrupted to protest my intimation that the military
> was running away with this war. He said, with great emphasis, that
> there never has been a war in our history that was more under
> civilian control than this one.
>
> I then shifted to say that in that case, the President himself
> would have to be blamed for the escalation just at the time when
> negotiations seemed likely. He said perhaps — if any blame was to
> be assessed.

(The restraint on the part of the Republican Representative
was remarkable, considering that his constituent was willing to
place the entire blame for the escalation of the war on the
shoulders of a Democratic President!)

> I left him with a copy of the brief (opposing the supplemental
> appropriation for the Vietnam war) and "The Politics of Escala-
> tion," plus the *Washington Post* quotes.

The visitor's impression of Rumsfeld was somewhat ambivalent:

> He is a thoughtful representative and worth cultivating, but I
> believe he goes along pretty regularly with the Republican view
> on appropriations. I have written him many times on subjects
> allied with peace and have always received a polite reply.
>
> He had a large picture of Dirksen in his own office, but I didn't
> see any of Percy.

The interview with Rep. Taylor of North Carolina was not
the kind a Quaker enjoys.

> He feels that at the present stage the war in Vietnam must be
> pursued with all the fire power we have, and that we must hit
> hard and get it over with. He agrees somewhat weakly that we
> have no right morally in being in Vietnam but feels that is not
> worth talking about now.

The brief statement makes clear that the interviewer held little
hope that Rep. Taylor would ever come around to the Quaker
point of view on peace.

"The churches are listened to only when it strictly is a church
issue," Snyder complained, "and when there is not so much
uncertainty — such as appointing an ambassador to the Vatican
or passing a prayer amendment." (The Quaker bureaucrat may
have defined the proper role of a church lobbyist much more
aptly than he realized.)

"There's nothing that will cool off an idea so quickly as to
say it involves church with state," he said. "I'm sorry about that.

Churches should speak to major problems of our society — war and peace, economic justice, racial justice. Because a clergyman is not in his area of expertise — theology — he is often discredited," he protested. "Very often moral arguments are brushed aside with the comment, 'We are talking about dollars and cents or harsh facts you know nothing about.' That kind of attitude leaves out a whole dimension of life."

Snyder was cutting close to the core of the matter. Politicians do need to consider the total man when weighing legislation in the balance. Conversely, the church lobbyist often fails to give legislators credit for possessing any spiritual perspicacity whatsoever. There are committed churchmen in Congress who feel they have as good a grasp on the moral dimension of a problem as does the professional church lobbyist. Churchmen do not seem equipped with any special insights denied others when they ascend to high governmental positions. John Foster Dulles headed the "Just and Durable Peace" Department of the Federal Council of Churches (now the National Council of Churches) before serving as Secretary of State under President Eisenhower. Needless to say, few of today's church lobbyists would agree with Dulles' moralistic approach to containing Communism. Diplomacy seldom can be reduced to such simplistic terms, and politics, the essence of which is compromise, often comes up in shades of gray rather than in black or white.

FCNL staff members have gotten caught in awkward positions in concrete situations. They have even been known to resort to euphemisms — calling the UN Police Force (FCNL is an avid supporter of the UN) a "police organization" rather than a "force." The pacifistic Friends also had some difficulty in backing the UN Congo military operations, but did support the move because the UN's existence was at stake.

The FCNL played a crucial role in establishing an independent Arms Control and Disarmament Agency late in 1961. Rep. Robert Kastenmeier introduced the first disarmament agency bill in the House in 1960. The proposal ran into stiff opposition, and the FCNL pulled out all stops during the legislative struggle to get the agency approved. The committee staff promoted 150 interviews with Congressmen urging passage, talked to ten Senators, thirty senatorial assistants and ten members of the President's staff, and testified at House and Senate hearings. The FCNL persuaded Friends from twenty states — as far as the West Coast — to come to Washington and testify.

Rep. Kastenmeier, after the legislation had been passed, complimented the FCNL. "One of the most important things done by these people," the Congressman declared, "was the spreading of information. Though lobbying is usually thought of as bringing pressure on people, I think of it as an education and information process, at which the Friends have done extremely well." It was a definition of lobbying that most church bureaucrats could endorse.

There are world issues which the Quakers find it difficult to get a handle on. Banning nuclear testing is one of them. In 1961, the FCNL submitted five arguments against the resumption of tests by the United States: (1) no proof existed that the Russians were testing; (2) the United States was ahead in nuclear weapons development, and resuming tests would allow the Russians to catch up; (3) testing would permit the development of even more terrible new weapons; (4) world opinion would be aroused against the United States; (5) the test moratorium had slowed down the arms race, and the United States should not be the first to break the truce.

Four of the five arguments went up in an ominous mushroom cloud when Russia resumed tests, demonstrating that world events lie beyond the control of church lobbyists with the best of intentions.

Raymond Wilson, dean of lobbyists, is not easily discouraged. "We have to work on long-time difficulties that don't get settled overnight," he admits. But he would be the last to underestimate the political clout of the churches. "If every Protestant and Catholic church and Jewish synagogue had a committee which would follow issues and see that the people were informed and articulate, you could pretty much change the whole climate in the United States," he believes.

CHAPTER XII

Generals Without Armies

If the flames of the Vietnam war could have been smothered by words, the religious leaders would have brought about instant peace. Congressmen and the President were aware that churchmen opposing the war represented only a segment of the church — and that a minority.

The apparent futility of issuing church statements which do not have the backing of the majority of the members in the pew is illustrated by the plethora of pronouncements released opposing the Administration's Vietnam position in 1965-66. In a significant number of cases, religious groups differed with the Administration in specifics as well as in general. And in counseling President Johnson there was no end. The following excerpts indicate different approaches favored by church groups:

> We protest the increasing reliance on military methods by all parties to the conflict and the resultant preparation for a longer, widening and more intensive war. [Resolution on Vietnam, General Board, National Council of Churches, February, 1966]

> We are deeply concerned that in the event the present halt in the bombing of North Vietnam fails to elicit the prayed-for response from Hanoi and the Administration feels constrained to resume these bombings, discouragement and frustration may alter the present character of the conflict as a limited war for limited goals, i.e., the integrity of South Vietnam. . . . We therefore urge the Administration . . . to steadfastly adhere to the principle that there cannot be a satisfactory military solution to this problem, and . . . not to permit a change in the restrained character of this conflict through military escalation. [Policy statement, Synagogue Council of America, January, 1966, signed by representatives of Central Conference of American Rabbis, Rabbinical Assembly, Rabbinical Council of America, Union of American Hebrew Congregations, Union of Orthodox Jewish Congregations of America and United Synagogue of America]

We urge the United States to halt the bombing of North Vietnam for an indefinite period in an effort to create more favorable circumstances for negotiations to begin. On humanitarian and moral grounds, we appeal to the United States to halt indiscriminate attacks on non-combatants in this densely populated country, whether by aerial bombing, artillery barrage or other means. [Resolution on Vietnam, General Board of Christian Social Concerns of the Methodist Church, Annual Meeting, Louisville, Ky., October, 1965]

[The 178th General Assembly] reminds United Presbyterians and the American public that neither abandonment of the struggle in Vietnam or escalation of military act will end the suffering and terror there. [Statement on South Vietnam, United Presbyterian Church in the U.S.A., 178th General Assembly, May, 1966]

We, the members of the Council for Christian Social Action and the board for Homeland Ministries of the United Church of Christ, deeply regret the resumption of bombing in North Vietnam and express our earnest hope that there will be no bombing of cities and villages. [United Church of Christ, Council for Christian Social Action resolution, January, 1966]

Others were even more specific in their objections:

... we protest our government's escalation of the war, its resumption of bombing, its practice of land defoliation and food destruction, its increase in troops and material. . . . [Resolutions on Vietnam War and on China, Church of the Brethren, General Brotherhood Board, March, 1966]

The Unitarian Universalist Association . . . urges the Government of the United States to negotiate with any and all principals in the conflict, including the National Liberation Front, in seeking a cease-fire, the holding of internationally-supervised free elections, and in aiding in the formation of a representative government of South Vietnam. [Resolution of the General Assembly of the Unitarian Universalist Association, May, 1966]

Even the President's own denomination issued a statement:

Therefore be it resolved that this Assembly of the International Convention of Christian Churches . . . urge our government to listen seriously to the voices speaking to us and about us from other nations and other groups not involved in this conflict, e.g., the United Nations, Pope Paul, the World Council of Churches, the Government of Great Britain, and citizen opinion in Japan.

A telegram the Mennonite Central Conference sent to President Johnson from its biennial session at Kidron, Ohio, on August 24, 1965, contained this question:

> Thus we must ask: However abhorrent Vietcong atrocities may be . . . has not the historical moment passed when the United States can hope to control world affairs by unilateral military intervention, particularly since in the eyes of the majority of the people of the developing countries this merely means new forms of colonialism?

One of the more humble statements was adopted by the Third General Convention of the American Lutheran Church, October 19-25, 1966. Called "Vietnam Involvement," the statement confessed:

> As a representative assembly of the American Lutheran Church, we have no special wisdom that enables us to propose specific courses for ending the war. . . . As an Assembly of The American Lutheran Church, therefore, we urge our people to study the issues and express themselves to their leaders in government. We urge our pastors, congregations, individual members, indeed, the nation as a whole, to turn to God in fervent intercessory prayer and genuine repentance for the widespread spiritual apathy presently characterizing our nation, recognizing that even though blame for this conflict is widely shared, nevertheless, no nation involved in its solution has a right to expect to find a sound course of action leading to an end to this or any such conflict apart from prayer, repentance and spiritual renewal.

All of "the stubborn ounces of weight" thrown on the scales of public opinion failed to produce a visible tremor of the balances. President Johnson, paying more attention to the Pentagon than the preachers, continued to escalate the war. With Gallup polls showing that he had the backing of the majority of the electorate, he would not be moved by the seemingly endless stream of church pronouncements.

* * * * *

The 600 delegates attending the sixth triennial National Council of Churches General Assembly in December of 1966 knew a statement had to be made on Vietnam. That was the issue before the nation, and the churches could not avoid it. But the delegates — mirroring the uncertainty of the American public — found it difficult to decide what to say. The convention provided a classic example of the political impotency of the churches when deprived of moral certitude. To leave Miami Beach without issuing some kind of statement on Vietnam was unthinkable. But what to say?

At the preceding General Assembly in 1963, the delegates also had been faced with an overriding issue — civil rights. The answer came easier on that one. Every American knew segregation was wrong. The politicians had taken the lead and introduced legislation which churchmen could support. And even the die-hard segregationists couldn't camouflage the fact that racial justice was more a moral than a political issue.

Allan R. Brockway, writing in the January, 1967, issue of the Methodist magazine *Concern* contrasted the dilemma facing the delegates in 1966 with the clarion call to action heard by their counterparts three years earlier:

> The Vietnam situation in 1966 presented neither of these certainties [moral certitude and proper political action]. The moral issue was clouded by indecisiveness over whether or not the war actually would accomplish what many considered to be morally valid goals of stopping communism, and whether the loss of men and resources was worth its accomplishment. Further, the Johnson administration was waging the war on the ground that it was the only morally correct way for the U. S. to conduct itself in Vietnam, while many in the churches believed the exact opposite to be true. The General Assembly was in a radically different situation than it had been three years earlier when the administration was on the side of generally acknowledged right.

The churches also had no legislation to bring the war to a halt behind which they could unite. (The Quaker would have disagreed. He would point to the appropriation bills in Congress which the churches could have opposed.)

The National Council of Churches got off to a slow start in the peace movement of the 1960's. The organization was so slow at the gate that, in July of 1965, the liberal *Christian Century* magazine castigated the NCC's International Affairs Commission for backing away rather than "confronting these fateful issues" of the U. S. intervention in the Dominican Republic, Cuba, and Vietnam.

The editorial pointed out that government bureaucrats seemed to be exerting influence on the NCC staff when it should be the other way around. "Influence can flow in either direction through such contacts, and it would be unfortunate if it led to the silencing of the Council's criticism of national policy," the editorial warned.

Dr. Vernon Ferwerda, an expert in international affairs who was then the director of the NCC Washington office, took a broad approach to peace rather than focusing on Vietnam. This upset some of the activists on the NCC staff and in member communions. Dr. Ferwerda outlined his views on peace in his remarks at the 1964 Washington Conference on Disarmament and World Peace:

In the National Council of Churches we work on education and action basis. Some of us think that education is the vital part, with action sometimes taking more general forms within the church. Perhaps the best thing we can do after educating people about the problems of war and peace is to guide them in the right direction — to support the United Nations as their priority; and as an activity, to join the local chapter of the American Association for the United Nations, and/or a local World Federalist group.

There is only so much we can do within the Church, because we have a large number of priority items — as, for example, the continuing support of world organizations and the rule of law.

Dr. Ferwerda later was dismissed in what he called a "profound reorientation within NCC." He took his own advice, however, and got another job with the World Federalist Association.

"I don't get much help from churches on human rights conventions and peace treaties because of Vietnam," Dr. Ferwerda lamented in an interview in March of 1967. "Preoccupation with Vietnam prevents churches from working effectively on treaties." He recalled that during his tenure with the NCC Washington Office, most of his time "was to literally daily examine joint proposals which came from Methodists, Quakers, and secular pacifists or Unitarians on Vietnam."

Dr. Ferwerda noted that the Quakers and other pacifist-minded churches "pulled in the United Church of Christ and the Presbyterians to throw in their lot with them in order to take some of the onus of pacifism off their action." It was a wise move, for the very persistence of Quaker peace efforts tends to dull Quaker testimony. Mrs. Helen Lineweaver, who had been representing the United Presbyterian Church, U. S. A., in Washington for eighteen years, said: "A Congressman said to me in an informal conversation: 'Ray Wilson is a fine man but when he comes over here to testify on disarmament it's just like rain on the roof.' "

By the end of 1965, the NCC began to increase the tempo of its involvement in the peace movement. The Council's governing board issued twelve policy statements and resolutions from 1965 to 1968. (The NCC still was not in the same league with the Methodists, who issued thirty-six statements, resolutions, or letters on Vietnam to governing officials over a two-year period from 1964 to 1966.)

The NCC's uncertainty blunted the agency's statement on Vietnam in 1966. Even the title of the statement — "Resolution

Concerning Vietnam" — which would have made it applicable to government officials as well as to member communions, was watered down to "An Appeal to the Churches Concerning Vietnam."

The self-flagellation, which became the trademark of church statements after 1967, was missing from the 1966 NCC resolution. The assembly overwhelmingly approved deleting a "Statement of Repentance" which confessed, in part:

> The Vietnam War is a war of atrocities on both sides. All this lacerates the Christian conscience, and in the face of it the churches can not remain silent.

> As members of our nation, we are unavoidably responsible for its actions. Some of us are in accord with present policies and others are opposed. But none of us rejoices in what is being done to our fellow human beings. We seek their forgiveness and the forgiveness of Almighty God for our involvement in this tragic conflict.

The moral uncertainty plaguing the delegates was reflected in such statements in the resolution as this: "The fact is that on every basic issue of the war, serious, sensitive, well-informed and highly motivated people disagree strongly concerning fundamental facts and policies related to them."

And the statement warned against an abrupt pullout of U. S. troops in these words: "At the same time, precipitate and unconditional U.S.A. withdrawal would open the road to even greater danger and suffering for people whose rights of self-determination, justice and peace the U.S.A. seeks to set forward."

Concerning the use of military manpower in Vietnam, the resolution balanced off with: "We question whether U.S.A. policy does not rely too heavily upon a massive military intervention. . . . We consider that the scale of the U.S.A. military intervention in Vietnam needs constant surveillance and reexamination."

The shrill demand for the U.S.A. to withdraw troops and let the people of Vietnam sort out their own problems was missing from the 1966 resolution. That would come later.

The document did recommend placing the Vietnam conflict on the agenda of the United Nations and urged the U.S. to give "the most serious consideration to a halt in the bombing of North Vietnam." The statement also criticized the lack of "candor on the part of those who make government policy in relation to Vietnam."

The Appeal recommended that member churches "mount a major effort to expand their study, debate, and action concerning

these issues within their own constituencies and cooperatively."
The General Assembly then approved a Priority for Peace pro-
gram for the next triennium on "Christian Witness on Inter-
national Affairs." The program was presented to the assembly by
Robert S. Bilheimer, director of the NCC's International Affairs
Program, who was determined to make influence flow from the
NCC staff toward government officials rather than vice-versa.

Vice President Humphrey, who had addressed a public gathering of the NCC Assembly, could return to Washington and report
to the President that delegates had neutralized the resolution
merely by changing its choice of target from the White House to
the churches.

James Hamilton, the genial secretary of the NCC Washington Office, conceded that the agency was coming under fire
from critics in the spring of 1967. "The activists say we are pussy-
footing on Vietnam," he said. "We don't see it as our major
responsibility. Rather than issuing statements saying it is wrong
for us to be in Vietnam, we have tried to raise some basic questions rather than rendering judgments."

The Washington office of the NCC helped raise questions by
co-sponsoring, with fourteen other denominational agencies, the
"1967 Churchmen's Washington Seminar" from January 31 to
February 3. Attendance was limited to 300 persons selected by the
participating denominations. Described as an "educational experience," a palatable synonym for lobbying, the purpose of the
seminar was outlined in a pamphlet:

> The seminar offers its participants opportunities for direct con-
> tact with government official personnel through personal or group
> interviews and panel discussions; for attendance at hearings be-
> fore congressional committees; for visits to some of the various
> government departments, such as State, Interior, Commerce,
> Justice, where conferences dealing with the functions of each are
> conducted on the scene.

In July of 1967, Allan M. Parrent joined the NCC Department
of International Affairs, to strengthen the Priority for Peace
program.

What many conservatives find difficult to understand is that
the National Council of Churches is not a "superchurch," but an
agency through which member churches believe they may bring
about changes in society they could never bring about alone. The
passage of a resolution by the General Assembly of the NCC does
not mean that the members of the churches in the NCC will

enthusiastically implement it. Even as late as February of 1968, church members would give little support to a U. S. de-escalation or pullout in Vietnam.

Eight major denominational magazines polled their readers in February in an attempt to discern the attitude of American church members toward the war. Seventy per cent of the readers of *The Lutheran* magazine (Lutheran Church in America) disapproved of the way President Johnson was conducting the war. But 62 per cent wanted to see the bombing continued and 58 per cent said they were in favor of an all-out military effort.

Majorities disapproving of the conduct of the war ranged from a low of 57 per cent for the Southern Presbyterians to a high of 76 per cent for the United Church of Christ.

But only among the United Church of Christ was there a majority in favor of stopping the bombing in North Vietnam, and that was a close vote of 53 per cent. In all other denominations the majority was against it. Ratios ranged from 55 per cent for Episcopalians to 74 per cent for Southern Presbyterians. Lutherans held a middle ground with 62 per cent against halting the bombing, 31 per cent in favor and 7 per cent with no opinion.

The question of whether the U. S. should use all strength needed for victory was answered in the affirmative by 72 per cent of the Southern Presbyterians (the most hawkish of the denominations), 63 per cent of the United Brethren, 61 per cent of the Disciples of Christ, 60 per cent of the United Presbyterians U.S.A. (Northern), and 36 per cent of the United Church of Christ.

A majority of church members indicated that they did not feel that "sincere protest should be defended by churches regardless of consequences." The Lutheran poll revealed a wide cleavage between the attitude of the clergy and the lay people to the war. While 85 per cent of the pastors believed protests against the war should be defended by the church, 58 per cent of the lay Lutherans were against it. In an editorial, *The Lutheran* said, "Officially the churches may coo like a dove but the majority of their members are flying with the hawks."

Another writer in the same magazine made this pertinent comment: "It seems, from the results of the poll and from the letters, that the church is going to be criticized no matter which way it turns on the predicament in Vietnam."

Dr. Arthur S. Flemming, president of the National Council of Churches from 1966 to 1969, wanted to place the Council in a militant stance for peace before his term expired. In June of 1969, the Council convened "a meeting of highly qualified people to consider the present stage of conflict." Eight of the twenty-eight highly qualified persons were staff members of NCC or associated with the Council. Four other churchmen also were present. The remainder included prominent educators, authors, and Republican and Democratic Congressmen.

In the 1969 letter to President Nixon, signed by all twenty-eight persons involved in the NCC-sponsored seminar, the indecisiveness prevalent in the 1966 Appeal was replaced by specific, strongly worded suggestions to "end, and not simply de-Americanize" the war in Vietnam.

Commending President Nixon for his decision to withdraw U. S. forces from Vietnam, the signers of the letter welcomed the President's "public commitment to accept any government in South Vietnam that results from the free choice of the South Vietnamese people, and not to perpetuate military bases in Vietnam or seek military ties with the future South Vietnamese government."

The preliminaries over, the letter then got down to "additional steps" the signers believed were required to end the war. Four areas of action were proposed:

(1) "To press vigorously toward an early negotiated settlement of the Vietnam war by simultaneously:

> [a] Replacing the strategy of maximum military pressure on the other side in South Vietnam with a policy reducing the scale of fighting in every possible way, looking toward the achievement of a standstill cease-fire, and

> [b] Seeking agreement through the Paris negotiations on an interim body which will be broadly representative of all political, religious, social and ethnic groups in South Vietnam (and not merely the Government of the Republic of Vietnam and the Provisional Revolutionary Government of South Vietnam), designed to lead to the creation of a government that gives full expression to the political will of the people of South Vietnam, this government to have, by prior agreement in Paris, the specific authority to 1) require the withdrawal of external military forces from South Vietnam, and 2) determine its future relationship with North Vietnam, and with other countries.

(2) "To make clear that the United States will not continue to support any regime in South Vietnam that is not broadly representative and does not extend normal political liberties to its people.

(3) "To make clear to the American people, as well as the Vietnamese, a specific date by which the United States will have completed the withdrawal from South Vietnam of all its military forces, and

(4) "To repeat again in clear terms the moral commitment of this country to help meet humanitarian needs in Vietnam, both North and South.

"In our judgment, Mr. President," the letter concluded, "the interconnected actions we have outlined are now politically possible here at home, and essential in Vietnam to any 'peace we can live with and be proud of.' Believing that the United States now has a unique opportunity, we pledge our whole-hearted support for such an honest ending of this war."

The committee boasted many of the best minds in the nation. The statement, however, contained serious flaws. In the first place, the committee failed to explain how to "create a government that gives full expression to the political will of the people of South Vietnam." The present government was elected but there are still those who doubt the honesty of the election and question how broadly representative it is of the populace.

Furthermore, to announce a specific date for withdrawal of all American troops undoubtedly would delight the government of North Vietnam. And one need not be overly astute in military science to imagine what impact an announcement of this type would have in North Vietnam. Seldom are enemy generals provided with such rare military information.

One of the constitutional purposes of the National Council of Churches is "To study and to speak and act on conditions and issues in the nation and the world which involve moral, ethical and spiritual principles inherent in the Christian gospel." The glaring omission among the recommendations put forth by the Flemming committee is any reference to the moral revulsion Americans should feel over waging a war in which we are forced to kill large numbers of helpless people along with enemy soldiers. The letter overlooks the moral implications of the war to focus on specific policy suggestions better left to military, political, and economic experts.

Instead of challenging the justification for our involvement in Vietnam, the signers appeal to the "demands of the American public, the repression in South Vietnam, and the meager progress in Paris" — pragmatic rather than moral criteria.

Rather than being overly eager to offer guidelines on how the

U. S. should conduct itself on the battlefield and around the peace table, could not the committee members at least have admitted, as did sociologist Peter Berger two years earlier, that "all sorts of dire results might well follow a reduction or a withdrawal of U. S. forces in Vietnam," but that *"morally speaking* (italics mine), it is safe to assume that no consequence could be worse than what is taking place right now"?

Few issues have so fragmented American society as the war in Vietnam. Clergymen critical of the conduct of the war often found they were alienating their own membership. The polarization extended beyond the pulpit and the pew. Even ministers within the same denomination clashed over the proper course the U. S. should be taking in Vietnam. Two of the best-known Presbyterian ministers in Washington, D.C., collided during a verbal showdown over Vietnam at a session of the Washington Presbytery in April of 1967.

The heated debate started with the introduction of a resolution on the floor of the Greater Washington Presbytery by the Rev. George M. Docherty of the New York Avenue Presbyterian Church, which boasts that nine Presidents, including John Quincy Adams, Andrew Jackson, and Abraham Lincoln, worshipped in its pews. Dr. Docherty, a former pacifist from the British Isles who possesses the eloquence peculiar to Scottish preachers, succeeded Peter Marshall as minister of the 2000-member church.

Dr. Docherty, who renounced pacifism in the middle of World War II but who finds the U. S. involvement in Vietnam abhorrent, introduced a resolution calling for a halt of the bombing of North Vietnam and immediate negotiations with the government of North Vietnam to discuss bilateral withdrawal of troops. He said his two-pronged plan would serve as twin "signals of our desire for participating in a peace conference for the re-establishment of international justice."

Dr. Docherty predicted that Hanoi would come to the conference table "as soon as the bombing ceases." He warned the Vietnam war will "smell in the nostrils of history for 100 years." The Presbyterian minister said the Vietcong will "win in the end. They will go on fighting for 25, 75 or 100 years. They will go on fighting for their soil for the next 1000 years if necessary."

The Rev. L. R. Elson, minister of the National Presbyterian Church, President Eisenhower's former pastor and later named chaplain of the U. S. Senate, rose to attack the resolution as ill-timed. Dr. Elson argued the Presbytery should make theology its concern rather than seeking to advise President Johnson on what weapons should be used and what targets should be struck.

Dr. Elson said "history has made a turning point in favor of American civilization" because the U. S. held the line in such places as Greece, Korea, Turkey, and Lebanon. "Things have been stabilized," he continued, "in Thailand, Indonesia, and elsewhere in Southeast Asia. Never in history have such steps been made to protect civilians in war as the U. S. has done in Vietnam."

Dr. Elson's stout defense of the American position in Vietnam was reflected in a vote which defeated the resolution 86 to 27. The Presbytery represents over 70 churches in the Greater Washington area.

The vote killed the resolution, but the debate was not over. In a sermon the following Sunday, Dr. Elson told a packed church that ministers who picket and protest do so from limited data and an arrogance of conscience.

Pointing out that he had a son-in-law in the Army and a son about to enter military age, Dr. Elson told his congregation:

> I do not want my sons commanded by officers whose targets are limited by a resolution, or whose weapons are restricted by an irresponsible resolution adopted by a church body. . . .

> It is one thing for an individual minister, or the professional pacifists, or the chronic protesters, or the convinced or concealed Marxists, to assemble unofficially and make demonstrations and exhibitions. It is quite another for the official Court of the Church in the nation's Capital to be the conduit of such sentiment to the President and his associates. . . .

> Not long ago a large company of clergymen came to this city from across the country for the purpose of petitioning the President to do what the resolution in our Presbytery would have asked him to do. These persons arrived with a pre-cast indictment of American guilt as though we were the sole offenders for the predicament in which the world finds itself.

> With an arrogance of conscience and a pretension to a higher morality than others, they had the formula: America is the guilty culprit and the criminal nation and therefore must abjectly repent and run. The truth is that America and Americans are guilty, but it is a guilt inherited and shared with other peoples and nations, and to indict America as bearing the sole guilt, or even the major guilt, at the very time we carry heavy responsibilities for the well-being of the whole world provides neither moral guidance nor practical statesmanship. Instead, such procedure

provides propaganda weapons for the opposition. And you do not make peace by furnishing weapons to the enemy.

On the same Sunday, Dr. Docherty declared that the Church, in its role as prophet, is to speak loud and clear on political issues. Later in an interview in his book-lined office, Dr. Docherty explained he had been a pacifist from 1935 to 1943 while living in Scotland. After an agonizing struggle with his conscience, he found pacifism an impossibility in wartime.

"Vietnam is different," he said. "You have a Marxist revolution — a nationalist revolution — going on there. We can't win the war. The Vietcong are being supported by the population.

"You can not win this war short of an atomic war. Finally, they are going to drop atomic bombs — and then we won't be America anymore."

Dr. Docherty emphasized that every minister should do his homework — and he obviously had — before speaking out on any topic.

"I agree with the Unitarians," he said, "that behind every political question there is a theological question. I also agree there is no clear-cut answer. Christians of equal integrity differ.

"You can't separate politics from religion. The war has made Saigon an escalated brothel. We are taking people out of their villages and burning their homes. For every combatant who dies on both sides, at least five civilians perish. This is a kind of policy that we cannot condone."

The differences of opinion expressed by the two Presbyterian ministers — both informed and committed Christians — pointed up the dilemma Americans found themselves in during the latter half of the 1960's. It was precisely that sharp split in society that church lobbyists found frustrating in their attempts to influence U. S. foreign policy.

U. S. Rep. Samuel S. Stratton, Democrat from the 35th Congressional District in New York and a member of the Armed Services Committee, described what might be termed the typical attitude of Congressmen toward church lobbyists in 1967:

> The Presbyterian Church has passed all kinds of resolutions which I think are out of place.
>
> I had a delegation of ministers call on me during the protest by the Clergymen and Laymen Concerned About Vietnam. They spent about three hours in my office. They were from my district, but they didn't change my thinking. Instead of making speeches

or giving sermons, many of these ministers come around quietly and ask, "How do you stand or will you go along with us on this?"

Harold M. Templeman, professional staff member of the GOP Policy Committee of the U. S. Senate, was more blunt:

> A minister is just another lobbyist. He used to be held in reverential attitude — but no more. The clergymen today are actually disliked.
>
> There is a tremendous amount of pressure on Vietnam. But they are digging their own graves. When a group of clergymen came to picket, one minister wrote his Congressman: "I will not be among them. I will stay at home and preach the Gospel."

There's the rub. Does preaching the Gospel imply "staying home" and not engaging in politics? Obviously, the church lobbyists don't think so. But as long as national leaders feel that the religious lobbyists are "generals without armies," the church spokesmen are going to be ignored.

Government officials are both sensible and sensitive enough to know whether a lobbyist represents a wide spectrum of opinion or whether he is speaking for a small class of church bureaucrats who have lost contact with their constituents.

Perhaps if churchmen expressed moral outrage, rather than proffering political and military advice, they would be more effective. The last three Presidents seldom have been in short supply of advice on how to end the war in Vietnam. There has never been an "advice gap."

The church lobbyist is never more true to his calling than when he forces our national leaders to re-examine U. S. goals in the uncomfortable glare of biblical morality. The most relevant thing a church lobbyist can do is to remind persons in high places that even nations stand under the judgment of God.

CHAPTER XIII

Registering Christian Opinion

Register Christian Opinion is more than the name of a political action pamphlet: It is a political axiom formulated by one of Methodism's most influential — and controversial — bishops, G. Bromley Oxnam. "If church people are to be effective on public issues, they must register Christian opinion with the persons making the decisions before they are made," Bishop Oxnam, a Washington clergyman whose political acumen gained him entree into the most smoke-filled of rooms, urged his fellow churchmen.

The Methodist-published pamphlet has wide currency among various denominations and has indeed become a blueprint for political action. Now in its 27th annual edition, it has stood the test of time. It is crammed with practical advice and with specific steps one should take to register Christian opinion. "Peace, freedom and justice are most likely to triumph when spiritually motivated persons use their political freedom effectively to translate their ideals into constructive legislation and national policies," it states.

"One cannot know all about everything; he will have to be selective regarding those issues that particularly interest him and focus his attention upon them," the pamphlet points out. Certain newspapers are recommended for political insight — including the *New York Times* and *Christian Science Monitor* — along with magazines ranging across the political spectrum from the conservative *U. S. News and World Report* to the liberal *New Republic*. Readers are also urged to watch television interviews, panel discussions, and documentaries to clarify national and international issues.

Armed with facts from the media and other materials, the church lobbyist is ready to set forth to do battle with the political powers. "There is no better way to express an opinion to a mem-

245

ber of Congress or Administration official than in a face-to-face encounter." A word of caution if you plan to visit a Congressman or Senator in Washington: "Be sure to phone for an appointment in advance."

While most constituents write letters to public officials, the pamphlet notes that "for the nominal fee of 88 cents" (this price subject to change) one can send a fifteen-word Personal Opinion Message to Senators, Representatives, the Vice President, or President by Western Union. "Such telegrams are delivered within 24 hours," the reader is assured.

When is the best time to write?

> If a certain foreign policy is being given serious consideration for implementation by the Administration, then that is the time to write the President or the Secretary of State. When a bill is introduced into Congress and assigned to respective House and Senate Committees, this is one of the times to write concerning the measure. Writing to members of the committee (especially if you are a constituent) may help get the bill on the agenda for consideration.
>
> One should remember that about 90 percent of the bills passed by Congress are adopted in virtually the same form in which they appeared when reported out of committee.

Under the heading "With Whom Does One Communicate," the pamphlet advises the reader to focus on the persons who have political clout:

> It is often most effective to send one's communication to the chairman of the committee in charge of handling the bill that interests you. A carbon copy sent to the ranking member of the minority party is also in order (this person would become chairman should his party achieve majority status in the future). On major issues, letters may also be sent to the top leadership of both bodies of Congress, that is, the Majority Leader, Minority Leader, the President Pro-tempore, etc. . . . . Further, one should not ignore the chairmen of certain key Sub-Committees of Congress whose reports are often given quick approval by the whole Committee.

The twenty-nine-page pamphlet devotes eighteen pages to listing printed materials dealing with public affairs and to listing the members of the Cabinet, the Congressional party leaders, the members of the Congress and Senate by states and Congressional districts, the Senate and House committees, the religion of each elected official, the members of the Joint Atomic Energy Committee, and the correct forms of address.

Having informed the church member how to take action, how to communicate effectively, when and to whom to write about what, the author of the political action pamphlet then sets the reader's conscience at ease:

> If one defines lobbying as "the use of moral and rational persuasion in a personal professional confrontation," then there is a place for Christian "lobbying" on Capitol Hill.

> But the activity described above is not lobbying in the sense of applying political and economic pressure. It is simply exercising responsible Christian citizenship. To do more than this might involve pressure tactics, but to do less would be to ignore our mandate — to subject all things to the judgment and redemption of God.

*   *   *   *   *

There are more than a dozen church-related agencies with offices in Washington serving as lobbying or information liaison centers. Eight of these are in a cluster near the Capitol, making up Washington's "Religion Row." The agencies more and more reflect a solid front on specific issues. The church bureaucrats constitute an ecumenical lobby of growing pressure and influence.

We have looked at the operation of a number of the church agencies and how they attempted to influence legislation or the administration of programs.

Each church lobbyist has his own reason for being in Washington and many of them shared their views with me during a series of interviews in 1967. They explained their overall operations, the division of labor within their own organizations, and most willingly revealed the size of their budgets. Their rationales may not be convincing to everyone — and they concede this point. Some could care less what the man in the pew feels. Others are concerned because they have not been able to communicate their viewpoints to their own denominational members.

The remainder of this chapter will be devoted to describing the organizational structure of the church agencies and the reasons given by the bureaucrats for their political involvement.

The United Methodists

The five-story, gray concrete Methodist Building gives the appearance of being an integral part of the Capitol complex — and in a real sense it is. Inconspicuously situated between the U. S. Supreme Court Building and the new Senate Office Building, and across the street from the Capitol, the Methodist structure serves as the operating center of lobbyists representing five major Protestant denominations and the inclusive National Council of Churches. The building itself is actually two buildings containing sixty income-producing apartments as well as church offices. The Methodist Board of Temperance bought the property and constructed the building more than forty years ago when Methodists were in the vanguard of the church-inspired Anti-Saloon League.

John Wesley, the Anglican priest who founded the Methodist Church, was a prince of preachers and a genius when it came to organization. There is good reason to suspect that beneath his clerical gown, Wesley wore a gray flannel suit. This flair for organization continues. There is a saying in church circles that "where two or more Methodists are gathered, there shall a committee be formed in the midst of them." Wesley preached personal redemption. But after a man's soul was saved, the convert usually found himself enrolled in some organization in a local Methodist church. This emphasis on organization has helped keep the Methodists near the top of the Protestant membership list.

The policy-making body of the now United Methodist Church is the 900-member General Conference, composed half of clergy and half of laymen. The conference meets every four years to hand down official position papers on issues ranging from alcohol problems (a Methodist perennial) to race relations and "Christian overseasmanship." The group charged with relating the church to government is the General Board of Christian Social Concerns, which operates out of the Methodist Building. This board, formed in 1960, represents a consolidation of three former boards – the Board of Temperance, the Board of World Peace, and the Board of Social and Economic Relations. The new board has a twelve-man professional staff in Washington, the largest Protestant lobbying group. The staff is assigned to three divisions of the board – Peace and World Order, Human Relations and Economic Affairs, and Alcohol Problems and General Welfare.

The Discipline of the Methodist Church says that "the board is expected to speak to the church its convictions, interpretations, and concerns. Recognizing the freedom of all Christian men," the document continues, "the board never presumes to speak for the whole church." In actual practice, the Washington staff members speak more to the government than to the church. On May 6, 1960, the General Conference called the attention of Methodists to the "twilight zones" that have developed in the relations between the church and state in contemporary American society. In traditional Methodist fashion, a Study Commission on Church and State Relations was appointed to study the problem. And on February 3, 1964, the commission completed its study and report and requested the General Board of Social Concerns to transmit its report to the General Conference.

The report noted that the possibility of government perverting its role always exists and that "against the perversion of governmental authority the church must speak its prophetic protest." The report also stated that "some stance of church toward government is unavoidable in any society." The commission made a total of twenty-two recommendations to the General Conference. One of the recommendations under the section entitled "Church Participation in Politics" stated:

> That the General Conference declare that any connectional unit of The Methodist Church (such as General Conference, Jurisdictional Conference, Annual Conference, local church, or general board or agency) shall continue to have the right to advocate government policies affecting standards of public morality, social justice, and human rights which it regards as essential to the maintenance of a good society.

The recommendation cautioned that any connectional unit exercising those rights should always make it plain for whom or in whose name it speaks or acts. Only the General Conference, it emphasized, can speak for the entire church.

Another recommendation urged church officials to do their homework. "In dealing with complex issues of public policy, it should also be recognized that good intentions and high ideals must be combined with as much practical and technical knowledge of politics and economics as possible," the report admonished.

It would be difficult to name an issue even in our highly organized society that has not come under the scrutiny of the General Conference. Under the quadrennial program of 1964-68, the church decided to speak to a range of topics reading like a United Nations work list. The issues were parceled out to the three divisions of the General Board of Christian Social Concerns as follows:

> (1) PEACE AND WORLD ORDER — Foreign policy, the United Nations and related international organizations, disarmament and nuclear weapons control, space control, economic aid and technical assistance, tariffs and trade, immigration and naturalization,

military policy and conscription legislation, conscientious objectors and the draft, and Christian overseasmanship.

(2) HUMAN RELATIONS AND ECONOMIC AFFAIRS — Race relations, civil liberties, public policy on education, church and state, civic responsibility, labor-management relations, agriculture, conservation, government and private economic policy and practices, technological change, unemployment, housing, migrant labor, reapportionment, and extremism.

(3) ALCOHOL PROBLEMS AND GENERAL WELFARE — Alcohol problems, narcotics, tobacco, gambling, pornography, traffic safety, mental health, medical care, problems of the aging, juvenile delinquency, crime and rehabilitation, population and planned parenthood, and general welfare agencies and policies.

Each of the three divisions of the General Board of Christian Social Concerns operates on an annual budget of $117,000. The associate general secretary in charge of a division in 1967 received a salary of $11,500 and $3,000 for house allowance. Out of the total $117,000 allotted for the Division of Human Relations and Economic Affairs, only $7500 was used for church-government relations in 1966-67.

The General Board of Christian Social Concerns defines a social action program as any "deliberate attempt on the part of church groups or individuals to bring about a change in the social structure of a community. The community may be local or worldwide in scope," it continues. Methodists are quick to admit that the first place to begin in changing the social structure of a country is in the capital.

Dr. Grover C. Bagby, associate general secretary in charge of the Division of Human Relations and Economic Affairs, represents the "new look" in Methodism's policy of emphasizing social concerns rather than moral issues. "We have a lot of people who think the church should not get involved in politics," he noted, rather wearily. "But they don't object to a minister preaching against liquor, gambling or Communism. They never think of that as political action."

The division director explained that policy-making is generally a two-way street between the governing bodies and the Washington staff. The board defines the policy, but often the policy is based on recommendations of staff members. "We are under strict regulations not to sound off on anything that is not church policy unless we make it clear we are speaking as individuals," Dr. Bagby emphasized. Church policy on social issues, which provides the authority the lobbyists need to act, also serves a useful function as a propaganda tool. Copies of policy statements often are sent to members of Congress or newspapers. Dr. Bagby doesn't believe in letter blitz campaigns but does encourage limited letter writing by influential church members to Congressmen.

"Our job is research, education and action on assigned social issues," he says. "We write to our social concern officials in annual conferences of which there are ninety-six. We give them information. We may or may not invite them to write to Congressmen or we may ask them to inform their constituents."

The Rev. Richard P. Edgar directs the department of social welfare in the Division of Alcohol Problems and General Welfare. "The church should be the stimulant, conscience, continually raising questions and keeping things stirred up," says the prematurely gray-haired minister. "But churches have a tendency to jump on the bandwagon rather than getting in on the ground floor."

Edgar often deals with unglamorous issues — such as a revision of the Social Security Act — which gains little popular support. Edgar is a proponent of rifle-shot lobbying rather than the scatter-gun approach, believing that a few carefully selected constituents making the right calls on the right people can most affect the outcome of important issues. When the House Ways and Means Committee held hearings in March of 1967 on Social Security, Edgar kept a continual flow of information going out to constituents of key members on the committee.

"This was a sneaky way of telling our people in the districts who the guys were they would have to work on," he said with a soft chuckle. "In this kind of operation, you don't have to contact over ten persons in each district. We work on the theory that Congressmen get very little mail on unemotional issues such as Social Security amendments. This means our efforts will have greater impact."

In seeking more liberal provisions in the Social Security Act, Edgar did not confine his campaign to Methodists. He formed alliances with other church and civic action groups to add strength to his political muscle. Edgar does not regard lobbying purely as a political power play because he believes there is a biblical basis for social action.

"This is one means by which we love our neighbors as ourselves today," he says, referring to his campaign to liberalize the Social Security Act. "If we leave it up to others, then political

and economic considerations, tempered perhaps with some humanitarian feelings, will predominate."

Edgar's lobbying for a more liberal Social Security Act was the
implementation of policy recommended by both the General Conference and the Executive Committee of the General Board of
Christian Social Concerns. The committee's recommendations
show that church bureaucrats can be as obtuse in their pronouncements as their government counterparts:

> We believe action is needed: (1) to bring the amount of public
> assistance payments throughout the nation up to a minimum
> American standard of health and decency; (2) to make possible
> comprehensive public assistance programs based upon need as the
> only relevant eligibility requirement; (3) to simplify eligibility
> determinant procedure; and (4) to extend the coverage and liber-
> alize the benefits under the social insurance programs, without
> jeopardizing the financial integrity of the programs.

All lobbying activity, however, does not stem from church pronouncements and recommendations. Edgar says that a divorcee
in Washington "kept bugging us about the restrictive Social
Security benefits to divorced women." It helped to prod him into
action.

Relaxing in a chair in his second-floor office at the end of a
hectic day, Edgar pulled a file out of his drawer to reveal his
master plan for lobbying on the amendments to the Social Security Act during the Ninetieth Congress. The first page outlined
the goal:

> To be effective politically, we must be well informed on the issues,
> we must know our representatives in the United States Congress,
> we must know the best means and time to encourage their support
> of needed Social Security amendments, and we must know how
> and when to secure support in the key House Ways and Means
> and Senate Finance committees.

> Obviously, direct action by a few individuals will not bring the
> public support needed. Therefore, we will need a network of
> contacts with informed persons throughout each state (Methodists,
> other denominations and faiths, and other similar-minded organ-
> izations) who will be ready to make their voice heard at the
> appropriate times.

> The task is not simple or easy. However, it must be done if we
> are to bring maximum benefit (economic, social, psychological and
> spiritual) to our neighbors who have come out on the short end
> of the benefits in our affluent society. It will take work, probably

over a period of many months, and possibly extending for both sessions of the 90th Congress [2 years].

Edgar's chart of command showed the department of social welfare and the national headquarters of other organizations acting in concert to direct the units under them. Edgar's office would secure basic information, make Washington contacts, keep track of legislation, and alert Conference Task Teams on times to act.

The duty of the Conference Task Team (the state-level unit) was to know key resources, secure contacts in each Congressional district, relay information to contacts, secure support for strategy. Five Congressional District Task Teams were attached to the Conference Task Team.

The churches played important roles in Edgar's plan. Conference Task Teams were to make contacts in state divisions of the Council of Churches and with influential members of the Methodist Church (bishops, Board of Christian Social Concerns). Panels explaining the proposed amendments and favoring their passage were held in local churches to drum up support.

The Congressional District Task Team also was urged to contact precinct captains or other party workers who could "write, wire, or telephone their Congressman, Senator, or a Congressional Committee member at key stages in the development of legislation."

The Methodist minister-lobbyist kept his field men informed through periodic reports. The reports were detailed in their description of the bill's progress and precise in suggested action for constituents. Edgar had learned his lesson well from *Register Christian Opinion*. He not only informed his field force on the status of the bill but outlined specific action to influence the legislation.

The Washington-based bureaucrat's first field order — labeled Report No. 1 — was mailed to his troops February 1, 1967. It is reproduced here in part to illustrate the thoroughness of Edgar's instructions:

> HEARING: Chairman Wilbur Mills, House Ways and Means Committee, has indicated that this will come second (after debt limit). Hearings are expected to start about March 1 on all parts of the Social Security Act. The first week will be given to government witnesses and the next two weeks to national groups. Individuals are not expected to be heard, although written testimony will be accepted.

ACTION: National groups should prepare for testimony and write the Ways and Means Committee, U. S. House of Representatives, Washington, D.C., requesting a time to be heard. Others wishing to submit testimony in writing can send it to the Ways and Means Committee. It is quite appropriate to testify on just one issue. Deadline for written testimony will probably be about March 22.

COMMITTEE ACTION: Consideration of the Social Security Act by the House Ways and Means Committee is expected to take about three months. Thus, key decisions will be made between March 1 and June 13.

ACTION: This is the best time to write the Representatives from your district, asking them for information or requesting them to encourage the Committee to take a particular action. If your Representative is a member of the Ways and Means Committee, this period is the time to secure many letters from his District supporting particular changes (see enclosed *Register Christian Opinion* for list of committees).

The report then gave a breakdown on the various titles of the Act to be amended and how the Administration's proposals stacked up against Republican alternatives.

Edgar believes that a successful lobbyist has to be specific both in defining his goals and in disseminating information because "then people have to make up their minds and decide for or against.

"We carry a liberal bias," he admitted. "We can't be objective."

He also said he had never before used the approach utilized in lobbying the House Ways and Means Committee. "We worked primarily through state legislatures before," he explained. "This really is an experiment for us."

The success of the experiment is difficult to measure. Several amendments were made in 1967 — one of which permits a woman divorced after twenty years of marriage and unable to work because of severe disability to get monthly benefits as early as age fifty.

"I don't know how to evaluate our programs — that's the problem," Mr. Edgar said. "I'm sure we could be more effective if we knew where we were making the most mistakes." The inability to assess the department's effectiveness in lobbying appears to be a minor problem, however.

"We are making a conscious attempt to increase our activity," the Methodist bureaucrat assured me.

Mr. Edgar obviously is a man in tune with the times.

The United Church of Christ

Dr. Lewis I. Maddocks, the pipe-smoking Washington secretary for the United Church of Christ's Council for Christian Social Action, cheerfully conceded that his role is an ambivalent one in the view of many members.

"Many of the critics of the church-employed Washington staff simply do not know what the staff are doing while others don't like what is going on even after they find out what it is," he said. "There are others who are disappointed when they find out that the churches' representatives in Washington are much more concerned with citizenship education than with the day-to-day activities called lobbying."

Dr. Maddocks is a good man with punch lines and he used a couple to illustrate the point above. "It is like a boy finding out that his father is employed by the FBI as a file clerk," he observed. "In fact, when I explain to the more militant social actionists that I am not well known among the VIP's of Washington, I begin to feel like an illegitimate child at a family reunion."

Dr. Maddocks came to Washington in July of 1961 and moved into the Methodist Building because the Council "thought there would be some advantages in a cooperative relationship with the Council of Churches." (The NCC's James Hamilton's office is just down the hall.) He is responsible to the UCC Council for Christian Social Action, composed of twenty-seven persons — one-third laymen, one-third laywomen and one-third clergy. Two-thirds of the members are elected by the church's General Synod and one-third is elected by the Council. On January 1, 1964, the Rev. Maynard Catchings, whose specialty is international economic development, came to Washington to represent the United Church of Christ and to assist the National Council of Churches in national affairs.

"I honestly believe," Dr. Maddocks said, "that the Christian Gospel speaks to all of life. I cannot separate the Gospel message from the economic, social, and political affairs of man. This does not mean that one position on a public issue is *the* Christian one and that the opposite is un-Christian. It means, rather, that two Christians can disagree.

"Opposition to the right of the church to speak would be better directed to opposition to the position taken," he continued. "When you take the view that some issues are 'political' and some are 'religious,' what criteria do you use to determine which are which? Who should make the decisions — the laymen? the clergy? the denominational executives? the conference?"

Dr. Maddocks sees a simple solution to the questions he raised. "If you see religious implications in all public issues, you do not have to try to determine which are political and which are religious," he said.

Dr. Maddocks doesn't believe the church should seek a consensus before it speaks. "It's not a matter of reflecting the dominant feeling of the church members," he explained. "The church has an obligation to be ahead of its members — to lead. Church leaders are not elected the way Congressmen are."

He admits that the average member of his communion is not even aware of his office. But, he says, there are two groups which are aware: the social action people who subscribe to the church's social action magazine and those who are opposed to political action on the part of the church.

"I suspect that the third group — which is not really aware of what is going on — may be the biggest of the three," he said, with a smile.

"The big issue going on in our church today is between those who say the church's job is largely one of serving the individual by making the people more spiritual — the vertical relationship with God — and those who say that the primary responsibility is a horizontal one — the church in the world.

"Now obviously neither one excludes the other. Everybody to a degree is vertical and horizontal but there is a matter of emphasis. The Council for Christian Social Action tends to place more emphasis on the horizontal than the vertical."

Arguing that the church must act on its principles to serve the powerless and the oppressed of our society, Dr. Maddocks commented: "In concrete terms this means, more often than not, political action — yes, it means involvement by the church in politics.

"Politics is activity by people and is concerned about people. It has been called the 'art of the possible,' which implies it is the art of compromise, the art of reconciling differences of viewpoints among people.

"In order to appreciate the Christian's responsibility in political action," he declared, "we need merely to recognize that Christianity is concerned with the welfare of people, and that politics in a democracy is based on government by consent of the people; therefore, Christianity, and thus the Christian, must be concerned with politics."

Dr. Maddocks explained why he does not register as a lobbyist. "If the church hired a person to spend full time in Washington attempting to influence legislators, to support or oppose pending legislation, such actions might very well be lobbying," he said. "As a result that might jeopardize the tax-exempt status of the church." Under the provisions of the Federal Regulation of Lobbying Act of 1946, he recalled, a lobbyist is defined as one whose "principal purpose" is to influence legislation. "Actually, I spend more time arranging seminars, speaking, writing articles, answering queries, interpreting statutes, and so on than anything which could be remotely called lobbying," he added.

The Internal Revenue Service grants tax exemptions to those religious and non-profit organizations "no substantial part of the activities of which is carrying on propaganda or otherwise attempting to influence legislation. . . ."

"Certainly no substantial part of the activities of either the United Church of Christ or even the Council for Christian Social Action are in an attempt to influence legislation or elect political candidates," Dr. Maddocks said. "In the first place, the Council for Christian Social Action receives only about 2 percent of the United Church of Christ budget." (Out of the church budget of approximately $11 million, the Washington office gets $30,000.)

Dr. Maddocks makes the argument one usually hears from the Washington-based church bureaucrats who contend they are not lobbyists in either the classical or legal sense. They come down particularly hard on the point that they are not motivated by self-interest. "The usual definition of a lobbyist is one who is paid by a group, such as business or labor, to urge passage of legislation favorable to and oppose legislation harmful to his employer," Dr. Maddocks said. "The church, however, is not interested in legislation which serves the interest of the institutional church."

On the other hand, Dr. Maddocks does believe that it is the role of the church to pass resolutions and then act on them to influence public policy. "Church resolutions, pronouncements, statements, and so on primarily serve three purposes," he said. "First, they force church leaders to face the truth that the Christian Gospel is related to the social, economic, and political affairs of man as well as his spiritual needs.

"The second purpose church resolutions serve is to promote within our congregations concern and discussion on the major issues of our day.

"The third purpose is to provide the basis for bringing the

influence of the church to bear on those in positions of political or economic power. If the church is to play a significant role as an agent for desirable change, it must act upon those who make public policy.

"The fact is," Dr. Maddocks concluded, "that in our highly pluralistic society, the voice of the church is only one among many heard by the makers of public policy, and at this stage it is merely to be hoped that that voice is heard at all and heeded even occasionally."

The National Council of Churches

James Hamilton, the genial attorney who heads the NCC office in Washington, believes his activity in behalf of civil rights in 1963-64 rewrote the answer to the central question of what is the proper role of the church on Capitol Hill.

"It is the task of this office to try to find ways to see that NCC policy has its day and that we have a hearing," he says. "We want to make an impact and not just pass resolutions and file them. We speak to specific situations. We flag a situation when it gets to the point where we ought to be feeding in our policy," he continued. "We watch committees, track hearings, help make arrangements for witnesses, answer inquiries from the Hill and make representations as needed."

In the early 1950's the statement of purpose of the NCC's Washington office contained these words: "The Washington office as such is not to engage in efforts to influence legislation." But that admonition was deleted after Hamilton served as key liaison man and full-time lobbyist in behalf of the Civil Rights Bill of 1964.

"I'm not personally afraid of the word 'lobby' but it is a word that might be easily misunderstood," Hamilton said, reclining in his thick-cushioned, black chair behind an L-shaped modern desk in the Methodist Building. "People read about the negative side of lobbying. We tend to speak more often of performing liaison or being a legislative representative of the church. Anybody familiar with this city and the facts knows you are lobbying," said the blunt bureaucrat.

"Most people have a low opinion of politics," he added. "By and large the vast majority of people on the Hill are very honorable, hardworking people who want to do what is right and moral. But they get into situations where they have to compromise and they have to make judgments.

"We have to do more than simply sit in an ivory tower and say this is moral and that is immoral. We have a responsibility to get in and help them with the decision they are having to make."

Hamilton says the church bureaucrat should not render moral judgment on the actions of a legislator. "It brings less conflict," he says, "when you recognize these people are in this kind of concrete situation. We don't render judgments and say you have to repair to this standard or else you are immoral. We don't do that. But it seems to me you are placing yourself in that position if all you do is make a moral pronouncement and then sit back."

Hamilton came to Washington on a patronage job in the early 1950's to work for Congressman Carson Hooven of Iowa — Hamilton's home state. He enrolled in George Washington Law School, graduated in 1956, and went to work in legal affairs for the Methodist General Board of Christian Social Concerns. "I was with the board for about three years, and I saw the potential of what the church ought to be doing in this area," Hamilton says. "Then I was given the opportunity to move into the NCC office." He was drafted by the NCC to work full time on civil rights. That job finished, Hamilton succeeded Dr. Vernon Ferwerda as director of the Washington office.

How is the NCC structured?

The Council has a General Assembly of 1500 persons composed of those selected by the groups that hold the ultimate sovereignty, the governing bodies of the member churches. And the Assembly can only elect those nominated by their own communions to the General Board, which consists of 250 persons. The Assembly meets only once every three years. Most of its powers are exercised by the General Board, which meets three or four times a year. Operating funds for the NCC are provided by boards and agencies of member churches, most of which operate virtually as free agents within their own churches.

As NCC officials are quick to point out, the organization is not a "superchurch." The only theological requirement is that all communions of the Council confess Jesus Christ as Divine Lord and Savior. The Council has no authority or administrative control over its members. Any member communion may register dissent or abstain from action if it so desires.

But the NCC usually reflects the position of member churches in its policies. A policy statement can be made only by the General Assembly or the General Board, and furthermore, the NCC seldom comes out with a pronouncement before several of its member communions have publicly pronounced a similar point of view.

The NCC's rationale for making statements in controversial areas is contained in a 1958 resolution which states that Christian churches and their councils

> not only have the right but also the duty to study and comment upon issues, no matter how controversial, in the realm of politics, economics and social affairs, in view of their common faith in Jesus Christ as Lord and Savior. For all matters of concern for human beings are matters of concern for the churches and to the churches' Lord.

An NCC pamphlet declares that policy statements are for the purpose of "influencing public opinion." And that is where the cherubic-faced Jim Hamilton in Washington comes in.

Hamilton, who at one time considered going into the ministry, knows he could make more money practicing law back in Iowa. "I don't feel abused," he says. "What I see here is more important to me than searching titles or drafting wills." He then picked up the telephone to answer the eight pink "call-back" slips that had accumulated on his secretary's desk during the interview. Life may be more hectic in Washington than in Iowa, but Hamilton is a man who likes his work.

The United Presbyterian Church U.S.A.

The United Presbyterian Church, U.S.A., began to double the strength of its Washington office in 1963 at the height of the civil rights struggle. Mrs. Helen Lineweaver had served as the church's Washington "listening post" since 1949. And the church's headquarters in Philadelphia sent H. B. Sissel to assist in the massive ecumenical assault to pass the Civil Rights Bill. (Mr. Sissel also testified for the Presbyterians at the hearings on the Elementary and Secondary Education Act of 1965.) He remained in Washington as the Secretary for National Affairs.

Mrs. Lineweaver described her role as keeping the church's Philadelphia office informed on issues being considered by Congress and administered by government agencies. "The Washington staff does not testify on issues," she said. "We would relay our information to Philadelphia and then if they wanted someone to come out they could." Her messages to Philadelphia were appropriately titled "Alerts." The Presbyterians' burgeoning interest in political, social, and economic issues was reflected in the appointment of a Secretary for International Affairs in 1967.

"Our denomination is not lobbying under the act as presently constituted," Mrs. Lineweaver assured me. "This doesn't mean we are not trying to bring pressure to bear on issues on which the church has spoken.

"We also have to anticipate what is coming up on the Hill so the church can speak," she said, referring to the church bureaucrat's practice of drawing up resolutions he wants his church governing body to adopt so he can follow through on them in Washington.

Mrs. Lineweaver gave an example how a church secretary may exert influence without lobbying. "Say a Congressman in the 12th District of Massachusetts is on the fence on an issue. I would call Philadelphia and ask if we have any Church and Society man in the 12th District who could give the Congressman a nudge," she said.

The Presbyterian Washington staff works closely with non-governmental organizations such as the Point Four Information Committee, the National Civil Liberties Clearing House, and the Leadership Conference on Civil Rights.

Mrs. Lineweaver admitted that Washington-based church officials have a tendency to get out of touch with their constituents. "The church bureaucrats have taken positions where they are not speaking for the churches," she said. "I think we could be at a turning point on the matter of lobbying." She said church lobbying may intensify or diminish — depending on whether the bureaucrats' or the more conservative church members' views prevail.

Albert Saunders, who works in an adjoining office, left his job as director of research and publications for the National Council of Churches in Washington to become Secretary for National Affairs succeeding Mr. Sissel in 1966. As the Presbyterian office is just down the hall from the NCC office, Saunders could make the change in jobs without even leaving the Methodist Building.

"Our function is primarily educative — but there may be a fine distinction between that and lobbying," Saunders explained. "Quite frankly, I don't consider myself a lobbyist. We do brush it closely, however."

"We do not go out of our way to button-hole Congressmen," he said. "We do not like to place a Congressman in any form of obligation. I don't want him to feel because he is a Presbyterian he owes us something." A slow smile appeared over Saunders' face. "However," he continued, "a Congressman who *happens* to be a Presbyterian and who *happens* to be involved, or who is an authority on a certain subject, we would contact him."

Saunders follows the operating principle of the church lobbyist to involve as many other communions as possible when dealing with an issue. "I prefer to work with other groups rather than having my own denomination going it alone," he said. "I do forsee seeking group support for Model Cities, firearms control, foreign aid, migrant labor, and assisting Indians." He sounded as if he were reading a church lobbyist checklist — and in a real sense he was. The issues he mentioned received top priority from activists during the remaining years of the 1960 decade.

The Presbyterian secretary relies heavily on written communications to educate his constituents — principally the *Washington Forecast,* mailed to all 193 presbyteries in the country on a regular basis; the *Washington Special Report,* issued intermittently as the title suggests; and the *Washington Advisory Memo* and *Washington Alert,* sent to those the church secretary thinks should be "advised" or "alerted."

The General Assembly of the United Presbyterian Church, U.S.A. (composed of an equal number of ministers and elders, representing the churches through all presbyteries), makes pronouncements on current public issues. The resolutions are then referred to churches and church members for study and action.

As to the force of the pronouncements, the 1958 General Assembly declared:

> That God alone is Lord of conscience; that the social deliverances of the General Assembly do not have the force of church law and do not bind the freedom of decision and action of any member or judicatory of the church; that they are intended rather to point the way to faithful response to God's action in the event of our times; that they cannot therefore be ignored or lightly dismissed but must be taken seriously as guides to Christian action....

The Washington office staff obviously take the pronouncements seriously and "Christian action" is the name of the game for the church lobbyist.

The Church of the Brethren

John H. Eberly, Washington representative for the Church of the Brethren, is a part-time church agent who divides his time between Washington and pastoring a small church in Carroll County, Maryland, sixty miles from the Capital. Eberly quietly explained the function of his office.

"I am not here because I think I can influence government," he began, modestly. "I am here primarily to raise the understanding of the people back home. Then as they become informed, they will become influential." (Somehow the indirect approach to influencing government coming from Eberly sounded more convincing than it did coming from some of his more brash counterparts in other communions.)

The Church of the Brethren, one of the nation's "peace churches," consists of about 200,000 members — more than half of whom live in Pennsylvania.

The church opened its Washington office in 1962.

"We were a bit isolated from the policy-making people of the world," Eberly said, "until we came to Washington; then we got a little more daring."

He emphasized that the Brethren pacifistic position is not a negative one. "We are not just against war," he said. "We are in favor of building a society in which wars will be less and less likely to happen. During World War II we decided we ought to do something constructive in lieu of serving in the military."

The church set up its Brethren Service Center in New Windsor, Md. Young men reported for basic training in welfare and social service work in much the same manner as other young men were sent to military basic training centers. (Actually, only about 10 per cent of the church's young men register as conscientious objectors.) The men worked for $10 or $15 a month in hospitals and as welfare workers in various communities. Today, young Brethren who object to serving in the military have volunteered to go to Vietnam to work in that war-scarred land.

The founders of the Brethren church came to this country before the Revolutionary War to escape German militarism. "We were all right until the Revolutionary War broke out," Eberly stated. "Then we hid our churches and kept the German language. For 100 years we were withdrawn from society and went to the extremes in isolationism."

The road to involvement in society was paved by education. (The church now has six colleges.) It was more an evolutionary process, however, than a revolutionary one. "Civil rights shoved the churches into political action as never before," Eberly said. "The Brethren had never been as active as some communions in civil rights. We were members of the Leadership Conference, however."

Eberly reflects the solid conservatism of his church.

"We have a history of conservatism which says 'If I work hard, I will earn a good living, and if other people will do the same, they will make a good living,' " he noted. "We're against poverty — but suspicious of the rich," he added, somewhat ambivalently. "Traditionally, we are Republicans. We're not too critical of government — except as Republicans."

The very fact he admitted he was a Republican made Eberly unusual. A Republican church lobbyist in the liberal climate of 1967 was as rare as a tuxedo at an LBJ cookout.

The National Association of Evangelicals

Although there has been much public concern over the impact of the religious and theological right wing, none of the religious groups identified with this viewpoint had Washington offices in 1967. The National Association of Evangelicals (NAE) Office of Public Affairs was the closest thing to a conservative voice. NAE lobbying was minimal during most of the 1960's; but in April of 1969, Dr. Clyde W. Taylor, NAE general director, urged conservatives to try their hand at influencing legislation.

"Some of the sins of our nation apparently can only be remedied at the political and legislative level," Dr. Taylor, who heads up the NAE Office of Public Affairs, told 1200 conservative church leaders gathered in Cincinnati for NAE's 27th annual convention. "Washington needs to hear more voices reflecting Christian convictions and telling Congressmen and Senators their concern over current issues." Churches that expect to have a "vital influence," the former-missionary-turned-bureaucrat said, will be "concerned over community relations, race problems, the welfare of minorities, especially the poor." It sounded like a call to social involvement, with the implication that political activism was not all bad.

Dr. Taylor told the convention he had taken part in recent Congressional tax hearings, testifying on those aspects involving the church. He also said the NAE Washington office had again opposed the appointment of a political envoy to the Vatican — a traditional target that conservatives and separatists zero in on with the changing of Administrations.

The delegates at the convention passed a resolution at Dr. Taylor's behest commending the "several branches of the Federal government which have given generously of both personnel and facilities to make possible the annual seminars on 'Christian Responsibility in Government' conducted by NAE for pastors and laymen." The NAE seminars evoke parallels with the United Methodist-sponsored seminars, although one has the impression the NAE is more sympathetic with the aims and goals of federal agencies than are the liberal churchmen.

Floyd Robertson, a retired Naval officer (Lt. Cmdr.) and an assistant to Dr. Taylor, told why the NAE staff did not register as lobbyists. "Our involvement in government affairs pertains only to those things which directly affect the function of the church and its activities — missions, chaplains, taxes, education, and freedom of speech as it pertains to radio and jail ministries," he said. "Our basis for polity is the Bible. Our basic authority is the Word of God. We believe that separation of church and state is taught in the Word of God." All NAE members must subscribe to a Statement of Faith which requires belief in the "Bible as the inspired, the only infallible, authoritative word of God" and a commitment to a well-defined category of fundamental Christian doctrine.

"The Bible teaches man's responsibility to God and government," he continued. "Only when the state infringes on a citizen's responsibility to God does a citizen have the right to defy the state.

"Most of our guidance begins with resolutions adopted by the plenary body which meets once a year at the annual convention," Robertson explained. "Then there is a Board of Administration with about 120 persons on it. The Executive Committee (12 persons) interprets policy and the Washington staff implements it."

Robertson continued: "We will not hesitate to give information about passed legislation and will encourage the introduction of legislation which we feel to be of particular interest to the church as a whole or to individuals as citizens." He said the information might include a suggestion they "write or contact a Congressman some way.

"The trend in the church [meaning the liberal wing, of course] is toward infringing on government," Mr. Robertson commented. "The churches do have a lot of weight that can be exercised. The church performing its proper role inevitably builds a tremendous potential for public influence, but when it exercises that potential through political channels it dissipates its strength. There is a point of diminishing returns. People very quickly begin to resent the church lobbyist and become anti-clerical in attitude.

"We don't think the church has the competence nor is it the proper role of the church to engage in political activities," Mr. Robertson said.

The NAE assistant director then revealed that the organization does have an intimate association with the national government. "We have a very close and pleasant relationship with the State Department," Mr. Robertson said. "We exchange confidential information and we attend seminars and backgrounders sponsored by the State Department. We may get calls from our contact in the State Department seeking information from a missionary back from the Congo who may know more about the situation than the government people," Mr. Robertson said with understandable pride. On the other hand, he continued, "The deputy assistant secretary of public affairs of the State Department sent over the other day legislation that would afford second-generation missionaries the same privileges for immigrations as extended to government employees."

The NAE claims a membership of about 2.5 million, but it boasts that it serves 10 million persons in forty small denominations. Organized in 1943, the NAE describes its role in public affairs as keeping "the churches informed of the actions of various branches of government and represents evangelicals to the government on matters of particular interest to conservative Christians. . . ."

The Lutheran Council

The Lutheran Council in the U.S.A., which succeeded the former National Lutheran Council in January 1, 1967, operates out of a converted mansion-apartment building at 2633 16th Street, N.W., far removed from the "Religious Row" of church lobbyists in and around the Methodist Building. The Public Relations Division serves as the educational-lobbying arm of the Council. Other agencies in the same building with interests in government operations include the Bureau of Service Military Personnel, the Chaplaincy Service Welfare Division, the National Lutheran Educational Conference and the Lutheran Service Commission.

The Lutheran Council brings together four Lutheran Churches — the Lutheran Church in America, the Lutheran Church — Missouri Synod, the American Lutheran Church, and the Synod of

Evangelical Lutheran Churches — and 96 per cent of America's Lutheran membership.

One of the stated objectives of the Council is this:

> To represent the interests of the Council, and the interests of a participating body so requesting, in matters which require common action before the American public, the national government and state governments, organized bodies and agencies outside the Lutheran Church.

The Division of Public Relations "has the responsibility of supplying the public with information concerning the faith and life of the Lutheran Church, and of publicizing the work of the Council. Through the Office of Public Affairs the division serves as liaison between the Council and governmental agencies."

Dr. Robert E. Van Deusen served a parish for ten years and was pastor to Lutheran military personnel at a service center for four years before being named director of the public relations office. Dr. Van Deusen received his master's degree in psychology from Syracuse University and was only a dissertation away from a Ph.D., at American University in 1967. His field was international relations.

"Our job here is information and interpretation, and not lobbying," he said. "This may not necessarily always be true. I think the church is going to take another look at the lobbying concept. The bugaboo may be bigger than its shadow. We must rethink our social responsibility."

Dr. Van Deusen explained that he works on a person-to-person basis with legislators. "We call up offices and talk issues with them," he said. "We are not trying to exert pressure but to take a look at issues. But, where the Council or a church body has passed a resolution . . . we feel free to pass it along to the legislators and testify before Congress. This is merely accepting an invitation from Congress to share a viewpoint," he said, giving a new definition to lobbying.

"I seldom do any testifying," Dr. Van Deusen added. "It is usually a man from our headquarters office in New York — and that not more than three or four times a year.

"We keep channels of communication open with government administrative agencies. Church leaders had a conference with State Department officials just yesterday. Dean Rusk called them in to talk foreign policy.

"We do not contact Lutheran Congressmen for the purpose of promoting select pieces of legislation," Dr. Van Deusen stated.

"We do try to keep in contact with them as people — we have a pastoral interest. And this often leads to a meeting where I learn more than they," he said, with a wide grin.

Dr. Van Deusen believes that there has been a dramatic shift in the role of the church in public affairs during the twenty-two years he has been in Washington. "Frankly, it was an experiment for the major denominations twenty years ago," he said. "We did it on tiptoes — except for the Quakers. I'm supposed to keep in touch with all of government, not just legislation, whereas the Friends are primarily interested in legislation."

"Most political decisions have some moral aspects and we shouldn't shy away from them because there are political implications," Dr. Van Deusen declared. "If you do, you leave a vacuum to be filled by amoralists. But the church is wise to major in issues rather than persons or parties."

The Lutheran official emphasized that the church view should never exceed the facts and that bureaucrats can never claim to represent the viewpoint of all the members of the church. Dr. Van Deusen mails newsletters to church officials and sends packets to various churches in the Council to be distributed to the social action and education leaders. "I get letters back sometimes from unhappy church members," he says. "The typical letter says 'You're not speaking for me, boy.'" He chuckled. "We are not attempting to speak for them." Dr. Van Deusen does admit, however, that the church has not "done as well as it might in filling the communication gap with its people.

"There are areas where church and state can justifiably cooperate," Dr. Van Deusen believes. "There is quite a difference of opinion among our members. The mood now is how far one should go — where to draw the line."

To help "draw the line," the Executive Board of the United Lutheran Church in America authorized the Board of Social Missions to appoint a commission to undertake a study on church and state relations in a pluralistic society. It released a forty-seven-page booklet called "Church and State: A Lutheran Perspective in 1963." It is a balanced, incisive, and scholarly document.

The commission, tracing the historical relations of church and state in this country, concluded that

> neither a state-controlled church nor a church-controlled state should be advocated by American Christians. . . . The biblical view of the sacredness of secular life leads us to reject this extreme position of an absolute separation of church and state. We dare not

forget that the same God is Lord of the nations as well as Head
of the church. By clearly distinguishing God's law of creation from
his gospel of redemption, the Reformers found a way by which
church and state could interact without being united and yet remain distinct without being divorced.

It was on this foundation that the Lutheran scholars set forth
their formula of "institutional separation and functional interaction of church and state in the U.S. and Canada."

The institutional function of the church was described as
follows:

> This one, holy, catholic and apostolic church manifests itself in
> the world through outward communities of organized Christian
> believers. The church militant is both a divine organism related
> to Christ and a human organization related to the state. As an
> ecclesiastical institution, its distinctive mission is to proclaim the
> Word of God in preaching and sacraments, worship and evange-
> lism, Christian education and social ministry.

> The purpose of the state is to establish good order, peace and
> justice in a sinful world. In other words, its might must be enlisted
> in the service of right. But Christians should not expect love to
> replace justice in the operation of government. . . . While persons
> can be transformed by the gospel, institutions can only be reformed
> by the law. We can "Christianize" politicians and statesmen but
> not politics and the state. They are ordained of God to remain
> secular. Hence, not faith and love but reason and justice are
> normative for the political realm. At the same time, faith can
> illumine reason and love can enlighten justice whenever Christian
> citizens meet their civil responsibilities.

The church relates to the state in a least five different ways, the
Lutheran study states:

> (1) By offering intercessory prayer in its behalf.
> (2) By encouraging responsible citizenship and government ser-
> vice.
> (3) By holding it accountable to the sovereign law of God.
> (4) By contributing to the civil consensus which supports it.
> (5) By championing the human and civil rights of all its citizens.

"The ethical and technical alternative in a given situation
may at times be clear enough to justify a definite stand on a
specific policy of the government in relation to a domestic or
international issue," the authors assert.

"The church strives," the study states,

> to help create a moral and legal climate of opinion in which solu-

tions to vexing political problems can take place more easily. In an age of corporate decision-making, the public witness of official representatives of the church-at-large can be particularly important in expressing the ethical judgments of the Christian community.

With the general principles outlined in the study, most could agree. The tension comes in where the "official representative of the church-at-large" fails to reflect in practice the consensus of the church-at-large and substitutes instead his own personal judgment. Unless the church bureaucrat maintains close communion with his constituents, he is merely a voice in the Washington wilderness speaking for, and to, himself.

The Reform Jews

"If there is no other word — and we do try to influence Congress — then we are lobbyists," said Rabbi Richard G. Hirsch, the director of Reform Judaism's Social Action Center at 2037 Massachusetts Avenue. The Center serves as a focal point for a variety of groups intent on gaining the attention of legislators through the ancient art of political arm-twisting. The Citizens Crusade Against Poverty, headed by UAW President Walter Reuther, the National Committee on Fair Representation, the National Council on Agricultural Life and Labor, and the United Negro College Fund are all housed in the Action Center.

"I don't make it my business to walk the halls of Congress," the rabbi continued. "That's too undignified and lacks subtlety. I do call and ask staff members of Congressmen if their man is going to co-sponsor a certain bill."

Rabbi Hirsch gave an example of how small favors can enhance one's rapport with the national legislators. "I helped a Senator's aide write a speech the Senator is going to give to a Jewish group," he said. "That helps me establish a closer relationship with the Senator's office."

The articulate rabbi limits his appearances before committees to keep from wearing out his welcome. "The title 'rabbi' can get you into many places and I don't want to demean that title," he said. "I find that anytime I want to get in contact with anyone, I can use that title as a wedge to get in. Whether it is legitimate or not is another question. I try to be responsible. I know whenever I do anything I cannot separate my person from my position."

Rabbi Hirsch wears two yamulkas — he represents both the Union of American Hebrew Congregations and the Central Conference of American Rabbis. The UAHC is the overall agency for all Reform Jewish Congregations and the Central Conference is the umbrella organization for rabbis. (He also was lay secretary of the Citizens Crusade Against Poverty in 1967.)

He has two full-time staff assistants, two office girls, and a $40,000 operating budget.

Rabbi Hirsch is an eloquent exponent of religious lobbying.

"There is a distinction between church and state and separation of church and society," he explained, often pounding his desk for emphasis. "Religion is a way of looking at life — not a separate compartment of it. Religion's role is to make better human beings by making a better society. You affect society by collective action through the source of power. Washington is the center of power. Religious groups, however, have to be realistic about their potential."

Rabbi Hirsch believes that religious groups by themselves could never muster enough political clout to achieve a specific legislative objective. He endorses the basic premise of most religious lobbyists that in coalition there is strength. And this means teaming up with nongovernmental agencies or so-called secular organizations.

Rabbi Hirsch takes his direction from a six-man advisory Committee of the Commission on Social Action for Reform Judaism. The committee consists of three laymen and three rabbis.

"When I decide I want to testify on an issue, I will send them a resolution covering the subject," Rabbi Hirsch stated. "I function within the resolution they pass. We don't take any action if we don't have a resolution for it."

The rabbi admits that the religious lobbyist at times appears to be taking a partisan position in supporting a specific issue. "I have never yet been able to find a satisfactory definition," he said, with a note of weariness, "of the difference between a generality and a specific.

"Let's say you have a resolution from your governing body supporting civil rights. But the civil rights bill is 25 pages long.

"Then the bill itself changes as it is considered by the House and the Senate.

"Then it comes time for a vote. People are going to ask you if you are in favor of the bill as it now stands. And you are going to have to make a decision — and that in itself becomes the utmost in specificity."

While most religious lobbyists found themselves allied with the Kennedy-Johnson Administrations in the decade of the

Sixties, Rabbi Hirsch warned that "religious groups should never become subservient to government.

"I would prefer that religious institutions not become welfare agents," he said. "I don't conceive the servant church as the primary role. If society wants to dispense a certain benefit, then there ought to be public institutions to do this and not the church or we lose our prophetic role. We should give society the vision but we should not become society's agents."

Rabbi Hirsch agrees that the religious lobbyist reaches his peak of power when he can transmute a political issue into a moral issue. "Religion adds its own unique dimension — the power of morality," he said.

It's the kind of power Rabbi Hirsch wields well.

The Unitarian Universalists

Robert Jones, executive secretary of the Washington office of the Department of Social Responsibility for the liberal Unitarian Universalist denomination, sat at his desk in a rather dowdy office in the three-story building owned by the Friends Committee on National Legislation. He was talking over the telephone to a friend at the Leadership Conference on Civil Rights who was trying to enlist Jones to serve on an inter-faith committee to help a school integrate its classes.

"I'll do what I can, but this week I'm on foreign policy," Jones said, brushing his hand over his thin, short hair.

Jones has headed the UU Washington office since its inception in 1964. "We are here to bring pressure to bear on the Federal government," he explained bluntly. "This applies to both the executive and legislative branch. We do lobby but we are not registered. We registered once under the old name of the Unitarian Fellowship for Social Justice. Then we became a department of the united church and our attorney advised against it.

"Frankly," Jones laughed, "I don't think he approved of our lobbying. We may register again. But I had a hard time registering in the first place. When I went over to the clerks' offices of the House and Senate, they could have cared less."

Unitarian and Universalist churches and associated organizations have long been involved in trying to change society. It was after the merger of the Unitarian and Universalist denomination that the Department of Social Responsibility was founded.

A denominational pamphlet states that the director of the Washington office is to "work closely with members of Congress, the Administration, the Washington press and diplomatic corps, and nongovernmental agencies located in Washington. The action of the Office," it continues, "is based on the accumulated resolution approved by the general assemblies of the association and its predecessors, although it furnishes information on a wider range of subjects."

Jones writes a one-page newsletter called *Window on Washington*, a part of a monthly packet of information mailed to UU groups from the Boston headquarters. "The packet demands a month's lead time and that makes it rough to keep current," Jones said, pointing up the problem of the church lobbyist trying to stay abreast of fast-breaking issues.

"We follow a few select issues," he said. "I will get a witness to testify before the appropriate committee. I will follow up the bill in committee and try to get letters to committee members stating our position.

"I will send carbons of the letters to ministers in the districts of the Congressmen suggesting the ministers to write.

"When the bill reaches the floor, I follow the same process."

Jones candidly admits that he both makes and executes policy. "I prepare statements and they [the general assemblies] adopt them," he laughs. "Staff always has to stimulate."

But Jones doubts if the UU Washington office has made a broad impact on either its constituents or government. "We don't have enough people to scare office holders at the polls," he said, "and we don't have large financial resources. [Jones operates on a shoestring budget of only $17,400, and both his salary and that of his secretary come out of that figure.] We can't command our people because our church operates under the congregational policy. We can only recommend social action.

"I don't think the average person in the pew knows we exist," he said with refreshing honesty. "I meet Unitarians all the time who never even heard of our office.

"And it's been very difficult in the atmosphere of the Great Society to get government officials to recognize there is a church-state problem."

The U.S. Catholic Conference

Undoubtedly, the U. S. Catholic Conference is the most formidable religious agency in Washington. It is, in effect, the closest thing to a central office for the Roman Catholic Church in the

United States. Officially, the Conference serves as the administrative arm of the National Conference of Bishops.

The Catholic Church is no stranger to power politics. Its long
history of political involvement gives the church invaluable
expertise in juxtaposing the spiritual with the temporal.

The Catholic bishops in America, however, did not organize
on a national level until World War I, when they formed the
National Catholic War Council. Up to that time, the American
bishops had met only twice as a collective unity in the entire
128-year history of the nation.

At the request of Pope Benedict XV, the War Council, formed
to "promote the spiritual and material welfare of the United
States troops at home and abroad," was continued, but the organization's name was changed to the National Catholic Welfare
Council. In 1923, the name was altered again by substituting
"conference" for "council" so as not to imply any legislative
power. The NCWC soon became well established and well known.

In November of 1966, the U. S. bishops met to revise their
organization in the light of the Vatican Council decrees. The
Council had ordered each nation to form its own national episcopal conference as part of a worldwide decentralization program.
Some powers were shifted from Rome to the episcopal conferences
as a result of the updating process.

The U. S. bishops formed themselves into the National Conference of Catholic Bishops, an ecclesiastical unit concerned with
spiritual matters. The NCWC was renamed the U. S. Catholic
Conference and incorporated under the laws of the District of
Columbia as a civil agency concerned with the temporal matters
confronting the church.

The Catholic Conference, sometimes referred to as the church's
"home office," is organized into eight departments:

(1) The Education Department oversees the Catholic school
system — the largest privately maintained school system in the
world.

(2) The Immigration Department serves as both an aid agency
and clearing house for Catholic immigrants. The department was
directly involved in the resettlement of thousands of Cuban
refugees during the 1960's.

(3) The Lay Organization Department includes the National
Council of Catholic Men, the National Council of Catholic
Women, and the National Council of Catholic Churches. The
department develops programs and supplies information to

Catholic laymen and -women on the parish and diocesan levels.

(4) The Legal Department, as has already been pointed out, concerns itself with legislative and judicial developments relating to the interests of the church. It is the actual lobbying arm of the church.

(5) The Press Department operates the National Catholic News Service. The agency services most of the English-language Catholic newspapers and periodicals in the United States and Canada and in many countries around the world.

(6) The Social Action Department "seeks to inculcate the Christian ideal in our rapidly changing society." It deals with interracial justice, social work, hospitals, international relations, and family life (for which there is a separate bureau).

(7) The Youth Department serves millions of American Catholic young people as well as the professional and volunteer adults working with them in approved Catholic youth groups.

(8) The Executive Department, as the name implies, supervises and coordinates the activities of all the other departments. Bishop Paul F. Tanner, general secretary of the U. S. Catholic Conference, heads the Executive Department.

Within the Executive Department there is a further maze of bureaucracies. These include the Bureau of Information, which serves the Catholic Church in the United States as an information and public relations agency on the national level; the Foreign Visitors' Office, which assists and orients foreign visitors to the United States; the Latin American Bureau, through which the U. S. bishops cooperate with and assist the Catholic Church in Latin America; and the Office for United Nations Affairs, which has an office near the United Nations and represents Catholic interests in UN affairs.

Other areas coming under the scope of the USCC are the Boy Scouts, rural life, charities, prison chaplains, Newman Clubs, the Pope's Peace Plan — the list is almost endless.

Bishop Paul Francis Tanner has the responsibility of overseeing the total operation and executing national Catholic policy as determined by the body of bishops. Bishop Tanner directed the Youth Department from 1941 to 1945, was assistant general secretary of NCWC from 1945 to 1958, and has been general secretary of the organization since 1958.

"The NCWC has grown like Topsy," Bishop Tanner explained. "And so has the Federal government. Now all social welfare programs are federally financed. Thirty years ago, a bishop could have his own social welfare program in his own diocese. But today, the local bishop is impotent to act against this colossus of a Federal government."

Bishop Tanner said that the rapid growth of the Federal government forced the U. S. bishops to act as a unit. "This approach made NCWC move from a very loose confederacy to an active, working system. Now since Vatican II, we have certain juridical power by a two-thirds vote of the bishops."

The Catholic Conference, the bishop continued, has twenty-six subdivisions "some of whom have relationships with government but most do not. We are trying to toss off as many agencies as possible not dealing with government. We are not the national headquarters of the American Catholic Church by any means," he insisted. "The Catholic Relief program, for instance, has its office in New York and immigration offices are scattered."

On the one hand, the bishop stated that "churches in the U. S. should not have political blocs. We have 50 million Catholics," he observed. "It would be ridiculous to say we can deliver all those votes." But on the other hand, commenting on the 1965 Elementary and Secondary Education Act, he remarked: "There were enough Catholics in the legislature in 1965 who said, 'If you're going to get your federal aid bill passed, we are going to get our 15 per cent' — so they [the Administration] bought it."

The bishop quickly added, "Catholics are entitled to a certain share, as the schools do more than teach religion. They also teach the other subjects required by the state."

He summed up his philosophy of church-state relations in this way: "In a given situation, you ought to make the views of the church clear to the legislators. The duty of the church is to attempt to define the principles that are involved and leave the implementation of those principles to the private citizens that perform the public service."

Profile of a Lobbyist: A Spokesman for the Poor

Father James L. Vizzard is a man of all seasons for all men who are poor, powerless, and in distress. A pioneer lobbyist motivated by love, he opposed the exploitation of migrant workers, the pollution of streams, and the abuse of soil long before those issues became popular causes.

The frail-looking Jesuit director of the Washington office of the National Catholic Rural Life Conference was a sick man spending long periods in the hospital when I first met him in the spring of 1967. His easy-going manner, his consuming concern for the poor, and his holy boldness in attacking controversial issues made him a man hard to forget and easy to like.

"I'm a lobbyist for justice," he told me in his small office at the U. S. Catholic Conference. "All I do is give a voice to the people who otherwise would be voiceless." His philosophy was simple: "If you love Christ, you love the poor."

Born and raised in San Francisco, Father Vizzard was shocked when he read John Steinbeck's *Grapes of Wrath*. He was appalled when he found a colony of "Oakies" in Prune Valley, only half a mile away from the University of Santa Clara where he was teaching English. He vowed then to try to right the wrongs being done to the wandering workers.

Because of poor health, including a bad back which required him to wear a brace, Father Vizzard never tried to get next to migrant workers by working with them in the sun-drenched grape fields. Instead he studied rural problems for a decade, came to Georgetown University, and began establishing friendships with legislators, labor leaders, and religious colleagues. He testified for the first time before a Senate committee in 1950, making the acquaintance of Senator Hubert Humphrey in the process. "He welcomed me to the long, long fight," he recalled.

In testimony before the Subcommittee on Migratory Labor of the Senate Labor and Public Welfare Committee, Father Vizzard spoke eloquently in behalf of the underpaid farm laborer:

> What right does a consumer have even to eat strawberries or tomatoes if the price of bringing them to the table is the most desperate of poverty?
>
> No group has the cards so stacked against them as the migratory farm workers. They receive the lowest wages in the American economy. They are unemployed on half of the days of the year. They are excluded from the protection of most of our welfare and labor legislation. For the most part they are not eligible for health and welfare services. They are human beings who are considered in a literal sense as a "commodity" to be bought at the lowest possible price.

That kind of talk made Father Vizzard politically influential but controversial. His consistent application of political pressure contributed toward the passage of the Migrant Medical Help Law, laws to provide more schooling for both adult farm laborers and their children, laws to reduce child labor on farms and to help provide migrants with better housing. One of Father Viz-zard's happiest moments came in 1964 when the Bracero Law was repealed. That law permitted Mexican labor to enter this coun-try and compete with domestic labor. The effect was to depress even further the wages of American migrants. Father Vizzard re-called with a broad smile how, after the law was repealed, a spokesman for the farm lobby stomped out of the Capitol, grum-bling: "The 'do-gooders' have put one over on us."

Like all effective lobbyists, Father Vizzard recognized that alliances give one political leverage. As chairman of the National Council on Agricultural Life and Labor, he headed a politically potent group made up of forty-two organizations from labor, farm, civic, social, and religious groups. He was the prime pusher of the National Campaign for Agricultural Democracy formed in February of 1967. The purpose of the organization is to lobby for legislation which will bring all agriculture workers in general and grape pickers in particular under the protective awn-ing of the National Labor Relations Act. Incidentally, the organ-ization typifies the interdenominational approach now so popular among lobbyists. The idea came from the head of a Jesuit, the organization is located in the Methodist Building, and the direc-tor is a United Church of Christ minister, the Rev. Eugene Boutillier.

Father Vizzard was quick to criticize his own church for what he considered unpardonable failures. While traveling with an interfaith group to Delano, California, to investigate a non-violent grape pickers' strike, he issued an independent state-ment citing Roman Catholic officials for being "frozen with fear" and "on trial" for not supporting the strikers. The Bishop of the Monterey-Fresno area accused Father Vizzard of "unadulter-ated disobedience, insubordination and a breach of office." Father Vizzard took the criticism in stride and continued working in behalf of the strikers.

In his small office on the third floor of the U. S. Catholic Con-ference building, the lanky priest recalled when he first came to Washington. "I came here in 1949 to study for my doctorate at Georgetown University," he said. "I began testifying before Congressional committees around 1950 or '51. The Friends [Quakers] were the only ones with a lobby then. The National Council of Churches did not have a man here. In fact there was a general Protestant-Jewish consensus that government was taboo. About the only reason any church body would have any relationship with the government was to defend its own special interest. The National Catholic Welfare Conference worked vigorously and long on war reparations for Catholic churches damaged during the Japanese invasion.

"But since 1955, there has been considerable growth in church representation and a significant change from so-called church interests to dedication to the common welfare. All of the other church representatives are personal friends of mine, and we constantly work on the same issues. There is no difference — not only in philosophy — but even in detail. We could have written each other's testimony in most cases."

Father Vizzard employed the old-fashioned, shoe-leather approach to lobbying, by visiting offices and making friends with the right people.

"This relationship is based on the understanding that I have no axe to grind and am not attempting to influence so-called church causes," he said, explaining how a lobbyist accumulates influence.

"After being around a while you get to know Senator X. You have lunch with him and talk to him over the telephone about the topics in which you are interested. But if he learns to like you, and trusts and respects you, he confides in you and you become an informed advisor to Senator X on a number of issues.

"As chairman of the policy committee of the Rural Life Conference, I am interested in food surpluses. This involves me in the food stamp program and that involves me in the Food for Peace project. This leads eventually to the whole foreign aid question. It's hard to know where to stop."

Father Vizzard learned early that a lobbyist's best weapon is grass-roots support. Once when testifying before a Congressional subcommittee on migrant labor, his position was questioned by Rep. Charles M. Teague of California.

"You say, Father Vizzard," asked Teague, "that you represent a broad Catholic view?" Father Vizzard said he did.

"Well," continued Teague, "about 25 per cent of my constituents are Catholics. I have not received one letter supporting your position. What do you say to that?"

Father Vizzard quickly confessed he had not done his job but promised: "I assure you it won't happen again." Upon returning to his office, the Jesuit priest started calling influential friends in Congressman Teague's district asking them to write letters and to telegram Teague. A few days later when he returned to testify,

Father Vizzard saw Congressman Teague looking out over a stack of letters.

"I see you did your job, Father," the Congressman grinned.

Well-written letters can change votes in Congress, Father Vizzard declared. He cited a dramatic example. For fifteen years Congress discussed a way of getting surplus crops into the stomachs of the poor but did nothing about it. The Catholic Rural Life Conference asked its members to join in a drive to get the Food Stamp Plan passed. The Council of Catholic Women in Rockford, Illinois, made it a project. When it appeared that the bill was beginning to show some life in Congress, Father Vizzard flashed the signal to the women in Rockford to begin writing their letters. Congresswoman Lenore Sullivan of St. Louis, chief sponsor of the bill in the House, succeeded in getting it through.

"The next morning she called and told me she never would have succeeded without all those letters," Father Vizzard said. "A thoughtful, sincere, polite letter can be more important than one's ballot."

Father Vizzard subscribed to the definition of lobbying given him by a veteran Jesuit priest many years ago. "When I first came to Washington, I asked this old priest where you draw the line on lobbying," he recalled. "He told me, 'The only distinction is whether your lobbying is successful or isn't.' I thought it was a good answer."

Father Vizzard coined the phrase "coalition of conscience and power" referring to the three-way alliances of churches, labor unions, and civil rights groups. "Those that possess the power cannot always be sure that their use of power is in the public interest and can be backed up by moral principle," he said. "Those that represent conscience, who have often felt they were prophets crying in the wilderness, need to have their convictions backed by power before they can have any impact on national legislation. Our biggest contribution, from a long-range standpoint, may be in helping to bring those two together."

CHAPTER XIV

Closing the Lobbying Gap

While some saw a lessening of tensions in 1968 and 1969 in our polarized society, the church activists took a different reading. The General Board of the National Council of Churches, meeting in San Diego, was convinced this nation was "in the midst of the most threatening domestic crisis of the last 100 years." And a special action program was initiated "to reorder, strengthen, accelerate and fully coordinate the resources of the churches and the NCC in the crucial struggle for justice in the nation."

The Special Order on the Crisis in the Nation declared that the "program is expected to continue as long as the crisis lasts." And in September of 1968, the General Board was given this report:

> The crisis facing this nation continues in all its gravity, intensity and threat of chaos. Since the number of riots has been greatly reduced this past summer, some people conclude the crisis is over. A deceptive calm offers a thin disguise for the explosive conditions within the nation. Blacks and whites carefully watch one another as fear, hostility and tensions mount higher and higher. The sale of every conceivable type of firearm to be stockpiled in city and suburb is increasing. The organization of gun clubs, vigilantes and para-military groups takes place in many suburban areas. Local governments incapable of finding funds for public welfare or education have no difficulty finding money to purchase the latest, most efficient, weaponry for their police force. A massive conservatism discourages even small appropriations for national welfare or OEO programs or prevents the adoption of a free food stamp program to feed the hungry. There is great reluctance to take up issues such as police brutality or violence as these are raised by the black community. For the foreseeable future liberal forces including the churches will continue under heavy attack from conservatives. The threats inherent in the campaign and November election illustrate this. A multitude of additional illus-

trations could be cited to underline further what should be obvious to all — the Crisis in the Nation is still with us. In view of this fact, the Special Order relating to the Crisis in the Nation should be continued.

Convinced that the Crisis in the Nation was unabated, the NCC board continued the Special Order.

The NCC machinery began tooling up immediately to deal with the crisis. A Communications Center was established in New York connecting the NCC headquarters with the Washington office, denominational offices, and seventeen regional offices, plus TWX linkage to nine regions. A phone recorder was installed at the NCC headquarters establishing an Information Bank of weekly reports from denominational and regional contacts not connected by TWX.

As time is of the essence in dealing with any kind of crisis, the NCC subscribed to Associated Press news service to gain a "valuable time advantage in responding to events." Apparently, the bureaucrats felt that relying on the daily paper was too time-consuming. A church paper *Approach* was sent out each week to 62,000 people with information pertaining to the Crisis in the Nation program.

The increased activity obviously placed heavy burdens of responsibility on the shoulders of the churches' Washington representatives. The Washington NCC office was strengthened with the addition of five persons supplied by the denominations. Responsibility for keeping close watch on legislation during the summer of 1968 was distributed. The Protestant church lobbyists gained a "new dimension of strength resulting from the close coordination and cooperation with Catholic and Jewish legislative committees which met with the Washington office on a weekly basis.

"The continuing crisis requires a massive long-term legislative program conducted through the Washington office," the NCC board was told in September of 1968. "There is no need to reiterate what has been said earlier about the conservative sweep bent on preventing the passage of more socially progressive legislation in the present or forthcoming session of Congress."

Unlike the Sixties when the lobbyists worked closely with liberal Administrations, the Seventies opened with a Republican Administration more intent on conserving the gains of the past than in introducing new legislation. And the NCC lobbyists saw the handwriting on the White House wall:

What is needed is not less but more strength in Washington to enable the denominations to mount a tide-turning legislative program. Staff and funds will be needed to allow for the development of grass-roots education and information regarding legislative issues. The churches cannot afford to ignore the urgent need for action in Washington; strong support for and expansion of the Washington office is imperative.

The strategy for 1969 called for initiating coalitions formed around special concerns:

Where individual denominations have particular interests or strengths for dealing with issues such as education, police-community problems, etc., they would be asked to serve as the nucleus around which the interests of all denominations might coalesce for program purposes.

The essential purpose of the program was stated boldly: "The Crisis in the Nation program has to do with the insistent and inescapable necessity for fundamental change in the structure and style of life in this nation."

Major concerns of 1969 were police and community problems, education, hunger, economic development and compliance with existing statutes on housing and employment.

The Washington office became the focal point around which much of the crisis program revolved. The NCC staff and constituent communions testified before Congressional committees. Communications were flashed across the TWX network. Action memos, phone calls, letters and personal visits were used to make contact with those "in the best position to really make an impact on the legislative process." NCC President Flemming wrote every member of Congress on several occasions. The church staff once again joined hands with nongovernmental agencies such as the Urban Coalition and the Leadership Conference on Civil Rights.

An Interreligious Legislative Conference in July of 1968 resulted in a two-day lobbying venture on behalf of the Kerner Report legislative recommendations and the legislative goals of the Poor People's Campaign. About 130 persons, drawn on an interreligious basis from fifteen selected states, spent the two days calling on their Congressmen and Senators following a briefing by the Washington staff. Acronyms are as profuse as cherry blossoms in the spring in Washington and WISC (the Washington Interreligious Council made up of staff members from various denominations and faiths) became familiar symbols in the ecumenical curia housed primarily in the Methodist Building.

The second Interreligious Legislative Assembly was held June 10-11, 1969. About 140 religious leaders of all three faiths from sixteen northeastern and midwestern states gathered in Washington under the auspices of WISC. The same format was followed as in the preceding assembly: the visitors were briefed by the Washington staff, then fanned out over the Capitol to talk with their Senators and Representatives. Welfare, the poverty program, arms control, housing and urban development, education, defense spending, hunger and civil rights made up the list of special concern.

The NCC Washington staff, reporting to the General Board meeting in Indianapolis in September of 1969, gave the following evaluation:

> This new style of action [that of the Interreligious Legislative Assembly], which is being refined and sharpened through experience, is planned to continue in the future with possible variations in format and substance according to the needs of the time. Two such assemblies are being planned in 1970 during the second session of the 91st Congress.

> IMPACT, an interreligious project to locate and organize grass-roots support in selected Congressional districts for legislation to meet the crisis in the nation, has moved forward during these months as its first full-time director, the Rev. Leon Riley, has begun work.

> High priority is now being placed by the Washington office on the further development of cooperative interreligious information gathering, planning, and action on national issues through the Washington Interreligious Staff Council.

> Central to this development is the functioning of some fifteen task forces on various issue areas through which the entire membership of WISC is kept informed of governmental developments related to these issues and enabled to plan concerted action on them where desirable and possible.

> These task forces, which came into being earlier this year, are an increasingly effective instrument for cooperative action in Washington, and the NCC Washington office bears the major responsibility for their direction and coordination.

For at least two decades, Quaker Raymond Wilson, dean of the religious lobbyists, has been lamenting that the churches have been doing about a tenth of what they should be doing in Washington. If indeed there has been a lobbying gap, the church bureaucrats seem bent on closing it in the Seventies.

*   *   *   *   *

There were storm warnings waving as the church lobbyists soared into the Seventies. A National Opinion Research Center poll taken in 1968 and released in August of 1969 showed that more than half of the American adults who knew of the NCC disapproved of church involvement in social and political issues. (The poll also revealed that among those who knew about NCC, 54.9 per cent had a favorable impression of what it was trying to do.) On the question, "In general, do you approve or disapprove of the churches becoming involved in social and political issues such as the urban crisis, Vietnam and civil rights?" 58.5 per cent said they did not while 36.7 per cent said they favored such involvement.

Interestingly, more Republicans and Independents knew and approved of the Council than Democrats, but Democrats were more likely to favor social action. This may help to partially explain why most church lobbying activity seems to have a Democratic tilt.

Among Protestants, more Episcopalians, Presbyterians, Lutherans and members of the United Church of Christ had heard of the Council than had Methodists and Baptists. The Methodists joined the former in being more favorably impressed with the NCC than the Baptists and the Disciples of Christ. Other Protestants were "most unfavorable," the poll found.

The NCC Establishment came under heavy fire from renewal radicalists at the 1969 General Assembly in Detroit. A group of white churchmen, called "Jonathan's Wake," demanded that NCC alter its priorities and devote its financial endowments to minority development. The group marched down the center aisles of cavernous Cobo Hall behind a flag-draped coffin bearing a sign reading "In Memoriam – NCC – 1950-1969." The NCC "body," however, refused to cooperate. It survived the assault of dissidents, proving the durability of church bureaucrats should never be underestimated.

Stephen Rose, editor-at-large of *Christianity and Crisis* magazine and a member of "Jonathan's Wake," made two astute criticisms of clerical activism in a lengthy article in the December 1, 1969 issue of the NCC magazine *Tempo*:

The first erroneous assumption is that the churches will attain relevance to the world only insofar as they engage in official commitment to specific courses of social action. In practice this quest for relevance has led to the clericalizing of social action, the suppressing of potential lay movements, the division between clergy and laity, and the failure to develop a strategy of ecumenical action in the world, particularly at the local level.

The second erroneous notion is that today's church is so conservative at its base that it is virtually unrenewable. Continued insistence on this belief within the denominational bureaucracies has helped to hasten the day of self-fulfilled prophecy. In practice, this insistence on local unrenewability has been used to defend existing denominational and conciliar establishments on the ground they are the only centers of avant-garde ministry within the church.

The bureaucrats showed signs they were beginning to get the message that a "general without armies" cannot win legislative battles. Admitting that the NCC has a communication problem, outgoing NCC President Arthur Flemming suggested: "It seems to me the conciliar movement has got to work at some kind of program which will make it possible for the NCC to communicate, at times, directly with the local churches."

There may be pragmatic reasons for attempting to establish grass-roots support. The NCC budget in 1970 was the lowest in five years.

The attempts by church activists to provide not only *direction* but *directives* to political society have helped to produce tension. (Church lobbyists have a tendency to write off all criticism as a vocational hazard.) Dr. Jeffrey K. Hadden, professor of sociology at Case Western Reserve University, wrote an important book in 1969 entitled *The Gathering Storm in the Churches: The Widening Gap Between Clergy and Laymen*. Dr. Hadden's research involving 7500 clergymen, together with a number of studies concerned primarily with laymen, shows that churches are entangled in a "web of crises" caused primarily by the action of clergymen in civil rights.

Dr. Hadden, who favors social involvement of clergymen, issued this warning:

> I do, however, have some serious reservations about some of the directions in which some of the new-breed clergy seem to be heading. It seems to me that a passion for specific issues has led many to pronouncement and involvement without paying adequate attention to the ethical and theological basis for their action.

Without at all implying that all the evidence must be in before one can engage in morally responsible or politically effective acts, I do believe that some clergy have been guilty of acting without having even the most elementary command of the issue.

If the church of Jesus Christ is to perform its unique role in the world, both the clergy and laity need to be hearing the same signals. Fundamental questions need to be resolved — or at least openly discussed.

Even conservatives concur that Christians have social and political responsibilities. They believe they should influence government, however, as citizens working through a political system. In an article in the September, 1968, issue of *Worldview* magazine, Quentin Quade, a political scientist at Marquette University, stated that the individual Christian should inject "what he takes to be some of the Gospel's implications into the politics of his nation or his world.

> He is, from one point of view, only another political actor pleading his special case at the bar of political opinion. But from another perspective, he may supremely and identifiably be a Christian: his motive (love), his method (convince rather than coerce), and his immediate objective (aid to the needy) may all reflect his interpretation of Christian commitment. . . . In these ways, the Church or religion may relate to politics, and relate crucially. But religion does not become politics, nor should it, if both are to maintain their integrity.

If the reader has detected a certain amount of cynicism throughout this book, he has not been misled. I believe that the church lobbyist, when he is speaking for a broad spectrum of the church (no one demands unanimity), has an important role to play. He should add a moral dimension to issues, however, rather than resorting to power politics. Church representatives in Washington have an unparalleled opportunity to use their moral authority and expertise in the Seventies for the betterment of all mankind. Suddenly in our technological society we find ourselves concerned about air and water — two basics we thought were inexhaustible. Smog is a threat to our cities. Our rivers are murky with pollutants from our industries. Conservation has become the business of everyone — not just of "nature nuts."

Our ecological problems lend themselves to ecumenical solution — indeed, those are the only solutions. The National Council of Churches in 1969 organized an action team to help churchmen assume responsibility on moral and technical aspects of environmental care. That group's importance will increase throughout this decade.

The Sixties saw a polarized society in America, split by racial prejudices, torn by conflicting attitudes toward Vietnam and wracked by riots and demonstrations. Now we're beginning to learn that if we are to live at all we will have to live together. Every man needs air and water to survive. Perhaps the commonality of these basic concerns will bring us together in the Seventies. The church lobbyist for the first time has the opportunity to speak for city dwellers and rural residents, the young and the old, the church and the unchurched. No one is going to criticize the church bureaucrat for lobbying for legislation to prevent our planet from being overcome by pollution.

The church lobbyist may be asked to play his most crucial role in the Seventies. Let us all hope he plays it well.

Index of Persons

Abernethy, Thomas, 24
Aronson, Arnold, 9
Ashbrook, John, 113

Bagby, Grover C., 250, 251
Baker, Donald, 61, 65, 82
Bell, Alphonze, 113
Bennett, John C., 206
Berger, Peter L., 207
Bernstein, Philip, 70, 71
Berry, Theodore, 69, 84
Biemiller, Andrew, 9, 22
Bilheimer, Robert, 237
Blake, Eugene Carson, 6, 7, 11, 34
Boone, Richard, 70, 84
Boutillier, Eugene, 278
Brademas, John, 123, 140, 148, 157, 193, 194, 196
Brickman, William, 141, 142, 143
Brockway, Allan R., 274
Buckley, Jeremiah, 188
Button, Dale, 165
Byrd, Robert, 54, 59, 60

Carey, Hugh, 113, 121, 132, 136, 140, 141, 142, 156, 158, 159, 164, 165, 166, 189, 196, 197
Carlson, C. Emanuel, 107, 108, 130, 169, 170, 171, 178, 179, 180
Carroll, Edgar, 82, 83
Carter, Hodding, 67, 69
Case, Clifford, 77
Cassidy, Robert, 61
Catchings, Maynard, 255
Cater, Douglas, 101, 174, 178
Celebrezze, Anthony J., 114, 115, 116, 117, 118, 119, 170
Climenhaga, Arthur, 163
Cohen, Wilbur, 104, 105, 106

Coles, Robert, 63
Connally, John B., 18
Consedine, William R., 101, 188
Conway, Jack, 9
Cooper, Owen, 67
Corbett, J. Elliott, 209, 218
Cotter, Paul, 51, 52, 57, 58, 59
Cronin, John F., 4, 5, 6, 19, 26, 30, 32, 38, 39, 41
Curtis, Carl, 30
Cutler, Nathan, 61, 77

Delaney, James, 104, 105
Dirksen, Everett, 3, 8, 25, 26, 32, 33, 38, 73
Docherty, George M., 241, 243
Donohue, James C., 102, 103, 186, 188, 190, 193, 199
Doran, Adron, 122, 123
Douglas, Paul, 36, 37
Douglass, Truman, 41, 78, 81, 82, 83
Dugas, Julian, 17

Eastland, James, 25
Eberly, John, 262, 263, 264
Edgar, Richard, 251, 252, 253, 254
Eisenhower, Dwight D., 4
Ellender, Allen, 54, 59
Elson, L. R., 241, 242
Engle, Clair, 1
Erlenborn, John, 190, 192, 195
Espy, R. H. Edwin, 173
Evers, Medgar, 8

Faubus, Orval, 4
Ferwerda, Vernon, 234, 235
Fiers, A. Dale, 173
Flemming, Arthur, 90, 126, 127, 128, 129, 169, 238, 283, 286

289

Ford, Gerald, 186, 187
Ford, William, 135, 158

Gallagher, Raymond, 70
Gardner, John, 177, 178
George, Bryant, 82
Gibbons, Ray, 12, 28, 29, 40
Golden, Charles F., 213, 214
Goldwater, Barry, 37, 91
Goodell, Charles E., 113, 114, 116,
  117, 118, 122, 123, 124, 125, 128,
  129, 132, 133, 137, 138, 139, 142,
  147, 148, 155, 159, 160, 161, 168,
  171, 180, 181, 187, 188
Gore, Albert, 36
Graham, Billy, 107
Green, Edith, 168, 169, 171, 172, 192,
  193, 194, 195, 197
Gunther, Violet, 9

Hadden, Jeffrey K., 286
Halleck, Charles, 9
Halpern, Sam, 106, 181, 182
Hamilton, James, 7, 9, 17, 22, 28,
  30, 39, 41, 82, 179, 237, 255, 258,
  259, 260
Hayden, Carl, 1, 33, 51, 54
Henry, Aaron, 50, 64, 69
Henry, Carl F. H., 268
Herbster, Ben Mohr, 28
Higgins, George, 208
Hilton, Bruce, 48
Hinton, Thomas, 46
Hirsch, Richard G., 87, 107, 145,
  146, 148, 149, 169, 180, 184, 185,
  270, 271, 272
Hochwalt, Frederick, 133, 134, 135,
  139, 170
Horn, Dawson, 57
Howe, Harold, II, 178, 187, 193
Hruska, Roman, 30
Hubbard, Stuart, 186, 187, 188, 189
Humphrey, Hubert H., 13, 25, 27,
  34, 80, 86, 206, 213, 277

Johnson, Lyndon B., 19, 30, 33, 39,
  89, 91, 93, 97, 98, 109, 132, 176,
  182, 184, 231, 233
Johnson, Paul, 47, 67, 72
Johnson, Philip, 130
Jones, Robert, 22, 42, 179

Kaplan, Marvin G., 9, 164
Kastenmeier, Robert, 229
Katzenbach, Nicholas deB., 9, 18
Keating, Kenneth, 17, 180
Kelley, Dean M., 99, 101, 127, 129,
  133, 167, 168, 169, 173, 174, 178
Kelly, William P., 61
Kennedy, John F., 8, 18, 19, 42, 93,
  105, 145, 204, 205, 206
Kennedy, Robert, 18, 32
Keppel, Francis, 103, 117, 121, 122,
  157, 158, 159, 160, 161, 162, 177
King, A. D., 7
King, Martin Luther, 6, 78
Kirk, W. Astor, 130, 131
Kramer, Herbert J., 44, 79, 80
Kuchel, Thomas, 27

Laird, Melvin, 186
LaNoue, George, 100, 155, 156, 167,
  198
Levin, Thomas, 49, 50, 82
Lewis, John, 34, 35
Lineweaver, Helen, 260, 261
Lippmann, Walter, 182, 183, 184
Lowell, C. Stanley, 163, 164, 165,
  170, 180

Maddocks, Lewis I., 13, 14, 28, 255
Maguire, David, 86
Malcolm X, 37
Mansfield, Mike, 1, 33
Marshall, Burke, 19
Mathews, James, 206, 207
McArdle, Edward, 133
McClellan, John, 33
McCulloch, William, 9, 15, 32
McDowell, John, 133
McGovern, George, 35, 210
McKay, Robert, 123, 124, 125
McManus, William, 133, 136, 137,
  138, 139, 140
McNamara, Robert, 213
McRee, James, 71, 82, 85
Mecklenborg, Paul, 188, 189, 190,
  200
Merchant, Joseph, 75
Miller, William J., 51, 52, 58, 60
Mills, Wilbur, 253
Mitchell, Clarence, 9, 21, 22

Moeller, Walter H., 88
Moore, Jay, 30, 38
Moore, William L., 15
Morgan, Charles, 15
Morse, Wayne, 98, 106
Mudd, John, 82, 83, 84
Mundt, Karl, 30, 35

Neigh, Kenneth, 81, 82
Neuhas, Richard J., 208
Nixon, Richard M., 87, 221, 239

O'Hara, James, 194
O'Neill, Thomas, 22, 105
Oxnam, G. Bromley, 245

Parks, Rosa, 4
Pastore, John, 36, 54, 55, 58, 59, 60,
    61, 62, 74
Percy, LeRoy, 67, 68, 75
Perkins, Carl, 98, 113, 117, 120, 123,
    124, 126, 128, 133, 147, 149, 150,
    156, 157, 159, 166, 193
Pfeffer, Leo, 151, 152, 153, 154, 155
Poage, W. R., 23
Poff, Richard, 23
Powell, Adam Clayton, 134, 135
Prinz, Joachim, 151

Quade, Quentin, 287
Quie, Albert H., 91, 98, 169, 171,
    182, 183, 184, 185, 186, 187, 189,
    195

Ramsey, Paul, 208
Randolph, A. Philip, 70
Rauh, Joseph, 9, 10, 18, 21, 26, 32,
    34, 79
Reed, H. D. (Jack), 114, 169, 175
Regier, Jon L., 70
Reissig, Herman F., 29
Reuther, Walter, 78
Ribicoff, Abraham, 86
Richmond, Julius, 61
Robertson, Floyd, 31, 265
Rose, Stephen, 285
Rumsfeld, Donald, 227, 228
Rusk, Dean, 210, 214, 215
Russell, Richard B., 2, 25, 37

Salinger, Pierre, 204
Saltonstall, Leverett, 55, 61, 73, 206

Saunders, Albert C., 86, 261, 262
Scherle, William, 191
Scheuer, James H., 143, 159
Schulz, Larold K., 70, 72, 81
Shaw, Rodney, 210, 211, 212, 221
Sherer, Morris, 141, 170
Shriver, Sargent, 44, 45, 47, 54, 61,
    62, 66, 73, 78, 79, 170
Shuttlesworth, Fred, 6
Sissel, H. B., 90, 130, 132, 260
Smith, Howard, 19, 23, 38, 175
Smith, Margaret Chase, 55
Smith, Merriman, 18
Smith, Richard, 130, 131
Snyder, Edward, 224, 225, 226, 227,
    228, 229
Speiser, Lawrence, 155, 156
Spike, Robert, 7, 19, 48
Spock, Benjamin, 206
Stein, William, 201
Stennis, John, 51, 54, 55, 56, 59, 60,
    61, 66
Stratton, Samuel, 243
Sugarman, Jules, 57, 82
Sullivan, Lenore, 280

Taft, Robert A., 94
Taft, Robert, 192
Tanner, Paul, 275, 276
Taylor, Clyde W., 264
Taylor, Ray, 227, 228
Teague, Charles, 279
Templeman, Harold M., 244
Thomas, Arthur, 49, 50, 51
Tower, John G., 37

Van Deusen, Robert, 267, 268
Vizzard, James, 276, 277, 278

Walmsley, Arthur, 17
Ward, A. Dudley, 213
Will, Herman, Jr., 205, 209, 213, 214,
    219
Williams, John Bell, 24
Willis, Edwin, 23
Wilson, E. Raymond, 222, 223, 230,
    284
Winn, Douglas, 68
Winstead, Arthur, 24
Wright, Marion, 53, 82

Yarborough, Ralph, 54

Index of Subjects

Alabama Christian Movement for Human Rights, 6
American Catholic Bishops, 5, 150
American Civil Liberties Union, 97, 155
American Jewish Congress, 96, 198
Americans for Democratic Action, 9

Baptist Joint Committee, 96, 107, 130
Birmingham, 6, 7

Child Development Group of Mississippi, 43, 47, 50, 51, 52, 58, 62, 63, 64, 65, 66, 71, 74, 84; National Citizens Committee for CDGM, 78
Christian Advocate, 48
Christian Century, 45, 234
Christianity and Crisis, 43, 70, 207
Christianity Today, 208
Church of the Brethren, 262
Citizens Crusade Against Poverty, 70, 82, 270
Citizens for Educational Freedom, 96, 186, 190
Civil Rights acts, 1, 2, 3, 9, 10, 21, 30, 38; cloture, 1, 2, 4, 33
Clergymen and Laymen Concerned About Vietnam, 208, 213, 243
Community Action Program, 47
Concern, 234
Congressional Quarterly, 21, 22, 32; *Revolution in Civil Rights*, 21, 26; *Federal Role in Education*, 93, 96
Coordinating Committee for Fundamental American Freedoms, 23
CORE, 15

Council of Chief State School Officers, 185
Crisis in the Nation, 281, 282, 283

Elementary and Secondary Education Act, 89, 91, 98, 99, 100, 110
Episcopal Church, 16; Department of Christian Social Relations, 17
Equal Employment Opportunities Commission, 26

Fellowship of the Committed, 12, 14
Fellowship for Reconciliation, 205
Friends Committee on National Legislation, 222, 223, 224, 226, 229

General Subcommittee on Education, 113, 126

House Rules Committee, 19, 21
HR 2362 (*see* Elementary and Secondary Education Act), 89, 90, 96, 114, 125, 126, 127, 141, 142, 148; marked up, 168; Senate subcommittee hearings, 169; passes House and Senate, 176

Interreligious Legislative Conference, 283, 284

Lanham Act, 92
Leadership Conference on Civil Rights, 9, 10, 19, 20, 21, 25, 26, 283
Lutheran Council, 266, 267, 268
Lutheran magazine, 238

March on Washington, 12
Mary Holmes Junior College, 47, 51,

293

52, 56, 64, 84
Morrill Act, 92
Mount Beulah Conference Center, 51, 56
Mississippi Action for Progress, 67, 72, 76, 84, 86
Mississippi Freedom Democratic Party, 43, 52

NAACP, 9, 50, 64, 65, 68, 131, 201
National Association of Evangelicals, 32, 96, 163, 264
National Catholic Welfare Council, 4, 6, 96, 133, 180, 274, 279
National Council of Churches, 7, 10, 96, 126, 129, 144, 173, 178, 231, 233, 234, 235, 236, 237, 240, 258, 281, 282, 285, 286; Commission on Religion and Race, 7, 11, 14, 30, 48
National Defense Education Act, 91, 92, 105, 131
National Education Association, 122, 123, 185
National Lutheran Church, 96
National Lutheran Council, 130
National Science Foundation Act, 131
National Security Council, 204, 205
National Society for Hebrew Day Schools, 141
Northwest Ordinance, 92, 142

Office of Economic Opportunity, 43, 46, 61, 64, 65, 66, 67

POAU, 96, 97, 163
Priority for Peace, 237

Race for Peace, 209, 210
Reform Judaism, 270, 271
Register Christian Opinion, 221, 222, 245, 254
Rust College, 12

Smith-Hughes Act, 92

SNCC, 48
Southern Christian Leadership Conference, 6
Synagogue Council of America, 231

Tempo magazine, 285

Union of American Hebrew Congregations, 87, 96, 107, 145, 210, 270
Unitarian - Universalist Association, 12, 96, 97, 165, 222, 232, 272
United Auto Workers, 9
United Church of Christ, 5, 7, 12, 26, 257, 266; Council for Christian Social Action, 7, 12, 13, 27, 232, 255, 257; Committee on Racial Justice Now, 7
United Methodist Church, 5, 31, 209, 210, 214, 247, 248; Board of Christian Social Concerns, 130, 205, 210, 213, 215, 216, 232, 248, 249, 250; Central Jurisdiction, 5, 30; Division of Peace and World Order, 205, 215, 216, 221
United Presbyterian Church, U.S.A., 6, 34, 232, 260; Board of National Missions, 70, 83; National Affairs, 130
U.S. Catholic Conference, 46, 102, 208, 273, 274, 275
U.S. Supreme Court — Brown vs. Board of Education, 4, 95

Vietnam, 208, 213, 214, 215, 216, 217, 218, 223, 224, 231, 234, 237, 239, 240, 241, 242, 243, 244

War on Poverty, 43, 45, 46, 47, 84, 97
Washington Study Program, 209
Wednesdays in Washington, 213, 226
Witness in Washington, 27, 29
World Council of Churches, 49, 208
Worldview magazine, 287